MW01609972

5-17

TRANSFER
OF
POWER

The War
of
1861

by

Elliott Germain

TRANSFER OF POWER

The War of 1861

ISBN 978-0-615-47978-1

Copyright © 1999

Elliott Germain

All Rights Reserved

PO Box 464 Hanover VA 23069

Republished 2011

libertynation.org

Printed in the U.S.A. by

Morris Publishing®

3212 E. Hwy. 30

Kearney NE. 68847

800-650-7888

www.morrispublishing.com

Introduction
by the Author

The "Transfer of Power" written of in this book is the transfer of political power from "We the People," as stipulated in the Original Constitution, to a "New America" wielding new unconstitutional powers. The New America was created in 1861, and by 1865, it converted our Constitution into an "evolving document" that seems to evolve only to serve avarice and greed.

The "Transfer of Power" that took place in 1861, actually was the culmination of efforts predating the war. One purpose of this book is to review the intrigue behind the people, organizations and businesses, in America and Europe, who instigated a political division of America.

This war should never be considered a simple case of North verses South. Instead, consider that an organization out of Ohio supplied tens of thousands of weapons to the pre-war South, not for profit but to instigate secession. Consider that the first deaths of the war were not at Fort Sumpter South Carolina but in Baltimore Maryland, and learn why. Learn why there were as many as 40,000 Northerners locked away in Northern jails under martial law during the Lincoln years for publically opposing the Transfer of Power.

It is not Mars who is the god of war, but mammon (money). Make the necessary connections to the economic motives behind the war. Within the same timeframe as America's most infamous war, there was a transfer of economic power in several critical areas. This centralization of the American economy served the purposes (and fortunes) of American and British bankers. The creation of a national currency, and a national banking system, and a debt-based money supply were the economic renderings of 600,000 dead soldiers.

The "Transfer of Power" required not only four years of war but also twelve postwar years of martial law over the South before the government in Washington D.C. could implement an irreversible legal system. The War of 1861 legally changed America forever; not in the sense most often recorded by historians, the freeing of slaves, but in the assumption of powers by a new Federal Government created during that timeframe. The political and social linking of "slavery" to the "old system" (the Constitution) has proved to be an effective tactic to conceal their Transfer of Power. Unlawful Constitutional amendments and subsequent Congressional legislation to free the slaves also contained deliberately hidden ulterior "power clauses" that can be interpreted to grant new powers to the Federal Government while discounting State powers and thus expanding Federal power over State citizens.

The "Transfer of Power" was hidden in "racial legislation" to create a political defense mechanism, that if a patriot challenged the new federal powers, he would be attacking the "racial justice" fronting the legislation and thus his attempts to restore the Constitution would be perceived as socially abhorrent. This defense mechanism remains in place, active and effective today.

The "political correctness" of today is the continuation of this racial defense mechanism undergirding the very foundation of the new Federal Government. The intent of this book is to present objective evidence to prove exactly how this Transfer of Power occurred, why it occurred, and in many cases, who were the perpetrators. However, providing evidence is only half the battle, the enlightenment also requires that the reader remain objective and not abandon his search for truth in those cases where the evidence falls victim to the stereo-typical cliches from the long-abused mantras issued forth out of the doctrines of political correctness.

Why are Americans today subjects of the Federal Government; where are the Original Rights? Why is America plagued with economic strife? Why is a fear and hatred of racism being perpetrated today by the establishment media? Is there a direct political linkage from the "uniting of sovereign States" back in 1861, to the "uniting of sovereign nations" today? Read this history of our nation and find out.

Contents

Chapters

Chapters

150 Year Commemorative Edition
1861 - 2011

Honoring the Directive of
General Robert E. Lee:

"Everyone should do all in his power
to collect and disseminate the truth, in the hope
that it may find a place in history and descend to posterity."

Lee also said:

"History is not the relation of campaigns, and battles
and generals ... but that which shows the principles
for which the South contended and which justified
her struggle for those principles."

Chapter 1

The True North

The truth behind America's War of 1861 must begin by dispelling certain myths, such as the myth that the war was fought over slavery and to view the war not as a war between North and South, but a war whose ultimate definition must be considered a war perpetrated by the Federal Government to consolidate all of the States into a central government. This war was a complex power-struggle as applied from three areas of operation: economic; political; and forces of international intrigue. The result of these three operatives was no less than the destruction of the U. S. Constitution, as well as the destruction of the State Constitutions and all of the rights therein guaranteed. In this effort to dispel the myth that the war was fought because Americans in the North vehemently opposed Americans in the South, it becomes necessary to make a closer examination of the "True North."

The purpose of this chapter is not to degrade the North, but to show that the social differences between the North and South were not enough to cause the War of 1861. There were truly differences between the two regions, the South being more Jeffersonian preferring an agrarian lifestyle, while the North tended to be more centralized around towns and cities and factories. The North had adopted a more Hamiltonian approach to economics, whereas the South, and the Democratic Party heeded Jefferson's admonition to avoid central banks and central economies. Also consider that Thomas Jefferson's grandson, George W. Randolph was a General in the Confederate Army.

Some Southerners today point out the cultural differences between the Anglo-Saxons of the North and the Anglo-Celtics of the South as being a main cause for social divisions, but that is a bit overstated. Probably the most conspicuous natural cause of separation was that North and South were geographically removed from each other and had developed into two separate cultures with two separate economies. The latter being the greater catalyst toward war, not so much as a war by the "people" but as a war for the bankers and industrialists.

Today's politically correct disinfectant history portrays the North as the savior of the Negro in America, but actually the North was not very different from the South regarding their feelings for the Negro. Slavery was popular in the South because the South was an agricultural region, particularly in the production of cotton. If the North had been agriculturally suited for cotton, there would have been just as many slaves in the North.

True States

History should more openly record that it was the Northern States that lobbied the Constitutional Convention to allow the continuation of the slave trade, insisting that Congress could not even discuss the slave trade until 1808 (Art. 1 Sect. 9, clause. 1). In fact the last slaver ship active in American waters was operating out of Massachusetts and captured at sea by the Confederate Navy in the War of 1861. Also, the one and only American slave trader ever executed in America was executed in the summer of 1862; he was from Portland Maine.

The North had 5000 men employed in the slave industry. One of these industries used sugar and molasses to produce the rum that was traded to the African chiefs in exchange for slaves. Also included in the northern slave industries were the crews of 700 slaver ships operating out of Massachusetts and Rhode Island. The fact that 13% of the slaves shipped from Africa to the United States died in transport translates to thousands of slaves dying at the hands of Northern businessmen, thousands more than ever died from mistreatment in the entire South.

In a last minute attempt to avoid the War of 1861, Wisconsin, as well as other Northern States repealed their own "personal liberty laws" thus favoring the controversial "Fugitive Slave Act" which allowed runaway slaves to be returned to their owners. The Union States of Oregon, New Jersey, Indiana, Massachusetts, Illinois and Ohio prohibited Negro settlers. Illinois' (the Land of Lincoln) prohibition of Negro immigrants was reenforced as late as 1862 with an added provision to their State Constitution prohibiting Negro immigration to Illinois. In April of 1862, Congress passed an Act that would give financial compensation for the gradual emancipation of slaves; but none of the "Northern" States adopted the provision. In January 1863, six days after Lincoln issued the Emancipation Proclamation, the Illinois State legislature drafted a resolution in opposition to the Emancipation, calling it a gigantic usurpation of power. In the Eighteenth Century, the punishment to a Negro for entering the State of Massachusetts was a public whipping. History, make a note; Hollywood do a remake: Yankee holding whip; Negro cries in vain.

Negroes were a small part of the Northern population in 1860, only 2%, however in the South, the percentage of Negroes was over 40% of the population. In those Northern States in 1860 there were over 36,000 slaves, repeat: slaves. The higher percentage of Negroes in the South played a major role in the postwar Negro suffrage; meaning under the postwar Reconstruction Acts, Negroes could vote in the South in 1865, but not in the North until the passage of the 15th Amendment in 1870. The Republican party, now unpopular in the North, could stay in power by getting that 40% of the Southern Negro vote that they created, while not affecting the political business-as-usual with the Negroes of the North. Actually, before the war, there were more free Negroes in the slave States that there were in the non-slave States.

True Politics

Congressional and political actions in the North also reveal that the causes of the War of 1861 were about anything but slavery. The same Republican Convention, of May 1860, that nominated Lincoln for President also proposed that there would be no extension of slavery into new States, but also said that there should be no interference with slavery in States where it already existed. After the war began, Congress, on July 25, 1861, passed a resolution stating that the purpose of the war was to preserve the Union and not to alter slavery. By January 9th, 1862, Congress suggested a means to colonize the slaves in some other area of the world while compensating their owners. Even as late as June 15, 1864, in the so-called war to abolish slavery, Congress voted against a resolution to abolish slavery. These Northern political actions, some made by the Party of Lincoln, reveal the vast gulf between the social and political realities of that time in history and the politically correct, agenda-based history of today.

Even the author of the original Civil Rights Act of 1866, Lyman Trumbull of Illinois, said this about his fellow State citizens:

"There is a great aversion in the West, I know it is so in my State, against having free Negroes come among us. Our people want nothing to do with the Negro. We the Republican Party are the White man's party."

The Northern Democrats spoke up as well. Senator Thomas Hendricks:

"We are not of the same race; we are so different that we ought not to compose one political community ... this is a White man's Government, made by the White man for the White man."

During the war, Democrats in the North began gaining seats in Congress. The Republican Party was being called the "War Party," so much so, that during the 1864 elections, the Republicans stopped using the name "Republican" and adopted the name "National Union Party," later, after years of public relations, the name reverted to the Republican Party.

The foremost leader of the Northern Democrats in Ohio was Clement L. Vallandigham, who was also the North's foremost "Copperhead." Copperhead was the name given to Northerners with Confederate sympathies. In May of 1863, Vallandigham was arrested for openly condemning the war and favoring the South, for which, he was given an unconstitutional military trial and sentenced to confinement for the duration of the war. Later, Lincoln changed his sentence to banishment to the Confederate South. Vallandigham ended up in Canada, where, in absentia, he received a Democratic nomination to be Governor of Ohio. That nomination could have made the North's foremost Confederate sympathizer a Democratic candidate for Ohio's highest office. Let these historical facts help reveal that the War of 1861 was not a war of "Northerners" against "Southerners" but a war in which the national government (referred to herein as the Federal Government) in Washington D.C. used 23 Northern States to defeat 11 Southern States.

Even the most vocal abolitionists made statements which revealed their own reservations. William Lloyd Garrison said he thought that the Negroes should have been educated more before given the vote. Thaddeus Stevens stated that the former slaves he had seen enter his State of Pennsylvania were not qualified to vote. Salmon P. Chase, who drafted the 14th Amendment and was President of the American Freedmen's Union said: "Let, therefore, this South be opened to Negro emigration ... and the blacks of the North will slide Southward." The author of Uncle Tom's Cabin, Harriet Beecher Stowe, after moving to Florida, also warned of the dangers of giving the postwar uneducated Negroes the vote. Her son, Charles Beecher Stowe later stated: "When the South drew the sword to defend the doctrine of States Rights ... certainly had on their side the Constitution and the laws of the land..."

True Lincoln

Abraham Lincoln cannot be left out of this discussion toward understanding the "True North." In 1847, on the floor of Congress, Abraham Lincoln said:

"Any people, anywhere ... have the right to rise up and shake off the existing government, and form a new one that suits them better."

If "honest Abe" was truthful in what he said, how was it, that four years later, as President, he denied that the Southern States had a right to "shake off the existing government?" Or perhaps this statement expresses his belief that "he" could shake off the nation established by the Founding Fathers; if so, then as early as 1847, Lincoln was already committed to the destruction of the United States Constitution and its federation of States.

The racial context of debates about the War of 1861 demands that a truthful depiction must present the facts that dispel the agenda-based interpretations of American history. In an 1858 political debate, Lincoln said:

"I am not nor ever have been, in favor of ... the social and political equality of the White and Black races ... nor ... in favor of making voters or jurors of Negroes ... nor intermarry with White people; ... I ... am in favor of having the superior position assigned to the White race."

History, please make a note: Lincoln, White supremacist.

In the Lincoln-Douglas debate, Lincoln said:

"Let us be brought to believe that it is morally right, and at the same time favorable to ... transfer the African to his native clime, and we shall find a way to do it, however great the task may be."

History, please make a note, Lincoln said send 'em back to Africa (or South America).

President Elect Lincoln said that he would support the first two Crittenden Amendments, which protected slavery in the States where it already existed, and would compensate owners for fugitive slaves that were not recovered, if the South would not secede. In Lincoln's inaugural address he said:

"I declare that I have no intention, directly or indirectly, to interfere with slavery in the States where it exists."

Even as late as August 1862, during the so-called "war to free the slaves" Lincoln said:

"My paramount object in this struggle is to save the Union and is not to save or destroy slavery. If I could save the Union without freeing any slave, I would do it."

In August of 1862, when speaking to a gathering of Negroes, Lincoln said:

"...we have between us a broader difference than exists between almost any other two races ... I think that your race suffers very greatly, many of them by living among us, while ours suffer from your presence ... It is better for us both, therefore, to be separated."

History, please make a note: Lincoln, racial separatist. Mrs. Lincoln inherited money from the sale of her father's slaves and had three brothers who fought and died for the Confederacy. Even as late as February 1865, with the nation sick of killing, Lincoln proposed to his cabinet that the Union pay $400 million dollars to the slave States if they lay down their arms by April First. Lee surrendered April 9th.

Emancipation was a political football being used to gain yardage for everyone involved. The concern for the Negro was seldom considered. For instance, as early as August 30th 1861, the Union General Fremont declared martial law in Missouri, an honorary Southern State, and in doing so, this California hero emancipated the slaves there. He was reprimanded by Lincoln who rescinded Missouri's emancipation on September 2nd.

In May of 1862, General Hunter, in the "Department of the South" (the Federal Government's bureaucratic name for their new fiefdom of Southern "rebellious" States) decided that he would emancipate the slaves in the conquered regions of the South. Lincoln again stepped in to make it clear that such decisions can only be made by the chief executive. Lincoln also modified the Congressional Confiscation Act of July 1862, to insure that only he, not Congress, could free the slaves in enemy territory. History, please make a note, the Great Emancipator repeatedly denied and rescinded the emancipation of slaves until he could take total and exclusive credit for it.

Is it not odd that in Washington D.C., the Capital city of the Nation fighting to free the slaves in the South, slavery remained legal for a year after the war started; how embarrassing. Congress finally got around to emancipating the 3,000 slaves in Washington D.C. in April, 1862, for which Congress paid a collective sum of one million dollars to their owners. Earlier, in 1847, when Lincoln first came to Washington D.C., he referred to the slave markets there as "a sort of Negro livery stable."

After the war, Washington D.C. became the first experiment for a referendum on Negro suffrage, in which the residents of Washington and Georgetown voted 7,369 against Negro suffrage, and only 36 for suffrage. Nevertheless, Congress, as the legal guardian of D.C., passed Negro suffrage lacking the consent of the governed. While Negro suffrage was being forced on the postwar South, Northern States continually declined having their own Negro suffrage. In fact, for the first three years after the war ended, every Northern State holding elections on the question of Negro suffrage voted to refuse the franchise to the Negro. This was the "True North."

When Lincoln finally did enact the Emancipation Proclamation, in January, 1863, under his war powers, it did not free any of the slaves in the North, nor in the border States, nor even in any areas of the Southern States occupied by the Union Army; such as several parishes around New Orleans, the bogus State of West Virginia, several counties in Northern Virginia and Tennessee. Lincoln only freed the slaves in the Confederate occupied South. As it was said in Britain: Lincoln undertook to abolish slavery where he was without power to do so, while protecting it where he had the power to destroy it. When Lincoln was asked by the "self-educated" former slave Frederick Douglas why he didn't free the thousand slaves living in the "Union" States, Lincoln replied: "It would be unconstitutional."

Was the Lincoln government protecting slavery? His Secretary of War, Simon Cameron ordered Union troops to enforce the Fugitive Slave Act by returning runaway slaves to their owners, except those slaves which had run out of the Confederate States. The Union's enforcement of legal slavery would include those slaves which Yankee General Benjamin Butler returned to their "loyal to the Union" masters in New Orleans, while putting the other "runaways" into work camps, declaring these humans to be the contraband of war. This also occurred in the "Department of South Carolina" under Union General Forster, who ordered the conscription of every able bodied Negro male over the age of thirteen. Some of these children were physically taken without notification to their parents, and some who resisted were shot. History, make a note: the Union Army was not a liberating army, it was a confiscating army.

True Resistance

Confederate troops fired upon Fort Sumter on April 12, 1861 (more details later), and on April 15, President Lincoln called for 75,000 volunteers from the non-Confederate States to fight what he termed an "insurrection." More than that number of volunteers responded. Was that because the Northern people had enough of the South, or was it perhaps the rampant unemployment rate in the North? If the President today called for volunteers to march against South Carolina, he would likely get 75,000 volunteers. Take a closer glimpse of the True North in their resistance to the Lincoln war machine.

Remember that border States were also slave States, but on April 15th, when Lincoln first called for volunteers, the North made no claims to be fighting the Confederacy to free slaves. Also remember that on April 15, the Confederacy consisted of only seven States, with its flag of seven stars. Virginia, Tennessee, North Carolina and Arkansas had not yet seceded. These and other border States did not respond to Lincoln's call for troops to serve in his private "Executive Branch" war.

The Governor of Kentucky, home-place to Mrs. Lincoln, offered this reply to Lincoln's request for troops to march against South Carolina:

"Kentucky will furnish no troops for the wicked purpose of subduing her sister Southern States."

Because of the governor's remarks and Kentucky's pro-Southern leanings, by August, Lincoln had established a Federal military camp outside of Lexington to insure "neutrality."

The Governor of North Carolina telegraphed the President stating that he could not respond to his call for troops because he doubted the President's authority to do so.

Governor Harris of Tennessee, doubtful of the constitutional powers of Lincoln's actions replied:

"Tennessee will not furnish a single man for coercion, but fifty-thousand, if necessary, for the defense of our rights or those of our Southern brothers."

Virginia, Arkansas, Maryland, Missouri and Delaware also refused to send troops. The Maryland legislature was considering a vote to secede and join the Confederacy until Mr. Lincoln moved troops into Maryland and arrested all those who spoke out against the new Federal Government's war regime.

Massachusetts was quick to respond; and the politicians of the New York Legislature immediately raised 3 million dollars toward attacking South Carolina. Only four days after Lincoln called for troops, the 6th Massachusetts Infantry had reached Maryland on their way to Washington D.C. Baltimore reacted with rioters armed with sticks and stones against Union troops armed with rifles and pistols. The 6th Massachusetts responded by killing 12 civilians on April 19th. The Marylanders responded by killing 5 soldiers. And remember, seven days earlier, during the exchange of artillery fire at Fort Sumter, no one was killed in action on either side. So, the first deaths of the war were inflicted by the Union Army against Baltimore civilians. And appropriately, the first Union soldiers to fall in the War of 1861, were killed by Maryland civilians in that same conflict.

The civilians of Maryland also severed the railroad link from Washington D.C. to points north, thus forcing any future D.C. bound soldiers from all points north to travel by ship up the Potomac instead. This resulted in Lincoln declaring martial law in Maryland. Citizens of the border States loved their freedom and their Constitutional rights as much as those in the Southern States.

By May 10th, 1861, riots broke out in Missouri which ended in a clash between Union soldiers and the Missouri Militia. Riots and protests spread throughout the North, and were always blamed on the Copperheads. There were also Northern newspapers writing in protest of the unconstitutional war declared by Mr. Lincoln. One such newspaper was the New York Hearld who sided with the South early on as revealed in this article dated November 11th 1860:

"The South has an undeniable right to secede from the Union. In the event of secession, the City of New York, and the State of New Jersey, and very likely Connecticut will separate from New England when the black man is put on a pinnacle above the white."

The lack of popular support in the North for the Republican's war against the South called for stronger measures directed against the Northern citizens by the new emerging Federal power.

On March 3, 1863, Congress passed the Federal Enrollment Act. This draft law was to raise an army by the drawing of names. On July 13, the New York draft office held the first drawing. This resulted in a mob of 50,000 New Yorkers storming the draft office; they killed its superintendent and burned the office of the Provost Marshall. The mob also beat a Union colonel to death and attacked the Mayor's home and burned the Tribune newspaper offices of the liberal Horace Greeley.

New York was already experiencing a resentment of the war which, by 1863, was being altruistically waged to enforce the Emancipation Proclamation. There was also an undercurrent of resentment against big New York businesses which had been importing cheap

Negro labor to work for starvation wages. These weren't slaves, just dirt cheap labor. You see the South had to house, feed, clothe and give medical care to their slaves, whereas in New York, "big business" could import Negroes, give them ten cents a day and wash their hands of any moral responsibility. Consider the words of the Hazard Circular which was distributed to American bankers during the American war of 1861, comparing the advantage of controlling wages over the use of slavery:

"Slavery is likely to be abolished by the war power and chattel slavery destroyed. This I and my European friends are in favor of; for slavery is but the owning of labor and carries with it the care of the laborer, while the European plan, led on by England, is capital control of labor by controlling wages. This can be done by controlling money."

The resentment of this employment practice by the resident workforce in New York caused the "draft riot" to turn into a "race riot." Negroes were hunted down and killed in the streets. An evacuated Negro orphanage was burned. Northern history plays this down but some casualty estimates go as high as 1,000 Negroes killed. Federal troops were called to quell the riot which resulted in a thousand more wounded or killed. The riot lasted four days.

The North was subject to continual internal, often violent resistance throughout the war. On March 28, 1864, Charleston, Illinois was the scene of anti-war riots which killed five and wounded twenty, and were the worst since the New York riots in 1863. There were people in the North who supported the war effort, as there always is in wartime, but in light of these facts, there is considerable evidence showing that this war was not fought on popular sentiment but was manufactured by special interests.

The lack of support by Northerners for Mr. Lincoln's declared war is also reflected in the fact that a Yankee could buy himself out of the draft with money, and that 116,000 Yankees chose to do just that. Yet, despite all of these set backs, there was in fact a Union Army; and a closer look at that Union Army will give a better understanding of the True North.

The True Union Army

Having discussed the draft dodgers, a review of those who did serve in the infamous war against the South would be in order. Out of every 100 Yankees drafted only 20 served. As early as 1862, the Provost Marshall estimated that there were 100,000 desertions from the armed services. Desertions between 1863 and 1865 averaged 1,250 per week; overall about 10% of the Army deserted. Desertions seemed to coincide with the battle patterns. The highest figure of desertions in one week was 5000. Bounties of five to thirty dollars were placed on deserters.

Out of desperation, in March of 1863, Lincoln offered amnesty to all deserters who would return to duty. Lincoln also recruited mercenaries from overseas. Most immigration came to America through the Northern ports. During the war years 764,000 immigrants came through Northern ports while only 191,000 immigrants came into Southern ports. Lincoln's need for (temporarily) warm bodies caused the North to offer citizenship to those who would serve in Lincoln's war. Some of these foreigners were the same "Union" soldiers who burned their way through Georgia, saving America, yet they couldn't speak a word of English (ominous and foreboding).

Lincoln's reason to invoke the Emancipation Proclamation was his hope that if he declared the slaves in the South to be free, it would cause an uprising of slave against master. The uprising didn't happen because Lincoln (and the Yankees) failed to understand the master/servant familial relationship that existed in the South. Lincoln also wanted to find some noble cause to excuse his treason against the U.S. Constitution. And third, out of his desperate need for replacements in his army, he decided to enlist Northern Negroes.

Weren't Negroes allowed in the Union Army from the beginning of the war? No. Up until 1862, Congress refused to let Negroes into the Union Army. In August of 1862, Lincoln himself, refused an opportunity to recruit two Negro volunteer regiments from Indiana. However in 1862, in Louisiana, Union General Butler did place himself in control over battalions of liberated slaves in work camps. Butler called the former slaves "contraband of war." Lincoln's Secretary of War, Simon Cameron, confirmed General Butler's use of human beings in his letter to Butler in New Orleans:

"President Lincoln desires the right to hold slaves to be fully recognized. The war is prosecuted for the Union hence no question concerning slavery will arise."

In the same spirit of General Butler, Congress, on July 12th, 1862, passed the "Confiscation Act" which, under the direction of Secretary of War Staunton, provided for the enlistment of Southern Negroes in the Union Army to be used primarily as guards for plantations and settlements. This pattern spread throughout the occupied South resulting in abuses of White civilians. The continuation of this policy after the war instigated the creation of the Ku Klux Klan.

Finally in May of 1863, the first Negro Northern Regiment was formed: the 54th Massachusetts Volunteers, which was sent to occupied Hilton Head, South Carolina to be trained. In July, 1863, this regiment attacked the Wagner Confederate Battery in South Carolina resulting in 1,511 dead Negro Union soldiers and 174 dead Confederates. White Union officers used the Negro soldiers as cannon fodder.

In the Union Army, which was fighting against the so-called racist South, Negro enlisted men always served under White officers. A White soldier of the rank of private earned $13 dollars a month, a Negro private earned $7 a month. When it became legal for Negroes to serve in the Army, White draft dodgers from the North began "buying Negroes" as substitute draftees, a practice that frustrated the Union Army so much that they passed a law stating that a White draftee could only be substituted by a White replacement. (It must have had something to do with being equal?)

Some soldiers resented the politics of Lincoln and paid the price. When Captain Tansill read Lincoln's inaugural address, he resigned his commission in protest, for which, he was arrested and jailed. Union morale began getting worse after the Emancipation Proclamation. After Lincoln read the Proclamation on January 1, 1863, hundreds of Union Officers and soldiers protested and left the Union army and went home. Remember that there were thousands of slave holders in the Union Army. Even General Grant was a slave owner who spoke out against fighting a war over slavery when he said:

"Should I become convinced that the object of the government is to execute the wishes of the abolitionists, I pledge you my honor as a man and a soldier I would resign my commission and carry my sword to the other side."

There was a family singing group that entertained the Union Troops named the Hutchinson Family Singers from New Hampshire. Some of their songs favored abolition. There were so many protests from McClellan's Army of the Potomac that the Commander of the Union Army forbade them to sing in Army Camps (Lincoln rescinded the order). There were also Union officers who refused to lead Negro units and were dismissed by the Army.

After General Butler was finally booted out of the Union Army, in part for his mistreatment of Negroes in Louisiana, he ran for Congress and became one of the foremost Congressional oppressors of the post-war South. During his campaign for elected office he introduced the first military service metal awarded to a Negro soldier, and like so many other White "Civil Rights" leaders, Butler was able to turn "slave contraband" into "political contraband."

Knowing the True North is essential to understanding the War of 1861; as well as realizing that the motives which governed the war were not the altruistic concerns for the Negro as implied in today's government education and media indoctrination. There is much more truth to uncover to fully reveal exactly how the Transfer of Power occurred during and after the Treason of 1861 and how it affects your life today. And for some necessary added depth to this subject, a presentation of the True South is required.

Chapter 2

True South
(Not Quite Dante's Inferno)

An entire definition of the Confederate States here and now, is not necessary in this chapter, but particular points about the South will remove the stereo-typical image that has been presented by the government and corporate media. This might be where it is expected that the author make a personal statement against slavery, and like so many other Virginians before me, I will. Slavery is wrong as a means of labor, it is wrong for the slaves and it is wrong for the non-slaves competing in the same occupation. The political use of slavery as a motivation or excuse to destroy the Constitution was also wrong.

Some persons and organizations in the South who were extremely vocal in favor of slavery during the 1850's and 1860's were acting in part toward the benefit of the very same foreign powers who introduced slavery in America and forced slavery on America. British Corporations such as the Virginia Company operated under the King's permission, and the King's government in the colonies forced America into permanent slavery. It is an error to believe that the War of 1861 was fought over slavery or racism.

During the War of 1861, General Halleck, Commander of the Union Army, ordered that no more Southern Negroes could be permitted behind Union lines because so many of them were acting as spies for the Confederacy. Why didn't these Negro Confederate spies just run away from the "evil Southerners" once they were behind Union lines? Because they were loyal to the Confederacy and were trusted by other Confederates. There were also Southern Negro prisoners of war held in Union prison camps.

There were more free Negroes in the South than there were in the North; 500,000 in the South, and 226,000 in the North. The collective value of property owned by the free Negroes of New Orleans alone was in excess of 15 million dollars. Virginia was the first nation in the world to outlaw the international trafficking of slaves on October 5, 1778. That was after Virginia became an independent nation but before Virginia joined in the federation of United States, when Patrick Henry was Governor. The Northern States that were trafficking in slaves lobbied the Constitutional Convention to protect the slave trade until 1808 from such actions on a national level, and they were successful as written in Article 1, Section 9, (clause one). However, with regard to Congress being prohibited from even discussing or stopping the importation of slaves, clause one states: "as any of the States now existing shall think proper to admit" meaning Virginia thought it proper to allow NONE: no international slave trade, and so, even with Article 1, Section 9, Virginia could continue to prohibit such importations. The 1808 limitation lobbied by Northern interests did not reverse Virginia's law prohibiting the international trade of humans.

Remember, discounting the slaves that the American Indians already owned before the White-eyes settled in America, the first so-called slaves that came to this country from Africa, came to Jamestown, Virginia in 1619. Those first 20 African Negroes were actually indentured servants who after seven years of servitude, obtained their freedom; such was the practice with indentured servants, Negro or White, in the colonies. Some accounts say that this practice was because the imported Negroes were made Christians, and "Christians" cannot be made slaves. These slaves were imported under the authority of the Virginia Company, a London based corporation.

One of the original 20 slaves, Anthony Johnson, was set free after his seven year servitude. He became the first Negro to own land in Virginia. After becoming free, Anthony Johnson began to buy slaves to work for him. When Mr. Johnson's Negro slaves served their seven years of indenture, they too sought their freedom, but Johnson refused. One of Johnson's slaves sought refuge at the home of a White Virginian name Parker. Johnson then sued Parker (Johnson vs. Parker - Northampton County, 1654) to get "his slave" back. The court, under the power of the English Crown, whose corporations had a vested interest in making slavery permanent, found in favor of permanent slavery, thus making a Negro (Anthony Johnson) and the English Crown the "founding fathers" of permanent slavery in America. By 1830, there were 10,000 slaves owned by free American Negroes. And at the beginning of the War of 1861, there were 3,500 Negroes who owned slaves.

The motives of the court and the Crown in the Johnson vs. Parker case were economic. The King's corporations needed permanent slaves to compete with Spain in the tobacco industry. Although slavery was already outlawed in England (don't bring them to England) in 1572, the King used slaves in America to make a fortune. In 1672, the King formed his own monopoly in the trafficking of slaves called the Royal African Company. No one else could traffic slaves into America except under the King's corporate flag. The King favored the New England shipping industry to carry on his evil trade in his name. In Virginia's Declaration of Rights, issued in May of 1776, when Virginia became a separate nation, it stated that one of the main reasons for their separation from Britain was that the King insisted on bringing slaves to Virginia against the will of the people of Virginia.

Virginia and other Southern States tried to solve the slave-race problem with attempts such as the American Colonization Society which had some success in giving Negroes their own destiny. Liberia became the first Negro Republic in the world whose first President, Joseph Roberts was a Negro from Petersburg, Virginia. In 1779, Thomas Jefferson proposed to the Virginia General Assembly that they purchase the slaves and settle them back in Africa, but the General Assembly did not have the funds.

After President Thomas Jefferson made the Louisiana Purchase, the Virginia General Assembly asked Congress to set aside a part of those lands as a nation for Negroes, Congress would not. There were other attempts made in the South, like the proposal that the State of Virginia purchase the children of slaves to end the cycle of slavery, but again, a question of money.

The Confederate Constitution also outlawed the international trafficking of slaves. In 1864, Duncan Kenner proposed a plan to the Confederate Congress which would have committed the South to freeing the slaves if Britain or France would give the Confederacy political recognition. Jefferson Davis and the Congress agreed but by the time Kenner got to London in 1865, it was too late. Also in 1865 the Confederate Congress passed, and President Davis signed a bill which would, upon agreement with each State, give freedom to slaves who would serve as Confederate soldiers. But all of this came too late to save the Confederacy.

Throughout the war, free Southern Negroes were serving the Confederacy on land and sea, in hospitals and as skilled craftsmen and laborers. Some Southerners today claim that Negroes served in the actual "military" but that claim falls short of providing documentation of any Negroes in service to the Confederacy as identified by a military "rank" which is essential in military service. But they did serve the "cause." As soon as the war broke out, free Negroes rallied to the aid of the Confederacy. On April 26, 1861, in Petersburg, Virginia, 300 free Negroes volunteered to work on fortifications. One of the Negroes, Charles Tinsley said:

"We are willing to aid Virginia's cause to the utmost extent of our ability." [And after receiving the Confederate flag, Tinsley said] "I could feel no greater pride, no more genuine gratification than to plant this flag on Fortress Monroe."

There are countless true accounts of Negro support for the South. Negro Churches after the war honored Confederate leaders such as Stonewall Jackson, as well as supporting Confederate memorials. There are accounts of European Journalists touring the South during, and just prior to the war, commenting as to how the slaves in the South were living better than the White factory workers in the North (not to mention living better than those imported Negro workers in New York who were working for starvation wages).

Out of a Southern White population of 5,450,000, there were 347,000 who owned slaves, and a very small number of those men beat their slaves, just as a small number of them beat their wives neither of which was condoned by Southerners, and it was not the cause of the war. How the General of all the Northern Armies (and slave owner) Ulysses Grant, felt about slavery is not well known, but the Commander of all of the Confederate Armies, Robert E. Lee freed his slaves before the war and declared that slavery was "a moral and political evil."

These facts are placed before you in an attempt to remove the moral high ground from being exclusively Northern, so that the true causes of the War of 1861 can be less emotionally brought forward. Neither will the facts presented attempt to cover the "sins of the South" which will also be discussed. The purpose in this writing is to objectively trace the who, what, when, where, how and even why questions and answers of America's Transfer of Power, and in doing that, let the chips fall where they may.

Chapter 3

The Money War

If wars have an engine, that engine is surely money. Wars are too often blamed on religion or ethics but if you dig deeply enough you will surely find that the root of war is money. But the seed that begat the root is more a matter of intrigue. The War of 1861 was fought because the American economy was a prize to be gained. There was always a Northern economy and a Southern economy. America's trade to Europe became a great source of wealth for both sides of the Atlantic. European financial interests (primarily Britain) looked to America as a young empire with great economic potential. The North and South traded with Europe separately. The European influences that came along with the trade deliberately directed the North and South into an economic collision in hopes that Europe could pick up the postwar pieces for a few pence on the pound.

The truth of history sometimes seems so discouraging, and to learn that one of the larger causes of the War of 1861 was money is one of America's saddest chapters. This war transformed the American economy forever. Buried within the military and political transfers of power, was a transfer of economic power employed to confiscate American monetary policy. Before reviewing the main contributing factors that caused the money war of 1861, consider some background on the Southern economy and how it was affected by the war.

The Confederate Economy

There is no doubt in international trade that cotton was the South's big money crop. In this arrangement the aristocratic cotton plantation owners, like the earlier tobacco plantation owners, developed a close relationship with British aristocrats. This relationship increased the distrust between Southern planters and Northern industrialists. By 1859, the annual cotton exports from the South were valued at $161 million.

The population of the North was almost 20 million, but in the

South, the White population was only 5.5 million, yet the South controlled over 57% of the total U.S. exports. The gross national product of the North was $1.9 billion; the GNP in the South was $820 million. So before the war, the South enjoyed a stable and good economic health. Whereas the North suffered from yet another contracting economy resulting from several factors, one of which was the end of Europe's Crimean War, which had brought European money to Northern industries through the sale of war necessities. The North had learned how to turn a buck on the misfortunes of war, an economic lesson they would remember in 1861. The end of the Crimean War in Europe, and the destructive effects of the inflation caused by the California gold rush, which too quickly ran dry, resulted in the economic panic of 1857 in the Northern States.

The Confederate "war economy" was planned out even less than their military strategy. In 1861, the American money system was based upon "specie" meaning precious metals (silver and gold) minted into coins. In the early part of 1861, there were $250 million dollars of specie deposited in Northern banks, whereas the South had $26 million of specie on deposit and an estimated $20 million of U.S. coin in circulation. The State banks could print their own paper money based on their equal deposits of specie.

The Confederate government also claimed three of the five U.S. mints in existence, North Carolina, Georgia and Louisiana. The combined contents of these three mints was $600,000 in bullion, hardly enough to produce the amount of specie it would take to finance a four year war. They struck some coins but very few. Some of the first Confederate paper money was printed in New York. The Confederate economy was healthy, but it could not survive a war economy. As bad as the economic prospects of secession were, staying in the Union would have eventually resulted in the economic domination of the South by Northern industrialists and bankers using the national government to gather tariffs from the South and spend them in the North, thus expanding the Northern economy as the expense of contracting the Southern economy.

The Southern Democrats were against tariffs, but the Northern majority in Congress wanted tariffs. Tariffs (gathered in Southern ports) would have meant Southern money going North, a taxation of the South by the North. That economic debate goes back to 1832 and South Carolina's Nullification Act, which was the political incubation of Southern secession and why the Confederate Constitution specifically limited tariffs.

The Northern majority Congress always legislated "pork barrel" internal improvement projects and government spending to benefit Northern industries, paid for, in a large part, with Southern taxes and thus, the Confederate Constitution also strictly limited taxation for internal improvements. Immediately after the Southern States seceded, Congress passed new tariff and internal improvement laws, which justified the Southern suspicions of Congressional "ear mark" spending. Years earlier, the Virginian George Mason, the genius behind our Bill of Rights, warned us:

"The effect of a provision to pass commercial laws by a simple majority would be to deliver the South bound hand and foot to the eastern States." (meaning New England)

When the Liberty Party, promoting emancipation of slaves, became a faction of the Republican Party, the Southern planters saw the election of Lincoln as yet another economic threat. If the 3.5 million slaves were emancipated without compensation to the owners, estimated value being 3.5 billion dollars, it would have been twice as bad economically as the Crash of '29, which created an economic depression that was ended by history's largest "war for money" experiment ever undertaken: World War Two. The South's economic concerns were justified and proved to be true, especially considering that 5.1 million of the 5.5 million White Southerners did not own slaves. Many of whom, like Robert E. Lee hated the evil. Slavery truly was not a "Southern" institution, but a legal dilemma between "emancipation" and "property rights" which needed to be resolved, but resolved in court. History has proved that the evil perpetrated against America in the War of 1861 was in no way the best solution. International bankers had more to do with starting the war than did slavery.

A German immigrant and banker named Christopher Memminger, residing in South Carolina, became the Confederate Secretary of the Treasury. It was Memminger who first convinced the Confederate Congress, in May of 1861, to print $20 million in fiat money (not backed by gold or silver). If the government issuing a fiat currency is honest and sound with frugal government expenditures, the currency would be as good as gold. Gold or silver backed currencies have problems with market hoarding and similar schemes which were attempted in the North during the War of 1861. Both systems are fine if used honestly. By 1865, the Confederacy had issued over $1.5 billion in paper.

The Confederacy also borrowed money by selling bonds, with many of the bonds backed by cotton. Fifteen million dollars in bonds were sold in Britain and France. The Confederacy had no mechanism for collecting a "national tax" because of their strong belief in State sovereignty. The Union had the South completely blockaded during the war which ended most foreign trade and devastated the Southern national economy. And because the majority of the war was fought in the South, it destroyed property, industry and homes. The culmination of these factors resulted in the total economic ruination of the South.

When Union General Sherman burned his way across Georgia, damages to property exceeded $100 million. In 1861, Georgia was free of debt, but after the war, after six years of rule under the carpetbagging Republican "Union" government, Georgia was $50 million in debt; and none of that was war debt; all of it was postwar debt generated by their martial law government. The war debt was repudiated by the 14th Amendment thus bankrupting all bond holders and driving the South into a hopeless economy totally dependent upon the New Federal Government.

The Confederate dollar was worth 1.6 cents when Lee surrendered; or as claimed by some historians, the South had a total of 9,000% inflation during the war. The South's war debt was $5 billion; the South's net worth after the war was $3.4 billion. If the South lost the war it would be bankrupt; but even if the South had won the war, it would be bankrupt. The South could not afford to "win" or "lose" the war; it simply could not afford war at all. Three years after the war ended, and after the confiscation of hundreds of millions of acres of privately owned land, and after driving every Southern State millions of dollars in debt, Congress levied a tax on cotton which extracted $70 million from the South in three years. The South was economically trodden down for a hundred years after the war as punishment for claiming freedoms guaranteed under the Constitution.

That is a thumbnail sketch of the Southern economy during and after the War of 1861. The people of the South had no grandiose plans to make money off of death. The Confederacy was never in a strong enough economic position to participate in the war-for-money game. In the South's attempt to secure their Constitutional rights, they were forced to endure "hate taxation."

The total net worth of the South in 1865, was less than the total net worth of their slaves in 1861. And for those who fought for State's Rights, well, as the Lincoln appointed Supreme Court Chief Justice Salmon P. Chase put it: State's rights died at Appomattox.

The War to Preserve the Union (Economy)

"…the Union must obtain full victory as essential to preserve the economy of the country."

Loyal Publication Society, 1863, New York.

The North had several motivations to enter a war against the South but the motivation that really delivered America into the War of 1861 was money. That does not mean that every Northerner was a war monger, but as a factor influencing the powers-that-be who have usually controlled the wars of history, the economy is the most traceable. The Southern economy was basic, constitutional and easy to evaluate, but the Northern economy is much more complex. The Northern economy represents much more power, primarily banking, and much of that power was European. The Northern economic landscape that waged war against the South included the industrialists, the railroad corporations, and the bankers, which includes monetary policy: the actual "currency" itself.

Horace "go west young man" Greeley, was a New York newspaper editor, who had dreams and schemes of his own. "Go west" was a way for eastern industrialists to create new markets, as well as establish pro-Northern populations in the western territories. However, there was a great resentment of the eastern establishment among the citizens of the "western" States of Ohio and Illinois. Many of those citizens left the Northeast to escape the horrible working conditions and wages.

There was so much immigration from Europe into the northern ports that employers were able to keep wages extremely low, it was the end of the American dream for the American working man. And because the economic powers-that-be won the War of 1861, you can observe that their immigration policies are still in full effect today. Things were so bad in the pre-war North that if a person quit his job, he needed a "permission to work elsewhere" note from his previous employer in order to be hired by another labor-inflated employer.

The West's resentment of the wealthy, corrupt eastern establishment led to the nomination of "log cabin Abe" for President in the Chicago, Illinois Republican Convention of 1860, instead of the eastern bankers candidate William Seward. Remember municipalities all across the North were going bankrupt, and unemployment was very high. The U.S. Government had its highest debt in 40 years (the earlier debt being the War of 1812).

The War Industry

When Lincoln took office he appointed several of his rivals into his Cabinet. Lincoln chose William Seward to be Secretary of State. It was Seward that first advised Lincoln that a foreign war would boost the failing Northern economy. Northern industrialists lobbied Washington to ease their great fear concerning the development of future western States. The natural route of commerce east from points west would be east to the Mississippi River and then Southward to New Orleans and then to Europe. Such a trade route would mean that the economies of the western States would bypass the North completely. That fact alone was a major reason for the war. The North wasn't satisfied that Northern industries produced 90% of the nation's manufacturing. Other economic advisors suggested controlling Southern ports to tap into the cash flow of the South even though the Southern ports were already sending millions of tariff monies northward. Someone once asked Lincoln: "Why not just let the South go?" to which Lincoln replied:

"Let the South go? Let the South go! Where then shall we get our revenues?"

The Northern industrialists were positioned to make their fortunes with cheap labor and endless natural resources. All they needed was a guaranteed market: a war. The total cost of the War of 1861, North and South, was $12.5 billion, some estimates vary, but at least half that amount was the Union's cost which would be at least $6.2 billion. The entire gross national product for the North before the war was only $1.9 billion. How could the North afford a war that costs $6.2 billion? The national debt in 1860 was $64.8 million. The Union debt in 1865 was $2.7 billion. That debt required some very creative monetary math:

U.S. Treasury 1860:	$ -64,800,000
Cost of War:	$6,200,000,000
Subtract Debt at end of War:	$2,700,000,000
War created wealth:	$3,500,000,000

Most of the money from the cost of the war went to Northern industrialists, $6.2 billion, and that's not counting paying off the 1860 debt. The $3.5 billion created was an economic coup. The military industrial complex, whether it was the War of 1861, World War One or Two, Korea or Vietnam, is an economic bonanza for the military industrial complex and for the money lenders. In 1863 alone, the U.S. military required 259,000,000 rounds of small arms ammunition.

The War of 1861 was the first American conflict to spawn a millionaire class of industrialists. Among these "richly patriotic" industrialists supplying the boys in blue (while making millions) were: Carnegie, supplying iron and steel; Bordens, supplying the new product: canned milk; Armor, supplying canned meat; Weyehaeuser, supplying the lumber; Remington, supplying the guns; Rockefeller, supplying the oil, and J.P. Morgan collecting the interest on the debt for the British Rothschilds. Many of the war industries gained such an economic advantage that they suppressed any future competition, and gained a favored contractor status with the U.S. Government, economically dominating America for a hundred years. You do recognize the names?

When the War of 1861 got underway, "king cotton" of the South was falling victim to the food shortages in Britain, and so the North used food sales, "king corn," to persuade Britain not to politically recognize the South. The separation between the United States Government and the giant favor-seeking corporations became permanently blurred. Our government "by the People" became "legislation for hire," and one of the worst-case abuses of money and power performed by the merger of the national government and big business was that of the railroads.

Railroading America

Before there was "big oil" there were the "railroads." That's where the big money was in the 1860's. A major economic problem of the industrial North before the war was that the Indian treaties made by the U.S. Government during the Presidency of Andrew Jackson, recognized the contiguous mass of land that went from Canada to the top of Texas, from approximately the Mississippi River west to the Rocky Mountains to be Indian lands. And with California and Oregon becoming States on the other side of that land mass, the only legal route that the railroads could take from the eastern States to those western States, without trespassing on Indian lands, was down to Texas and then west through the pro-Southern States of New Mexico and Arizona. This was the lawful route proposed in the U.S. Senate to the railroads before the war by Senator Jefferson Davis. In the contra-position, Illinois Senator Stephen Douglas was proposing a Northern route, which was the hidden Northern agenda driving the Kansas and Nebraska debates.

The American railroad network before the War of 1861 was a rail system going from one city to another city; with each city connection being established and carried to the next city by separate corporations. For a railroad company to own 200 miles of track was considered big industry. In 1860 there were 30,500 miles of railroad. The North possessed 72% of that mileage. Even during the depression of 1857 to 1860, railroad mileage was growing at almost two thousand miles a year. The railroad industrialists were typically in the political class of Southern Democrats who were formally Whigs, or the Northern (monied) Whigs who, after 1852, migrated to the Republican Party.

Eventually two (almost) completely separate railroad systems developed, one serving the North, the other serving the South. The Southern rail system went from Richmond, Virginia to Florida, and most points west. The Southern system consisted of 112 different companies.

As the railroad grew in the North, larger companies bought out smaller companies and gained more and more power and became larger and richer. By 1853, New York was connected through to Chicago, but using several different companies. By 1856, the Illinois Central connected Chicago with New Orleans. Railroads became big business and began attracting bankers.

The reputation of railroad corporations suffered as they became larger and more corrupt; a reputation that added the derogatory term of a person being "railroaded" to the American vocabulary. The real economic power of the railroad was that they controlled commerce through transportation. This lead to price fixing and favoritism. One example was the arrangement between certain railroads and Rockefeller's Standard Oil.

John D. Rockefeller (the first), while still in his teens, was a commissions broker in Cleveland, Ohio. In that capacity he witnessed the potential of the quickly expanding oil industry. By 1861, the U.S. was actually exporting over a million dollars worth of petroleum to Britain. Rockefeller bribed and coerced a rebate arrangement with the Pennsylvania, Erie and New York Central railroads, where the railroads would pay Rockefeller a rebate for every shipment of oil shipped by himself or shipped by his competition. This drove his competition out of business. Such underhanded business practices were also happening between the railroads and other industrialists in coal, meat or anything big.

These monopolistic business agreements led to an economic system that altered business management and ownership. Due to contrived economic downturns, small business owners and stockholders signed away their corporate voting powers to the banker-industrialists who secretly controlled the trusts. By 1890 Rockefeller controlled over 90% of America's refineries. It was the unethical business practices of the industrialist millionaires, who began their wealth in the War of 1861, that culminated in the anti-trust legislation at the turn of the century. The offenders of the anti-trust laws of the 1890's were the same powerful railroad corporations, the same military industrial complex, and the same bankers holding the national debt, who centralized (nationalized) their economic control during Lincoln's war to preserve the Union (economy).

Just as soon as the Confederate States pulled out of the Union,

Congress passed new higher tariff laws, and "ear marked" those funds for internal improvements, justifying the fears of the South. The most grandiose internal improvement was to go to the richest of the corporations, the railroads. Certainly national development is good. The North favored Hamilton's (pre-Keynesian) economic policies, while the South preferred Jefferson's policies of not allowing the national government to operate outside of its Constitutional economic limitations. The failure of Hamilton's (or Keynes') theory is that it fails to recognize the likely corrupting influence over Congress by the "money powers" seeking the lucrative government contracts.

On April 15, 1861, three days after Fort Sumter was fired upon, Lincoln took upon himself, new unconstitutional powers, and with those powers he could do things that no President before him had ever done; Lincoln began an irreversible Transfer of Power. By May 25, his Secretary of War, Edwin Staunton, ordered railroads to give first priority to military needs. These Union railroads connected into States sympathetic to the South; some of the border State railroads were not too cooperative toward being drafted into Lincoln's war against South Carolina. Missouri, though not always considered a "Confederate" State, was formally admitted into the Confederacy by the Confederate Congress on November 28, 1861, one month later, the President declared martial law over the railroads in St. Louis and throughout Missouri. Mr. Lincoln, having been a railroad lawyer in Illinois, and backed by the railroad influenced Republican Congress, became the biggest railroad man in history. Let the corruption begin!

In 1862, Congress started granting cash and lands to the railroads. During the war, the Union Government granted 2.6 million acres to the Illinois Central (Land of Lincoln). Then the Illinois Central turned around and sold one-third of that land (over 800,000 acres) to settlers before the war had even ended, and made a handsome profit (subtracting the payoffs to lobby Congress, it was all profit).

In July of 1862, the Congressional Pacific Railway Act chartered companies to build railroads. The first one was to be the "Union" Pacific. The Union Pacific was to begin in Omaha, Nebraska and head west toward San Francisco. The Central Pacific was to start in San Francisco and head east toward Omaha. This was the pipe dream of the Northern Whigs before the war. How would building a railroad to California help the war effort?

Lincoln's "New America" government gave $27 million toward the construction of the Union Pacific Railroad. Investors came up with $23 million (bonds sold). The construction company was Credit Mobilier. They built the Union Pacific for $50 million and the brains behind the scam watered down the stock and presented the venture as a $73 million capital investment, and thus pocketed $23 million. They used some of the watered down stock to bribe Congressmen. In 1864, Congress chartered the Northern Pacific Railroad to go from Lake Superior to Puget Sound (Seattle). Eventually there were 4 great railroads in the west built with borrowed government money and give-away government land. Before it was over, the government gave private corporations 130,000,000 acres (three times the size of New England).

Oh yes, during this great economic expansion, there was a war going on, men dying, lives being ruined, property being destroyed. And as the North conquered portions of the South, they rebuilt the Southern rail systems. The Union Army was a railroad-building army. Most Southern rails were a different size than the Northern rails, so the conquering Union Army brought the Northern railroad system into Dixie. Eventually they rebuilt one-third of the Southern railroad mileage. In 1865, the largest railroad company in the world was the "U.S. Military Railroads" with 2,105 miles of track, 419 locomotives, and 6,330 cars. In 1866, one year after the war ended, the "Union" government got out of the railroad business and sold everything for 25 cents on the tax dollar invested. To whom did they sell the railroads in the South? Well, on paper, they were "Southern" companies. But the South was in economic ruins and under martial law. The Southern Democrat-Whigs acted out the part of being the "local" owners, but money and control came from the North.

The Government of Alabama, after the war but before the carpetbaggers could set up and take over, tried to revive their own railroad system. They issued bonds in an attempt to keep the Northern railroad from taking over. Alabama had invested so heavily in saving their railroad system that railroad bonds were Alabama's largest debt. In spite of this noble effort to retain local control, they were out maneuvered by the big money and legalese of a railroad corporation out of Boston. The South didn't have a chance.

Andrew Johnson (Democrat), who became President after Lincoln, was an honorable man at a dishonorable time and in a very dishonorable city: Washington D.C. He spoke openly against the Federal Government giving funding and land grants to the railroads, predicting that it would become a series of "endless corrupting legislation," which it did. In contrast to the Honorable President Andrew Johnson, the next President, Republican Ulysses Grant appointed two railroad attorneys to the Supreme Court. Congress impeached President Johnson (but failed to kick him out), while Grant's face is on the fifty dollar bill.

The railroading of America during the War of 1861 altered American industry forever. But the railroads were not the most powerful economic force vying for control of our new continent. The bankers were a money-power greater than the railroads. Industrialists cut the throats of their competition and bribed Congressmen to get their mighty dollar; but the power of the bankers redefined the dollar itself, they altered United States monetary policy to place themselves at the economic helm of America. And yes, this banking coup was also part of the Transfer of Power in the War of 1861.

Banking

The United States Constitutional economic system centers on gold or silver coins, which are called "specie." The Constitution gave Congress the power to "coin" money. That literally meant that "coin" was to be the only federal money. The pre-1789 States had a bad experience "paper" during the Revolutionary War when the Continental Congress printed unbacked "paper dollars" as money. And just as with the Confederate dollar after the War of 1861, the final post-Revolution value of a paper "Continental" was one cent on the dollar; thus the expression: not worth a Continental.... The use of paper money was discussed at the Constitutional Convention and it was specifically forbidden to be used as the "money" of the United States. However, a State bank possessing "specie" (coin) reserves could issue paper money based on a 100% redemption back into specie upon demand (coins were awkward to carry).

At the time of the Constitutional Convention there were only three national banks in the U.S. They were located in Massachusetts, New York, and Pennsylvania, all three were "Union" States. The first Secretary of the Treasury was Alexander Hamilton complete with his dreams of "internal improvements" at the expense of the taxpayers. Hamilton decided that America should commission a private-yet-government central bank to improve commerce. That has always been "the sell," jobs, jobs, jobs, while the "cream of commerce" floats to the top of the food chain: bankers. Therefore Congress granted a 20 year charter to the first "Bank of the United States."

The first Bank of the United States opened its doors in 1791, in Philadelphia. It had eight branches and began with a capital investment of ten million dollars, which was fifty times larger than what was then considered "big business." Two million of the ten million dollars was put up by the U.S. Government, while eight million was put up by investors. Remember, paper money had to be backed by specie on deposit at a bank, and the start-up money for the new central bank placed between one-third and one-half of the nation's specie in the hands of the first Bank of the United States. Strict Constitutionalists, such as Thomas Jefferson, were concerned that this quasi-governmental arrangement created a danger of a powerful corporate (and international) control over the American economy. And when Americans discovered the extent of the bank's ownership by foreign banks, particularly British banks, (our number one enemy at that time), and because of dirty banking tricks against State banks, the charter of the Bank of the United States was allowed to expire in 1811. Britain's attempt to conquer our post-revolution nation back through economic deception failed.

The central bank's currency was removed from circulation creating a monetary shortage, and Britain then attacked the United States in the War of 1812. These combined military and economic tactics undermined public confidence in the remaining State currencies which were made weak by the central bank and there was a run on the banks to exchange paper for specie (gold and silver coins). Banks suspended specie payments in the economic chaos. This war-induced panic conveniently set the stage (recession) for another attempt to convince the public that they needed another national central bank; just what Britain wanted.

The next central bank was also called the "Bank of the United States," but history refers to it as the second Bank of the United States. Instead of starting with a capital investment of ten million dollars as did the first bank, in a war torn, bankrupt nation the second bank invested an astronomical $35 million, and this time the national bank had twenty-five branches reaching into the South and West. The second Bank of the United States implemented policies that deliberately devastated the competition: the small State banks. The second bank policies caused yet another economic panic. This was an assault by the giant centralized national bank against the State banks for the purpose of gaining economic control over the entire nation. The comparison of this "banking war" to the War of 1861, is to reveal that Lincoln's new national government not only fought to centralize State governments into a national government but also fought to centralize State banking into a national economic system.

Andrew Jackson became President of the United States in 1828; he was the international bankers' worst nightmare. Jackson was a Southerner who opposed the centralization of American monetary policy. Jackson was well aware of the economic domination that the second Bank of the United States was gaining over America. Jackson accused the second bank of printing more currency than it had in specie reserves, which was true (they printed millions of fiat dollars). The President of the second bank, Nicholas Biddle, and the President of the United States entered into a very public head to head struggle concerning America's economic future, a struggle history calls the "bank wars."

The (monied party) Whigs feared that Jackson would not sign the renewal bill for the extension of the second bank's charter, which would expire just after the 1832 election. The Whigs made banking an election issue. The people spoke and Jackson won. The renewal legislation for the second bank did pass the House and Senate, but Jackson vetoed the bill, and the veto stood. President Jackson and his Secretary of the Treasury Roger Taney then withdrew the government's deposits of specie from the second Bank of the United States because the bank was floating more (fiat) currency than it had in specie reserves which meant that the nation's deposits were threatened if there was another public run on the banks to exchange paper for specie.

The aggressive lending policies by the second bank's branches in the South and West resulted in the economic ruin of individuals and State banks. The most egregious tactic was that when the "national" bank made loans to persons in those States, the interest monies (which were not provided in the national loan) would have to come out of the "State" currencies which the "national" bank would then exchange for the State bank's specie, thus absconding with the gold and silver of the State banks. So when Jackson took the U.S. deposits of specie out of the second bank, he deposited them throughout many State banks that had been "robbed." The banker controlled media called these State banks, Jackson's "pet banks." Spin-controlled history paints Jackson as a smooth politician who damaged the American economic system. America should expect the very best, most cleverly enunciated pro-banking "authoritative" spin from the "best scholars money can buy."

In July, 1836, President Jackson required that payment for government lands be paid in specie and not in "bogus banker bucks." Jackson's reason for this was that the second Bank of the United States was printing money without backing, lending the fraudulent money to settlers who paid it to the U.S. Government to buy land. And so, for zero cost to the second bank, the bank obtained the mortgages of thousands of farms and homes. The second bank would also make loans which they knew would fail, so they could repossess the land, keep the down payment, and sell the same land all over again. This money scam profited millions of dollars to bank stockholders. Jackson's demand that all future government purchases be made in specie "called the hand" of the bluffing second bank to match its "paper" dollar for dollar with "specie." The second Bank of the United States was exposed as fraudulent, proved insolvent and quickly went under. How Jackson's face came to be on the twenty dollar Federal Reserve note is surely the biggest irony in American banking.

Andrew Jackson saved the American monetary system, at least until the War of 1861. And the next time that a "central bank" raised its ugly head again in America it was called the Federal Reserve Bank which began operation in 1914. Jackson set the bankers back 30 years, but the European bankers and their American agents were working day and night to establish a central bank. They kept their eye on the prize, and if they had to destroy America to get it, they would. If they had to use deceit to get the North to fight the South, they would. If they had to create the worst war in American history and destroy the Constitution, they would. They could always redeem themselves later, by hiring hundreds of credible, intelligent, mercenary scholars to rewrite history to put themselves in a better light (which they did); and today, their history is the history that our children are learning in school and from television.

War of 1861

The Endangered "Specie"

On April 12th, 1861, at Fort Sumter, South Carolina, Confederate and Union armies exchanged cannon fire. On April 15th, that fateful day, perhaps the darkest day in American history, Lincoln called for troops. The war began, and to pay for that war, the Federal Government (which was bankrupt in 1860) needed a new economic system to finance their New America. The bankers had been waiting in the wings for this moment since the days of Andrew Jackson, a day for which they had long planned. They had secretly financed and politically staged certain events leading to this moment, using their occult forces. Their goal was to introduce a debt-based currency, which endangered America's Constitutional specie-based monetary supply.

The Secretary of the Treasury, in the Lincoln 1861 cabinet, was Salmon P. Chase. Chase became the central player working within the government to create a new economic system. In 1861 he began agitating Lincoln for a new banking system. Lincoln needed money right away for his war, and Chase was able to secure loans from his friends in the eastern banking establishments. Salmon P. Chase was a friend and associate of the banking house of Jay Cooke. Jay Cooke became a major player in the economic War of 1861.

Salmon P. Chase was authorized in July, 1861, to borrow up to $250 million. History records that Chase secured loans to the government at 6 to 7%; but suppressed history says that some banks charged as high as 19%. Lincoln rejected future loans and devised a plan of his own. Lincoln decided to print fiat money, that is, money not backed by specie or precious metals. These fiat dollars were called "greenbacks." Fiat currency had been used in America before, but only during the worst recessions, such as when former President Jefferson advised President Madison to introduce fiat currency to protect the nation from the destructive effects of the vengeful first Bank of the United States in the recession and war years of 1812-1814.

Lincoln's first greenbacks, were issued in 1861, these were "demand notes," or simply put they were "trust me" dollars from the government. Chase issued 60 million in 1861, and to control the inflation

34

caused by an expanding money-base of fiat currency, in August 1861, Congress passed the first ever National Income Tax bill, which taxed all income over $800 at 3%. This first attempt at an income tax was deemed unconstitutional and never went into effect.

During the War of 1861, just as in the War of 1812, public confidence in paper money was falling. And so when these unbacked demand notes entered the economy there was a rush to exchange them for coin (specie). This put a strain on the Constitutionally required specie reserves held by the banks, and it also absorbed the coins in circulation. Responding to this shortage, in 1861, the U.S. Treasury introduced "fractional currency" or paper "coins." At the beginning of 1861, there were 250 million dollars in specie held in Northern banks. By the end of 1861, there were only 102 million dollars in specie in those banks, and that was to supposed to provide the lawful backing the 184 million dollars of Constitutional currency. It is easy to see that the 60 million unbacked demand notes (greenbacks) were turned into coin and strained the specie reserves and thus left the lawful currency without backing. So in 1861, Lincoln's new government suspended the specie redemption requirement.

The value of greenbacks continued to fluctuate wildly, in 1864, a greenback was only worth 40 cents in gold. As soon as greenbacks were introduced, people refused to accept them as money. The President and Congress had to adjust the new money to make it "acceptable." Congressman Spaulding introduced a bill in late 1861 that mandated acceptance of the greenbacks. The Congressional bill was called the "Legal Tender Act" which made it a law that you had to accept the fiat money, and thus made it "legal" tender, and "illegal" to refuse. With this law in place it also called upon the Treasury to issue $150 million more greenbacks. The Legal Tender Act is still in effect today, read your dollar: "This note is legal tender for all debts, public and private." This law went into effect in July 1862.

The Legal Tender Act raised public confidence enough that the Treasury sold $500 million in additional bonds which paid 6% interest, giving the North more money to fuel the war (or build railroads). This Act was accompanied by the creation of an Internal Revenue Act to enforce the newly created income tax. The first try failed, but in June of 1864, Congress passed the Internal Revenue Act which did take effect though it was a violation of the Constitution (Art. 1, Sec. 9, clause 4).

The Income tax proposed in July 1862, was a graduated income tax: 0% tax from $0-$600; 3% from $600-$10,000; and 5% on income over $10,000. It has often been said by those who seek the truth in history, that the graduated income tax is the U.S. Federal Government following one of the ten planks of the "Communist Manifesto," in which Karl Marx called for: "A heavy progressive or graduated income tax," (published in 1848). Before the war, Horace Greeley, who supported Lincoln in 1860, and had close affiliations with Salmon P. Chase, was editor of the New York Tribune and was publishing (and paying for) regular articles in his paper written by Karl Marx. Greeley was nominated for President in 1872 by the "Liberal Republicans" and also by the "Liberal Colored Republicans" and received 40% of the vote in 1872 against Grant.

The Legal Tender Act and the new income tax subtlety manipulated America toward economic centralization. The amount of power being assumed by the President and Congress brought up Constitutional questions that challenged their legal authority. Such questions were not brought up before the Supreme Court during the war, because Lincoln had declared martial law and emergency powers (which if valid, were only valid during the war). However Chief Justice Taney, who had dealt with bankers as Andrew Jackson's Secretary of the Treasury during the "bank wars" and who had been vocal against Lincoln's abuse of power in Baltimore, (Taney was from Maryland), had prepared a statement which discussed the problem at length. Supreme Court Chief Justice Taney's opinion (out of court) was that the Legal Tender Act was unconstitutional.

Taney's thoughts were that the Congressional power to "coin" money did not grant the power to "print" money. Nor did the "power to borrow" grant the power to force irredeemable notes on private creditors. Taney knew that the Constitutional Convention had specifically struck down any power of Congress to emit bills. Lincoln threatened to put Taney under house arrest. Unfortunately, Chief Justice Taney died in 1864 and was never called upon to decide the money issue after the war.

However, in 1862, the "money people" were scrambling to devise legislative tactics to circumvent Taney's Constitutional arguments. The total amount of greenbacks printed was $450 million, plus $50 million in unbacked "fractional currency," (paper coins). The money powers now needed to create yet another money system. It became obvious that the greenbacks did not receive strong endorsements from Chase or his supportive banking community. In 1863, Chase introduced a totally new banking system that the international bankers endorsed (and probably designed).

On February 25, 1863, Congress passed the National Currency Act. But still, Lincoln, Congress and Chase had to eventually face the Supreme Court about this new currency, and Chief Justice Taney's opinion was that legal tender was unconstitutional. They needed a legal foundation for their new national currency. Five months earlier, Lincoln had placed the entire nation under martial law (for various offenses) on September 24, 1862, but it did not meet Justice Taney's Constitutional criterion, Lincoln needed to partner-up with Congress to out maneuver the Judicial Branch. So, before the Treasury issued the new (unconstitutional) Treasury Notes, and only a week after passing the National Currency Act, Congress on March 3rd, passed two bills simultaneously: one, suspended the Writ of Habeas Corpus in every State (martial law), the other was an "emergency" financial bill to rescue the federal economy by issuing Treasury Notes. The "New Money" for Lincoln's New America was created out of a financial emergency.

The seditious nature of such legislation undermines America's economic foundation, especially when considering that these martial law changes were designed to extend beyond wartime. Paper money was not constitutional, so Lincoln and Congress, claiming powers under martial law, took America off of the Constitution to issue their bogus bucks. Martial law can only exist during times of war, and emergency powers can only govern during an emergency, and without a war or an emergency, such legislation is null and void. The Lincoln government abused its use of martial law in America and created permanent unconstitutional changes in American law and provided bankers with the mechanisms to centralize the American economy, which had been the bankers' goal since Hamilton.

Salmon P. Chase designed the Transfer of Power for American banks: the National Banking System, designed after the New York Free Banking System, where all New York based bank currencies had to be backed by government bonds (debt). The New York system was adopted by Chase to create a new national currency called "Treasury Notes" to be based on a national debt. These Treasury Notes were also branded with the "Legal Tender" provision which mandated their acceptance by the public. The new currency was based on government bonds. Government bonds mean government debt, so the money supply of Lincoln and Chase's New America was based upon a national debt. When people today complain that the Federal Government has a five trillion dollar national debt [1999], they should blame Lincoln and Chase for creating a debt currency.

There was a separate issue of currency in 1863 called Gold Certificates, which was backed 100% by gold deposits. Those certificates were not part of Chase's system of new money, but were a conservative hedge against the "trust me" money. They also filled a requirement of the money lenders; interest on government bonds was not to be paid in unbacked currencies but in gold backed dollars. The bankers gave America a debt money supply, yet they insisted (by law) to be paid their due interest in gold.

Because the new Treasury Notes were backed by government bonds it created a bond market to finance the war against the South (or the expansion of railroads). At this point, the North's economy was based upon destroying the South. It should be noted that the Union cost of the war in 1863 was as high as two and a half million dollars per day, and because the Northern economy was now based on war bonds, sales were brisk. The federal Treasury created over 2 billion 620 million dollars (of debt). That made the United States the greatest debtor nation in the world; in debt mostly to the bond buying bankers.

In the Transfer of Power that occurred in 1861, America sold her soul, and now we see to whom. And when people today cry about our "national debt" being over five trillion dollars, they must remember, our currency is based on debt and without that debt we have no economy (the Chase-New York Free Banking system). Our currency is always paying interest on the debt to those who hold government bonds, whether it is "ma and pa" or international bankers.

One of the most revealing examples of the many treasonous government-banker collusions can be observed in the relationship between the U.S. Secretary of the Treasury, Salmon P. Chase and the banking house of Jay Cooke. Chase an associate of Jay Cooke's brother, Henry, was lobbying in Washington for Jay Cooke's Philadelphia bank. It was through Cooke that Chase had secured the war loans in 1861, Cooke created a new banking firm at the exact time of these loans.

The international bankers lobbied for the new national currency because it promoted centralization of the economy, which always favors the giant banks. So in Chase's plan, approved by Congress, it specified, that the sale of government bonds had to be handled by a private bank, that bank was Chase's old friends at the Jay Cooke House. And for this service, Cooke would receive a modest 3/8 of 1% commission, which at first sounds reasonable. Well, in just one day, Cooke's bank sold $853 million in bonds which would provide a $3.2 million commission for one day's work. Some sources say that out of the $2.6 billion of bonds sold, that Cooke sold $2.5 billion which if handled at the same fee rate, would make Cooke's commission $9.3 million (in the 1860's).

After the 1863 National Currency collusion, Cooke needed somewhere to put his profits. So in 1864, Congress passed the second major railroad bill creating the Northern Pacific Railroad to run from Lake Superior to Puget Sound (Seattle). Jay Cooke helped finance this "internal improvement" and was able to become a railroad robber baron, being given millions of acres of land and money by Congress as mentioned earlier. Cooke hated Lincoln's successor, President Andrew Johnson and helped end Johnson's career in public service. Why? Because Johnson told it like it was, when he said: "The war of finance is the next war we must fight."

Jay Cooke bankrolled U.S. Grant for president in 1868 and 1872, after which Grant appointed two pro-railroad men to the Supreme Court. Cooke's fortune had its ups and downs because his financial empire was undermined by J.P. Morgan and the Kuhn Loeb (American-German) banking firm who were both acting as American agents for the British Rothschilds the richest banking family in the world. J.P. Morgan and Kuhn Loeb entered and eventually controlled the U.S. bond market and 90% of railroad ownership. Cooke financially collapsed in 1873 but due to his "insight" on a Congressional Act in 1872, which backed greenbacks 100% in gold to take effect in the year 1879, Cooke's bank hoarded the greenbacks which were discounted everywhere, and regained a fortune.

The National Banking Act
Monetary Centralization

The National Banking Act was made law on June 3, 1864. This Act gave a preference to "national" banks over "State" banks, it actually created a National Bank system. The Act required that State banks that wanted to use the "national currency" must deposit government bonds in the U.S. Treasury for which they would be given 90 to 100% of their value in the new National Bank Notes. This part of the new American currency scheme was to "bait" banks into the national system, and for them to abandon their State banking systems. Technically, the legal truth of the War of 1861, was that it was not a war between Northern States and Southern States, but a war between all of the States and the new central government. The National Banking Act was the Federal Government establishing its economic domination over the States.

The immediate result of the National Banking Act was the creation of 584 "national" banks in 1864. It would be modified (fine tuned) in later years, usually following tactical money supply panics. Having completed his banking tasks with the June 3, 1864 passage of the National Banking Act, Chase resigned as Lincoln's Secretary of the Treasury on June 30th, and started campaigning with Horace (Karl Marx) Greeley and Benjamin (spoons) Butler, each having Presidential aspirations to run against Lincoln.

Chase had run for party nomination against Lincoln in 1860, and again briefly in 1864, and again unsuccessfully against Grant in 1868. Lincoln appointed Chase as Supreme Court Chief Justice, after Taney's death in 1864. Salmon Chase's new mission, as Supreme Court Chief Justice and master manipulator, was to bring the Judicial Branch of the U.S. Government into the new "martial law" regime.

It was not mandatory for all State banks to join the National Banking system and naturally, some refused. The final death blow to State banks came with an Act of Congress in 1865, which took effect in July 1866. Congress put a 10% tax on all State banks. Notice, this was not a tax only on Southern State banks but on all State banks. A 10% tax on a bank makes it non-competitive. The tragic results of this (postwar) economic centralization can best be observed with a look at the numbers:

National banks		State Banks
1860..............	0	1,562
1866.........	1,582	297

The spin-historians and the best economic experts money can buy all say that this was good news: Chase was the father of the American banking system, but this system isn't new, it's older that Babylon. It is the same banking system that has conquered all of history's pilgrims who fled out of the many collapsed Babylon's of the past whether it was Babylon, Mesopotamia, Persia, Greece, Rome, Europe, or Britain and now it is America. Only one empire can remain: Globalism, Babylon the Great! Chase, under the guidance of international bankers brought America into an economic system that must expand until it bursts. Chase later realized his mistake and admitted it; Chase:

"The greatest financial mistake of my life was in what I had to do with the passage of the present National Bank Act. It ought to be repealed...."

The National Banking system of 1864 continued basically unchanged until 1914, when the bankers concluded that enough time had passed since the days when Andrew Jackson exposed their fraudulent monetary system, and it was time to reinvent the central bank. The Federal Reserve System (FED) was superimposed on top of Chase's National Bank System. This revised system was designed by the German born banker, Paul Warburg who was part of the European Rothschild-Warburg international banking cartel. The Rothschilds had financed the mutual destruction of the North and South in the War of 1861, and in 1914 along with a few other international bankers took complete charge of our Federal Reserve Bank and by 1935, the FED controlled America's monetary policy.

National Banks created under the Chase system were forced to become members of the FED by buying FED stock equal to 3% of their capital and assets. In return, the FED had to buy their National Bank notes from the member banks and had to buy their government bonds which had been used as security for those notes. The international bankers used the National banks' own assets to control them. The FED was a private non-governmental system. Eventually, the currency changed from National Bank notes to Federal Reserve notes. And then to eliminate the remaining independent banks who would not join the FED but could use National Bank currency because they could back that paper with "securities" (deemed lawful some years earlier), Congress insisted that all banks back their currency 100% with gold.

This conquered the remaining National Banks into the Federal Reserve System, and with gold outlawed in 1933, and American currency taken off its gold backing completely, the previous system could never unseat the architects of the FED: the Rothschild, Warburg, Kuhn-Loeb, J.P Morgan, Rockefeller international banking cartel.

After making gold deposits mandatory for all banks, and after all independent banks capitulated, President Roosevelt relieved the FED of the unprofitable necessity of backing its notes with gold. This occurred in 1933 when President Franklin Roosevelt followed Lincoln's lead and declared an "economic emergency."

Roosevelt initiated the Emergency Banking Act on March 9th; and by June 5, America was completely off of the gold standard. All gold, gold certificate currencies, and amounts of gold or silver coins in excess of $100 was confiscated (redeemed for FED notes). The "endangered specie" was now extinct. Congress and the FED had no intention of staying on the gold backed money system, except to back the U.S. dollar with gold for the international central banks. Roosevelt and the FED used the confiscated gold to establish the U.S. dollar as a world currency. So after all of the dust settled, America had one private internationally controlled central bank printing "paper" without any specie backing, and Congress forced it on America as "Legal Tender."

Benjamin Franklin:

"The inability of the colonists to get the power to issue their own money out of the hands of George III and the international bankers, was the prime reason for the Revolutionary War."

Chapter 4

1861
The Union "Blue-Coats"
Invade
The Indian Nations

Think of the logic: In 1861, when the bankers and industrialists began their plan to use the 20 million people of the North in a war against the 7 million people of the South, to confiscate their 465 million acres, why not also use the same federal army to conquer the 250,000 Indians between the Mississippi River and the Rocky Mountains and confiscate their land too, over one billion acres?

First consider some relevant historical background. Before the "White-eyes" came to America, Indians tribes would war against each other. The members of the losing tribes often became slaves; the winners became their "masters," the victors also took their land if they wanted it. That was the law in America before Jamestown. So next, the "White-eyes" showed up on the shores of America and a contest between the two cultures led to cultural conflicts. The Europeans defeated the Indian and settled the land, but also, in the European tradition, the "White-eyes" made treaties with their adversaries.

During the Revolutionary War, the former British colonies became independent nation-states. The Indians living within each respective State fell under the jurisdiction of that sovereign nation-state; this was before the "United States" but after the Revolution. Those nation-states entered into a mutual compact called the U.S. Constitution. Under that Constitution, the national government was prohibited from dividing an existing State for the purpose of creating another State without that State's permission (Art. 4, Sec. 3, cl. 1).

After the States united, some of the Cherokees in the South intermarried with the Whites. Their children were taught both worlds, including the English world of written law. Some of those educated English-Cherokee sought to rescue their Indian parents from the cultural conflict caused by living in, and being controlled by, the legal jurisdictions of the States. Attempting to preserve their culture using the "new" European rule of law, they held a Cherokee Constitutional Convention and wrote a Constitution. Then they sought the assistance of the federal government for permission to become a separate nation within the southern State of Georgia.

President Andrew Jackson brought this issue forward before Congress in 1829. He admitted that his hands were tied by the Constitution: "that no new State shall be formed or erected within the jurisdiction of any other State ... " without that State's consent (and the consent of Congress). Jackson asked if anything could be done to "preserve this much injured race?" Jackson made a proposal to Congress:

"As a means of effecting this end. I suggest, for your consideration, the propriety of setting apart an ample district west of the Mississippi ... to be guarantied to the Indian tribes, as long as they shall occupy it: each tribe having a distinct control over the portion designated for its use. There they may be secured in the enjoyment of governments of their own choice, subject to no other control from the United States ... "

Congress passed such an Act and provided $500,000 to help with the transition. Jackson insisted that the move be voluntary, with a warning that those who remained in any State would be subject to the laws of that State. The Congressional Act included this statement:

"The United States will forever secure and guarantee to them, and their heirs or successors the country so exchanged with them."

There is "The Great Promise" made by the pre-1861 United States Government. This treaty did not put the Indians on a "reservation," it created sovereign Indian nations. The nations were to be located west of the Mississippi River and not in any existing State. The location for the new Indian Nations was the area now known as Oklahoma, Nebraska, and Kansas. The Jackson Administration was fair to the Indian Nations and respected their separate cultures. The Cherokee tribe, with 17,367 total population, received 13 million acres, which equals 748 acres per person. The Osages, with a population of 5,000 received 7,564,000 acres, which equals 1,512 acres per Indian. The average amount of land granted to the other relocated "eastern tribes" equaled about 1000 acres per man, woman or child. In the Indian culture, the ownership of land was tribal, not individual. The lands, west of the Mississippi obtained for the relocation of the eastern tribes were lands obtained through the recognized owners as transferred through negotiations with the western tribes, who preferred living on their lands further north.

The western Indian nations shared the land from Texas to Canada, and from the States along the Mississippi to the Rocky Mountains. Basically, it was the Louisiana Purchase which was the land that Jefferson bought from the French so that the U.S. could deny any French claim to the land, yet continue to allow its original owners, the Indian Nations, to keep it; it was theirs! The French did not "own" that land, they could only claim that it was their land; and Jefferson's Louisiana Purchase paid to settle that claim. That Indian preserve, which was home to 250,000 Indians, including the relocated ones, equaled about the same amount of land that was home to 28 million "White eyes" (counting slaves). This means that the average land held per American Indian was 3,000 acres, while the average land held by European Americans was only about 33 acres per person. Establishment history refers to this "relocation" of the Cherokee as the "Trail of Tears" but considering that those Indians received 100 times more land than the "White eyes" it could be said that the pre-1861 U.S. Government was very fair to the eastern and western American Indians prior to 1861, and prior to Lincoln.

There were some individuals and even some groups who crossed the western Indian lands, some as early as the 1830's. They were the settlers going to Oregon and California, but they were just passing through, often paying the Indians for passage rights. The federal government attempted to help the Indians establish their tribal boundaries on maps so that the settlers would know which tribe controlled which western route. The federal government even negotiated with tribes to place Army forts along the pilgrim trails; these way-stations were granted by the Indian Nations. There was no attempt by the pre-1861 U.S. Government to steal Indian lands.

The Mormons crossed the Indian preserve to Utah in 1846 followed by the federal army that went to Utah to control the Mormons. It was impossible for the U.S. Government to stop free individual Americans from going west. That would have been like trying to prevent a person from traveling anywhere else in the "unknown" world. In 1859, gold was discovered in Colorado, and although individual prospectors violated the Indian national boundaries, it was not a government policy to violate Indian lands.

In 1819 Congress had authorized the President to provide services to the Indians to "prevent their extinction." In 1834, Congress created the "Bureau of Indian Affairs." In 1849, Congress created the "Interior Department" and placed the Bureau of Indian Affairs in that Department.

Indian history, as presented by Indians, records that the unceasing military attempts of genocide against the Indian Nations came from the "Blue-Coats" beginning in 1861. It was Lincoln's government that shared the "Indian relations" of the Interior Department with the War Department. The new, martial law, national government used the War of 1861 to invade the Indian Nations and void the Congressional promise of sovereignty.

Indians and Negroes today have been taught to hate the White man and to blame their past and present unfortunate status on a "race," the White Race. The real shame is that those two peoples will never solve their "hate" problem nor receive any social justice until they realize that it was not the "White man" to blame for their present sorrows; it was bankers and corporations. And notice regarding today's media-spin-history that it is the giant corporations that pay for the television portrayals of Indians and Negroes being the victims of the "White man," whether it is "Public T.V." or "Hollywood." But in real life, shouldn't the oppressor be identifiable by his accumulation of wealth? Blame your stolen heritage on wealthy corporations; not on persons of White.

In the Transfer of Power of 1861, corporate America bribed, bought and choreographed the White House and Congress. Their military-monetary strategy was to conquer the South and the West. The prize for corporate America in the West was an economic bonanza which included gold and silver discoveries, Northern routes for transcontinental railroads, land sales and home mortgages, mining, and new business loans. There were only two obstacles in their way: the Confederacy and the Indian Nations. The unfettered capitalists needed a plan to circumvent the Indians' deed to the land; that "deed" was the promise of lands given by the pre-1861 U.S. Government to "forever secure and guaranty to them, and their heirs." Violating Indian treaties was no harder for the post-1861 Federal Government that was their destruction of the U.S. Constitution.

Corporate America made sure that the South was set up for the fall, and the Confederacy was doomed from the beginning. It was a double bonus for the industrialists to use the same Army during the same years to destroy the Southern State governments and begin the longer war against the Indian Nations. How?

Albert Pike, a member of a secret society called the Illuminati, moved from Massachusetts, the Northern State where much of the secession was planned, which - no coincidence - was also the origin of the radical abolitionist movement. Pike, as per plan, moved to Arkansas in an attempt to get that State to secede from the Union. When the war between the States broke out, Pike was able to get the Creek, Cherokee, Chickasaw, Seminole, and the Choctaw Indians to raise an army of 3,500 to fight on the side of the Confederacy.

The Confederacy (proper) did not trick the Indian Nations to enter into their war against the North, it was a plan out of Massachusetts, a plan of conspirators like Pike. This agreement between Pike's Indian soldiers and the Confederacy "fortuitously" violated the earlier agreement with the "Great White Father" in Washington. Pike lead the Indians in the first battle west of the Mississippi. In fact, when the Confederate Army Command asked General Pike to bring the Indians into the States, Pike refused and resigned, after only one year of service. His assignment was complete; he raised an Indian army against the North, which gave the North an excuse to void all treaties holding all those Indian lands.

It was more natural for the Indian tribes to side with the South than with the North because the South respected cultural sovereignty. On the very first day of the Confederacy, the Choctaws declared their loyalty to the C.S.A. While the South made friends with the Indians in 1861, the northern industrialists began scouting the western frontier for that northern railroad route proposed in the Senate years earlier. The Indians were allies with the South until the end, in fact, even though Lee surrendered on April 9, 1865, the last sizable Confederate force to surrender was on June 23, with the surrender of a Confederate-Cherokee battalion under Brigadier General Stand Watie. [The last Confederate force to lower the flag (and stop attacking ships) was the CSS Shenandoah on November 6, 1865. Bad news travels slowly at sea.]

The Cherokee flag was identical to the eleven star Confederate

National Flag (not Battle flag) except that in the center of the Confederate stars were five red stars, to represent the Five Civilized Indian Nations, as they were called. Even Indians who chose not to relocate to the Oklahoma Indian Territory served in the Confederate Army. Two Army Companies of the 69th North Carolina were Cherokee Indians from the Carolina Mountains.

There were other western tribes who avoided entering the war on either side. In 1862, as the nation tore itself apart with war, Congress chartered the railroads to begin efforts to unite Atlantic railroads with Pacific railroads. The first charter began laying rails west from Nebraska and expanding the system within Kansas. By 1863, Buffalo Bill was serving in the Union cavalry fighting the Kiowa and Comanche Indians, who just happen to be located right in the proposed route of the Union Pacific railroad. The Union Army protected the Union Pacific rails. The more Indians that could be tricked into the war, the more treaties could be voided, with more profits to be had.

Some Indians were living nowhere near the Confederacy and only wanted peace. The Sioux and the Dakota Nations were located in the Dakotas and Minnesota area. The more-northern railroad that Congress chartered was Jay Cooke's Northern Pacific, which was to run from Puget Sound (Seattle) to Lake Superior Minnesota, Indian land. That spells Indian trouble. Although Congress didn't finalize the deal with Northern Pacific until 1864, the Union Pacific Act in 1862 gave the green light for the Northern Pacific rail system. The railroad scouts surveyed the Indian territories and chose the land they wanted to be "granted." As the railroad gangs headed west, they killed the Buffalo, destroying the food source of the Sioux and Dakota tribes who struck back beginning in August of 1862.

In September of 1862, the Sioux and the Dakota tribes went on the "warpath" killing 450 and capturing 550. That was very "fortuitous" for the industrialists in solving any "treaty" problems. In fact, they used the same technique over and over again: pushing the Indians until they struck back then reacting with genocide. It was the railroads that encouraged the settlers to move west to "push" the Indians off their lands. As a result of the 1862 "unprovoked" Indian massacre, Lincoln, the master of American martial law, ordered the execution of 38 captured Indians. The hangings took place in Mankato, Minnesota on December 26, 1862. It is the largest execution in American history (so far).

When the War of 1861 finally ended, the "Five Civilized Tribes" that sided with the Confederacy lost their long-standing treaty made by the Andrew Jackson Administration. The new Federal Government gave the Indians what they gave the South: a Transfer of Power, that is, all power is transferred to the Federal Government. There can be no pretense that this was fair; the Indians were fighting on their land, and of course, the entire War of 1861, South or West, was a set up. Remember the guarantee of the Congressional Treaty proposed by President Andrew Jackson in which it promised:

"The United States will forever secure and guarantee to them, and their heirs or successors the country so exchanged with them."

The new Federal Government provided those heirs with a new treaty, they had to relinquish half of their land. Some of their land was used by the Federal Government to relocate postwar Indians from all over the West, from wherever they were "in the way." This was the birth of America's new "reservation" system, not sovereign nations as before the War of 1861, but only reservations. The remaining portions of their promised-to-be-perpetual lands were given away in the Oklahoma land rush in 1889. There were many treaties with many tribes, some fared better than others; sometimes monies changed hands to make it look proper and those who benefitted, looked the other way.

One of the most disgusting elements of the War of 1861 was that when it ended in 1865, it really didn't end. The undeclared war of martial law powers continued against the South and against the Indians. It just changed tactics, from military destruction to military occupation, from martial law to martial law rule. In 1867, Congress created an Indian Peace Commission (double-speak 1867). They placed General Sherman and General Terry as the senior military advisors on this "peace" commission.

Union General William Tecumseh Sherman had some experience with "peace negotiations" during the war in the South such as his famous "March to the Sea" campaign in May 1864. In Sherman's memoirs he describes his method of peace:

"One hundred million dollars of damage has been done to Georgia; Twenty-million dollars injured to our benefit, the remainder simply waste and destruction."

Sherman took 100,000 Union soldiers and destroyed everything from Tennessee to the Atlantic Ocean (through Georgia). His theory for peace can be summed up in his words to General Grant in January, 1865:

"We are not fighting against an enemy army, but against an enemy people; both young and old, rich and poor must feel the iron hand of war in the same way as the organized armies. In this respect my march through Georgia was a wonderful success."

Nothing describes genocide any better than that statement. Sherman had deliberately turned his Union Army into a band of murderers and rioting thieves. After his burning march reached the sea in Georgia, he turned his locust army northward, of which he remarked:

"The whole army is burning with an insatiable desire to wreak violence upon South Carolina. I almost tremble for her fate."

General Sherman is found at the bottom of that odious barrel of war criminals. Yet, remaining in the competition of bottom dwellers is General Grant who said that the "rebellion" can only end by:

"the complete subjugation of the South ... by destroying their means of subsistence, withdrawing their means of cultivating their fields, and in every way possible."

The destruction of the subsistence of the entire Southern population would be nothing short of genocide. Sherman believed that he was fighting against a "people." Perhaps he had not heard of America's "rule by the consent of the people." The "government by the People" dream died in 1861, or at least by 1865. It was this genocidal maniac, General Sherman, who was chosen for the Indian Peace Commission because his "peace initiative" for the South revealed the possible solution for the Indian nations. Sherman's Southern plan:

"Until we can repopulate Georgia, it is useless to occupy it, but the utter destruction of its roads, houses, and people will cripple their military resources ... I can make the march, and make Georgia howl."

Another statement showing Sherman's "peace process" for Southerners was in his letter to his fellow war criminal, Secretary of War Edwin M. Stanton, in which Sherman wrote:

"There is a class of people, men, women and children, who must be killed or banished before you can hope for peace and order."

The Sherman Peace Process: kill men, women and children! Peace? Sherman was a shining example of New America's man of peace, and that is why he was chosen to lead the new military wing of the "Indian Peace Commission." That explains why the Federal Government's "final solution" for the Indians resembled their "final solution" for the South.

Also inserted into this benevolent chain of command, below Sherman and above Terry was Union General Sheridan. Sheridan's human rights mentality was a perfect fit for the Peace Commission as expressed in his official report describing his campaign against the people of Virginia:

"I have burned two thousand barns filled with wheat and corn, all the mills in the whole country, destroyed all the factories of cloth, killed or driven off every animal, even the poultry that could contribute to human sustenance. Nothing should be left in the Shenandoah but eyes to lament the war."

After the war against the South, Sheridan was moved to make peace with the Indians. The Union Army savages roamed free while men of honor were locked up like animals; men such as Constitutional scholar Jefferson Davis. Compare Davis' directive for warfare engaged by the Confederate Army while within Northern battle areas, a directive from a code of honor that he learned while attending West Point. President Jefferson Davis instructed his soldiers:

"The rules taught at West Point were: 'Private property can be seized only by way of military necessity for the support or benefit of the Army of the United States. All wanton violence, pillage or sacking, maiming or killing is prohibited under the penalty of death or punishment adequate for the gravity of the offense."

Was that just talk? It was not just talk according to Charles Francis Adams, son of President John Quincey Adams and Lincoln's Minister to Britain during the war who stated:

"I doubt if a hostile foe ever advanced in an enemy's country or fell back from it in retreat leaving behind it less cause for hate and bitterness than did the Army of Northern Virginia."

When the war ended, Indian fighter Buffalo Bill left the Army and in 1867 went to work for the Kansas Pacific Railroad, who happen to be laying tracks over the dead bodies of the Kiowa and Comanche Indians that Cody killed during the war. What was William Cody's job with the railroad? Killing buffalo. The railroad plan came right out of the play-book of the Sherman and Grant peace plans for the South: conquer "by destroying their means of subsistence." It may be hard to tell if Sherman's policy of genocide was being carried out by the industrialists or vise versa.

The Kansas Pacific Railroad was the "NGO" of its time, a non-government organization used to perform the "non-military" removal of the Indian's means of subsistence: the buffalo. Their policy of killing buffalo to achieve the genocide of the Indian Nations, making Indians dependent on the Federal Government, took years to achieve. The pre-1861 buffalo population was in the millions, but by 1884, that population was reduced down to a couple of hundred. What a success, the food source was gone. The Federal Government could then safely step in to supply the Indians with the three "B"s: booze, blankets and beans. The Indians soon learned to "know their place" and stay on the reservation and beg the "Great Federal Father" in Washington when they needed something.

General Sherman advised his Peace Commission to stop making treaties with the Indians. By that time, there were over 370 treaties with Indian Nations. By 1871, the government had placed the Indians on more further removed, more remote reservations. New America had set up schools where Indian children, taken from their parents, were forced to speak English. Indian dress and Indian dance were outlawed on all reservations. The Federal Government destroyed America's "natural diversity" as fast as it could. [Historians-for-hire could rewrite that later and blame the White-eyes.] Churches would lobby Congress for franchises over Indian reservations which granted exclusive "religious territorial rights" to specific churches be they Catholic, Lutheran, Methodist, or Episcopalian. If the government delegated a Catholic priest to a tribe, then that tribe would be Catholic.

Next the railroads started negotiations with the Indians which brought in a new wave of deceit and fraud. One railroad acquired 800,000 acres of Cherokee land in a rip-off that the Governor of Kansas called "a cheat and a fraud in every particular." The railroad then turned around and sold the very same land to White settlers for a sinful profit. On one occasion, the U.S. Secretary of the Interior had to step in to prevent the sale of 8 million acres of Indian land to the railroad for 20 cents an acre. Previously, Indians had not individually owned land, and so the sale of land was a foreign idea.

Next consider the fate of George Armstrong Custer. Custer was more of a soldier than a bona fide war criminal. He graduated from West Point one month after the War of 1861 began. By 1863, at age 23, he was America's youngest General. It was Custer who cut off Lee's retreat from Appomattox and accepted Lee's surrender flag (a towel). Some Southerners consider all "Union" officers who led troops against the South as war criminals; but as war criminals go, Custer falls into the lesser category of soldiers who thought they are doing their job. Custer was not to be counted among those Union generals who hated an entire people.

When the war ended, Custer, like so many others, was reduced in rank. In 1866, as an army captain, he was sent to Kansas where he was courtmartialled and kicked out of the service for a year. During that time he went to Mexico and fought for Benito Juarez. Generals Sherman and Terry were chosen as the senior military advisors in the Indian Peace Commission in 1867, which allowed Custer to return to Kansas for duty in the army. Custer's regiment guarded the surveyors of the Northern Pacific Railroad, war financier Jay Cooke's railroad.

U.S. Grant was still General of the Army in 1867, but he had presidential aspirations. He was preparing to run for President of the United States in the 1868 election and Jay Cooke was his financial advocate, which translated means: the railroads had to be protected by Grant's Union army. When Grant became President, he appointed William T. Sherman as his General-in-Chief replacement. Sherman was stationed in St. Louis, to be closer to the Indians. On May 10, 1869, the union of the eastern and western railroads finally drove the connecting "Golden Spike" at Promontory Utah.

The next thing to go wrong for the Indians was that gold was discovered in the Black Hills of Dakota in 1875. The Black Hills were sacred to the Sioux and the Cheyenne. The government had promised that the Indians' possession of the Black Hills would be inviolate. But that was before gold was discovered. The Sioux and Cheyenne were confined to smaller and smaller reservations (which they could not leave). However, both tribes did leave the reservation for Montana.

General Terry, from the Indian Peace Commission, serving under Sherman, sent a message to Sitting Bull (and Crazy Horse). It was dead winter, 40 degrees below zero. Terry's message ordered Sitting Bull to return to the reservation by January 1st, (1876) or "I'll come looking for you." Well, Sitting Bull remained seated, he didn't run, and Crazy Horse was probably the bravest Indian that ever lived. This created another timely and fortuitous "irrepressible conflict."

Meanwhile, back to the fate of Custer. From 1867 to 1876, Custer was an Indian fighter and during the early seventies, he wrote his memoirs. Politically, soldiers should be seen and not heard. The railroad's plan for America's future had no room for compassion of, or respect for the Indians (that would come after the deed changed hands). Custer's memoirs, written in 1874 and '75, contained comments that could indict or at least embarrass the powers-that-be. Custer wrote:

"If I were an Indian, I would certainly prefer to cast my lot ... to the free open plains rather than submit to the confined limits of a reservation."

The railroads were not yet finished robbing Indian lands so there could be no compassion for the Indians yet, particularly from a cavalry soldier and Indian fighter. Custer's candid writings were a public relations set-back and would simply not go away.

Spring, 1876, Sitting Bull's deadline had come and gone. Who could General Terry send into the Big Horn area against thousands of defiant Indians? It was that same year, when the Indians had finally realized they must unite against the Blue-Coats if they were to ever regain their liberty. The Indian Nations joined forces. False rumors circulated about horrible Indian massacres in an attempt to garner public support for the necessary end game of genocide. The "Peace Commission" knew that if the Indians ever inflicted a real massacre, with the correct media coverage, the Indian Nations would be doomed.

Spring, 1876, Colonel Custer became involved with a criminal investigation. The army awarded contracts for post trader franchises, like today's army "PX" (post exchange). Members of President Grant's family were implicated in the sale or leasing of these franchises. Colonel Custer was an outspoken critic of the Grant Administration. In fact, Custer had been a supporter of former President, and Southern Democrat, Andrew Johnson. Colonel Custer testified before committees in Washington D.C. about the franchises; his testimony implicated members of President Grant's family. Grant ordered his removal from the service. But, for political reasons, that did not happen.

There were certain other anonymous "military authorities" who advised Grant to take a different course of action to handle Custer. From the top down, Custer's chain of command basically goes like this: President Grant; General-in-Chief Sherman, of the Indian Peace Commission; General Sheridan, Grant's other General at Appomattox; and Brigadier General Alfred Terry, also of the Indian Peace Commission. The events that followed shed some light on the mystery of Custer's Last Stand.

After the hearings in Washington D.C., Custer's commander, General Sheridan gave Custer the field command of the 7th Cavalry. He was sent to serve under General Terry who had stirred up a hornet's nest of Indians in Montana with his back-to-the-reservation ultimatums. Scouting for the Army to find the location of the Cheyenne was Indian fighter Buffalo Bill Cody, who, that same year, had killed the son of the Cheyenne Chief.

Colonel Custer had located an encampment of Indians at the Little Big Horn in Montana. At a safe distance back, General Terry ordered a Regiment of 650 men, to split into three columns; Custer leading 225 (some say 265) men toward Little Big Horn. General Terry was to catch up with him two days later. On June 25, 1876, Custer's 225 man column encountered 2,500 warriors, Custer and all of those soldiers were killed. There could have been more details of this tragedy but the official records vanished.

The massacre of Custer's column was the much needed "Fort Sumter" justification to eliminate the Indians from the railroad's empire. Crazy Horse had opposed the corporate attempt to "civilize" the Indians. He said that surrender by the Indians meant the doom of his race. After the Little Big Horn battle, Crazy Horse and his Braves were hunted men. And in January of 1877, Army Colonel Miles tracked down and killed Crazy Horse and the remnants of the Indian dream. The year 1877 marks the end of any hopes that the Indians had for preserving their culture. It also marks the year that the Federal Government lifted martial law in the Southern States. The War of 1861, was two wars, a war against the Southern States and a war against the Indian Nations. Martial law (military rule over civilians) lasted 16 years and the price that the Indians and the Southerners paid to be part of this glorious "Union" was their cultural genocide.

In 1871, an Act of Congress took Sherman's advice about not making any more treaties that recognized any Indian Nations; the law read:

"No Indian nation ... shall be recognized as an independent nation, tribe or power with whom the U.S. may contract by treaty."

In 1885, Congress passed the "Major Crimes Act" which imposed federal jurisdiction over all Indian reservations.

In 1887, the Dawes Act partitioned the reservations into 160 acre tracts divided up between individual Indians, who being tribal in culture, did not fully grasp the notion of private land ownership. Many sold their land to railroads and land speculators who turned around and sold it to incoming settlers making great profits. This finally left the American Indians "homeless."

In 1968, the Indians finally became part of America's great "assimilative community" under the Civil Rights Act. The sad irony is that the corporate powers which took the lands, livelihood and freedom from the Ikcewicasa (Natural Man), are the same corporate powers financing the teaching of today's Indian to hate the racist White man. Let not the

Indian forget that the Indian and the Grey-Coats both fought and lost to the corporate-banker financed Blue-Coats. Will we remain forever defeated?

When people sit back and watch the forging of their chains, yet discern it not, they have likely been taught to accept a myth about their past and sadly do not know their own history. America has two histories: Easy (corporate governmental) History, and Rare (patriot preserved) History.

The Easy History is the one you can easily find by turning on the television. Easy History is the one we were taught in school at no charge. Easy History is funded by large corporations and the government to put their spin on history. Easy History is the history that portrays all non-White cultures as victims of the White race, teaching that the White race has destroyed the "Edens" of all other cultures. Easy History is a curriculum designed to insight other cultures to dismantle and destroy the greatest threat to the corporate empire: Western Patriots.

The Rare History must be sought out. You must seek it. It is not financed by the wealthy; it is not taught in the schools, and it will rarely if ever be seen or heard on television. There are "secrets" within the rare history, without which, your conclusions about history will be erroneous, sometimes with dire results.

Because you have sought out THIS rare book, which will not be found in your local library, please continue reading, to review as much of this Rare History as these pages allow. The secrets of history require you to penetrate into the shadows and behind the closed doors in order to give you a glimpse into the "inner circles" of people and organizations who precipitated the War of 1861. You cannot fully understand the War of 1861 until you understand the men of mystery operating in their illusive world of intrigue.

Chapter 5

Intrigue
The International Enemy

The United States of America was 72 years old when it died in 1861. The individual States themselves were slightly older when they died. Virginia became a nation in June, 1776, and so the State of Virginia was 89 years old when it was conquered in 1865. The age of these systems were young compared to the earlier European models, some of which had survived through centuries. By 1860, most of those European nations had fallen from their long lived governance. Europe had fallen victim to certain ancient political and religious rivalries that bitterly fought through the centuries. America's War of 1861 was, in part, a spill-over of those ancient European rivalries.

America's experiment in democracy was new to the world. It was based on the noble idea that men should be self-governed by a body of laws that they-themselves created; a government of principle, by a consent of the majority. However, democracy has at least two serious flaws.

One flaw is that the election process quickly fell under the control of political parties. Proponents of political parties claim that they too are "representative" of the people and thus a natural intermediary of democracy. However, because political parties are themselves corporations whose main goal is self-perpetuation, the "will of the people" takes a backseat to political brokering. Included within this organizational flaw is the fact that the public's political opinion is shaped by a corporate media. This flaw puts the leadership and direction of the "peoples' government" under the control of a small clique of self-perpetuating media, political, and lobbying corporations.

The second flaw is that elected officials only serve a two, four or six year term of office. Some people today advocate going to limited terms of office. Short, or limited terms of office would be helpful in purging harmful politicians (though in practice, this falls short). The flaw of having short or limited term elected officials is when you do get good honest ones in office, they cannot employ an agenda long enough to counter the ill effects of the private, perpetual "ancient rivalries" which brought down the governments of Europe. A limited two year Congressman would hardly have the time to safeguard America's freedom against the dynastic political-religious intrigue coming out of Europe.

There are four categories of European political-religious power groups. Sometimes they scheme together and sometimes against each other. It is essential to understand the international intrigue surrounding America's War of 1861. The four categories of ancient rivalries are: The Church of Rome, usually to include the Jesuits; Cabalistic Judaism; European Dynasties, whether monarchies or banking families; and Secret Societies.

The following indictment of these four categories of occult political agencies is in no way an indictment of all Catholics, Jews, Kings or members of fraternal organizations. When this book over-simplifies these groups by referring to them as "Jews" or "Catholics" etc. it is because that is how they are referred to in written history. Yet when taken in its most accurate reality, this review will be referring to specific persons who have hidden themselves within these groups, and these groups did offer them cover.

The Dynasties of Europe were involved with the War of 1861, but were not the master of America's fate. Queen Victoria was sitting on Britain's throne during the War of 1861, and agents of her government were heavily involved with the war, but the connections to the Queen were keep low profile. The British Dynasty, as a true sovereign power, for all intents and purposes had already fallen with the severed head of King Charles in the days of Cromwell; the English-British monarchy never fully regained its former status as a true sovereign.

The Royal Dynasty that had retained its sovereignty up to and beyond 1861 was the Russian Dynasty, the Czars of which were related to the British Dynasty. During the American War of 1861, the Czar sent two fleets of ships to the American coasts to restrain any unwanted European interference in the American war. The Czar, friendly to America, was well aware that the ancient power-hungry European rivalries had their lustful eyes on America. The Czar wanted to prevent the occult powers from conquering America the way they conquered Europe by 1815 (and who later conquered Russia in 1917).

Cabalistic Judaism was composed of certain international radicals operating out of Jewish communities throughout Europe. These

Jewish radicals followed an ancient text called the Cabala (or Kabbalah), they were part of the occult forces behind the French Revolution, and the specific influence that the Czar was trying to keep out of America. Their Cabalistic powers included the control of banking, medicine, and occult religion. The Cabalistic agenda followed an ancient plan for world domination. These so-called "Jews" did not control a nation of their own but were scattered throughout many nations. Their "internationalism" enabled them to use one nation against another, their banking abilities allowed them to finance wars or revolutions to install new Kings who would implement Cabalistic policies designed to amalgamate sovereign nations into a one world government; or overthrow monarchies and install republics.

The Church of Rome had been the religious foundation sanctifying the monarchs of Europe and sharing their power. For a thousand years, from Charlemagne to Louis XVI, the Pope crowned the Kings of Europe. From the year 800 to the year 1500, the Pope was in equal standing to any King of Europe. But when the Cabalistic "Jews" financially backed the Protestant movements started by Martin Luther (1517) and John Calvin around 1533, it became an irreversible downhill slide for the Church of Rome. Martin Luther, a good an honest Christian, learned of the Jews' motives to gain power by creating religious divisions and wrote a polemic against them.

The Amsterdam banking Jews benefitted most by the Protestant movement in Northern Europe because the Church of Rome prohibited lending money at interest, and wherever the Church was allied with the Kings of Europe, there could be no usury. The Cabalistic French Revolution of 1789 destroyed France, the most powerful Catholic nation in Europe. The revolutionary government confiscated all church properties and used its value to back a new currency. These and other actions including the Napoleonic Wars finally placed the Vatican in check; and by 1861, the writing was on the wall.

The Society of Jesus, (the Jesuits) is a "Catholic" society of militant priests. It would be incorrect to say that the Jesuits are one-and-the-same with the Catholic Church. It is critical that you know the difference in order to understand the role that the Jesuits played in America's War of 1861. In matters of intrigue, the Jesuits must be considered a secret society within the Catholic Church but operating against the traditional Catholic Church.

The Jesuits were started in 1534 by Ignatius Loyola, who was accused by a Church commission seven years earlier of being a member of the Alombrados, a lesser Spanish version of the Illuminati. The Illuminati secret societies advocated a world government and were anti-Catholic. The rise of Luther in Germany, and Calvin in Switzerland, provoked the misinformed Pope to sanction the Jesuits as a military wing of the Catholic Church to counter the Protestant movement.

The first major project of the militant Jesuits was the Thirty Years War, deceptively enacted as a war of Protestant verses so-called Catholic but the protracted war was actually a war to divide Northern Europe religiously and economically from Vatican dominated Southern Europe. Their war killed half of the German population. The grotesque level of destruction put upon Germany in this European war was inflicted upon America over three hundred years later by the same competing forces of European intrigue.

The fourth group among these ancient rivals also operated as a secret society: the Masons. There are today, Confederate organizations that are heavy laden with Masons in their ranks, and with this book being mostly pro-Confederate, it might make popular-sense to delete the Masonic role in the War of 1861, but truth is the best servant of history. Patrick Henry, George Mason, Andrew Jackson, and Jefferson Davis, four of the greatest Americans that ever lived devoted their lives to the truth. That devotion must continue today. The Masons are, and have been for hundreds of years, an organization of talented and intelligent men, and being such, they were infiltrated by occult forces and used to obtain political power; first in Europe then in America.

When the Jewish bankers of Holland dethroned the last real King of England, Charles I, in 1649, they moved their center of operations from Amsterdam to England. From 1717 to 1789, the Cabalists in Britain and Europe infiltrated fraternal Masonry to influence the Anglo-Saxon powers that controlled all of Europe and particularly France. France was the "superpower" of Europe at that time, but France was Catholic. The French Revolution was a battle between the two teams of ancient rivals, the Jewish Cabalists allied with the Masons, verses the French Monarch allied with the Catholic Church. With the beheading of Louis XVI in 1793, the Cabalists and Masons won France. It is obvious that the motto of the French Revolution is also the motto of the Masons: Liberty, Equality, and Fraternity.

With the fall of the French Monarchy, Vatican influence was finally removed from Northern Europe. With France out of the way, the Jewish-Masonic co-op set out to establish "Republics" throughout Europe during the mid-1800's. These ancient rivals next turned their eyes to America. The monarchs are of little concern by 1861, and the Vatican is all but a memory, except for the Jesuits. In America, the occult forces that did the most damage were the Cabalistic Jews and the Scottish Rite Masons.

An in-depth understand of America's most destructive war also requires some insight on an international secret society called the Illuminati. When the British based "Templar" Jews set out to fill all of Europe with a sect of pro-Jewish Masonry, they had to unite competing factions of existing Freemasonry, such as how German Masonry was opposed to French Masonry. Prior to 1776, the highest degree (grade level) in Masonry was 32 degrees, (not counting some lesser Masonic organizations in other countries with up to 90 degrees).

Masonic national organizations were independent and not centralized. So, in an effort to unite all Masonic organizations throughout the world, certain members invented a new "secret" higher than the secrets held at the 32 degree level. The occult organization that created this claim of a higher secret was the Illuminati, founded in Bavaria in 1776 by the Jesuit trained, Adam Weishaupt. Weishaupt recruited the most progressive cosmopolitan-minded 32 degree Masons into his Illuminati. One of these progressive globalists was the famous French Mason named Voltaire. The Illuminati was discovered by Bavarian authorities in 1786 and suppressed, and, as official history proclaims, the Illuminati never resurfaced.

Although it was the end of the Illuminati in Bavaria, Voltaire had already returned to France with the "new and higher" secret to create the 33rd degree of Masonry (the Illuminati). At that point the 33rd degree took on the title: The Ancient and Accepted Scottish Rite. This can also be called "Templar" Masonry after the ancient 14th Century Knights Templar, which provided the mystic drama needed to back the claim of its 18th Century discovery in Bavaria. This rediscovered "ancient" higher secret was the namesake for the "Ancient" and Accepted Scottish Rite" of the 33rd degree. From that time on, the 33rd degree can be considered the home of the Illuminati. This was the brand of Masonry behind the French Revolution. This new radical form of political terror, now hiding within conventional masonry, was exported to America in 1789, at the beginning of the French Revolution and the year our first Congress was convening.

Germany and Britain, not France, were the providers of the new occult politics. Also consider that in 1714, three years prior to Masonry officially entering Britain (1717), the German King George of Hanover ascended the throne of Britain. This new "Templar" form of masonry was exported to America in 1789 to infiltrate the thirteen independent Masonic organizations within the thirteen American States. The funding of these Templar agents came from wealthy European corporations such as the East India Company, with their British and Amsterdam banking connections, and funding from the Hudson Bay Company. It will be extremely instructive to note that the first "Knights Templar" organization in America took root in Newburyport, Massachusetts.

There were many Masons in America before the Ancient and Accepted Scottish Rite came here. These young colonial Masons were considered country bumpkins compared to the Intrigue of the Europeans. And because most American Masons were patriotic, it presented a "cultural problem" to ask American Masons to perform deceitful intrigues against their own nation, in fact, Masons like Washington and Jefferson opposed Templar Masonry. Templar Masonry brought to America the "dream" of working to create a world government to replace the national governments, but Americans loved their national government.

This inner conflict also existed in European Masonry. There was an in-house power-struggle for control of European Masonry between the Anglo-Saxon Masons and the Jewish-Anglo-Templar factions of Masonry. This may seem like old baggage to drag out but this baggage is necessary to understand the intrigue behind the War of 1861, and without which you cannot.

Aaron Burr, Vice President under Jefferson, and like-minded brother-in-law of Benedict Arnold, received his Masonic insight through the Masons in the British Army before and during the American Revolution. In 1804, after Burr's involvement with several pro-British secessionist attempts in New England, Massachusetts and New York, and after killing Alexander Hamilton in a duel, Burr fled to Charleston South Carolina, which was the prominent Southern nest of Templars or Scottish Rite Masons. Burr's migration to points south helped established the secessionist seed in the South. It was then that the two "poles of political intrigue" were established: Charleston South Carolina and Newburyport Massachusetts; both controlled by the "Templar" Masons, both would provide the loudest trumpets for war.

Aaron Burr continued southward to New Orleans, which became the Southern-most hotbed of Scottish Rite Templars. Burr received "northern" occult reinforcements, he was followed to New Orleans by Edward Livingston, the Masonic Deputy Grand Master of New York who became the Masonic Grand High Priest of New Orleans. Livingston and Burr hired mercenaries in an attempt to create a nation within Jefferson's recent Louisiana Purchase. Their plan was too grandiose, they failed and were tried for treason by Thomas Jefferson and Justice John Marshall. Burr agreed to move to Britain, while Livingston was allowed to continue his law office in New Orleans. The name Livingston still represents power in Louisiana today, as does the name Slidell.

John Slidell, son of the President of Mechanics Bank of New York, moved to New Orleans in 1819, and trained under Edward Livingston. Slidell became a leader in the secessionist movement in Louisiana and a leader in the Democratic Party. It was Slidell's brother-in-law Pierre Beauregard, a Templar Mason, who, as a general in the Confederate army, commanded the firing on Fort Sumter and began the war of secession.

Slidell's niece married August Belmont, the private secretary and official U.S. agent for the Rothschilds whose British bank, financed the South during the war, while the French Rothschild bank financed the North. Slidell also brought Belmont into the Democratic Party where he became its national chairman during the controversy that split the party into Northern and Southern Democrats of 1860. John Slidell also brought Judah Benjamin into his law firm. Judah Benjamin, a member of a Jewish secret society, came to New Orleans from Charleston South Carolina. Benjamin became Attorney General for the Confederacy, and later became its Secretary of War, and then Secretary of State.

The question to be asked by pro-Southern Americans [like myself] is whether those British financed secret societies really wanted the South to successfully secede, only to come under more and more British control; or was the secession just a scheme to divide America and conquer both North and South? Those Americans who believe that the United States survived the war of 1861 might say that the British attempt was crushed, but after discerning the changes made in American monetary policy and Constitutional law, as reviewed in this book, it will become evident that the Original United States was indeed vanquished. The British attempt to divide and conquer both North and South was successful. Consider the motives of our post-1861 national actions: we entered World War One because of Britain, and we entered World War Two because of Britain. Britain said jump, America asked "how high." Yes, things have changed since World War Two, but that's another story.

Cabalistic Judaism

During the chaos after the French Revolution, but before the Napoleonic Wars, in 1799, Napoleon was leading an expedition in Egypt. It was there that he suggested he capture Palestine as a homeland for the Jews. He returned to France overthrew the Revolutionary Directorate and became Emperor for life. He spent the next few years conquering Europe. In 1804, Napoleon, having overthrown the revolutionaries that suppressed Catholicism, was to be crowned King of France by the Pope in the Church's effort to reassert its power in France. The Papal ceremonial crowning of kings was a thousand year old European tradition, but because Napoleon was a Mason, and Masons being anti-Papal, he took the crown from the Pope's hands and crowned himself successor to Charlemagne, (the first king crowned by the Pope in 806 AD). This ended the Papal-Dynasty alliance which ruled Europe for a thousand years, from 806 to 1804.

As Emperor of France, Napoleon again suggested that Palestine be made a homeland for the Jews. The Paris Sanhedrin declined the offer. At this time there was an inner conflict between White Masons and Cabalistic Jews. This inner-Masonic power-struggle led Napoleon to change his opinion of Jews and by 1808, he called them "the most vile nation in the world." Napoleon's change of heart eventually led him to Waterloo in 1815, where he was crushed by the British.

Years before Waterloo, during the Napoleonic Wars, Napoleon, knowingly or unknowingly, was serving the agenda of the Templar Masons which also served the agenda of the Cabalist Jews. That agenda was to make war against every nation in Europe to destabilize and weaken them. After which, at the Treaty of Vienna in 1815, all of the nations fell under "Republican" control. Republicanism was the Masonic replacement for monarchies, that is, all except the Czar of Russia. That is why the Czar sent war ships to America in 1861, to protect us from the forces that he knew destroyed Europe, the forces who, in 1861, turned their "eyes" upon America.

The in-house struggle for supremacy over Masonry between Jews and Caucasians was refined in 1811 when the German patriarch of the Jewish banking family Meyer Rothschild started the first "Jews only" Masonic lodge called Order of Asiatica. The name of that new order confirms the writings of Judah Halevi in his 12th century book that reveals that the people living in Europe who had come to be known as Jews, were actually an Asiatic-Oriental mix and were not the descendants of the Biblical Semites or Tribe of Judah. The upper degrees of "Caucasian" Masonry, who claimed their origin from Judah, via King Solomon, knew about this false claim, but instead of exposing them, they joined with them in their convoluted world of mysticism. And even though this mysterious partnership continued and the Templar and Asiatica lodges worked together, each secretly worked to control the other through Intrigue.

Meyer Rothschild had five sons, with whom he established the most powerful international banking family in the world. Each of his five sons established a Rothschild bank in five different nations: Germany (actually inherited his father's bank), Britain, Italy, Austria, and France. The three Rothschild "nations" most involved with America's War of 1861 were Britain, France and Germany.

The Rothschilds of Britain, who by 1830 controlled British Banking, had made great strides toward controlling the British government behind the scenes. The head of the British Rothschilds was Lionel Rothschild, who became the first non-Christian member of Parliament in 1858, after years of being denied that seat for not being a Christian. His son Nathaniel, was the first non-Christian to enter the House of Lords in 1885. Lionel Rothschild advanced the political career of Benjamin Disraeli who became the first Jewish Prime Minister of Britain in 1868. And yes, all of this is related to the War of 1861.

In 1857, the leaders of the Rothschild family were gathered to celebrate the wedding of the daughter of Lionel Rothschild to her cousin, the son of James Rothschild, of the French Rothschilds. Benjamin Disraeli, as a guest at this gala event, proclaimed:

"Under this roof are the heads of the family of Rothschild; a name famous in every capital of Europe and every division of the globe. If you like, we shall divide the United States into two parts, one for you James, and one for you Lionel."

It was these Rothschilds that financed the mutually assured destruction of both the American North and South in 1861.

Although the British Rothschilds had gained economic prominence over their kindred Rothschilds in other countries, they were all united in their goals. Frankfurt Germany was home to the first Order of Asiatica lodge, founded in 1811 by the Rothschild patriarch a year before his death. Out of Frankfurt, a number of movements were spawned in the 1840's and were sent out into the world to serve the goals of the occult, which loosely defined would be the centralization of economic and political powers.

Moses Hess, founder of Zionism, began his mission in Germany in the 1840's. Zionism was designed to centralize the people calling themselves Jews into a global political and religious power. One hundred years later they established the Mideast nation of Israel. Hess co-authored a book, The German Ideology, with his fellow Jewish German, Karl Marx. In 1862, Moses Hess wrote a book titled Rome and Jerusalem which spoke openly about his new form of revolutionary "Judaism" which would move the seat of world power from Papal Rome to Jerusalem. Hess revealed the ancient conflict between Judaism and Catholicism when he wrote:

"Papal Rome symbolizes to the Jews an inexhaustible well of poison."

Out of Germany came Karl Marx. Marx was the father of Communism, having published the Communist Manifesto in 1848. Remember, Karl Marx wrote articles for Horace Greeley in the New York Tribune; Greeley who ran against Grant for President. Karl Marx was using the International Workers organization to promote world communism based upon a rhetoric of serving the working class. Marx co-authored the constitution of the International Workers organization with Giuseppe Mazzini.

These facts reveal that there was direct lineage from Rothschild's German Jewish faction of Masonry to Mazzini. Giuseppe Mazzini was a leader, if not the leader, of the European Illuminati. Whether Hess and Marx were members of the Illuminati is not known, but the Rothschilds were supporting all three of these revolutionaries. Hess, Marx and Mazzini were wanted by the law throughout Europe for fomenting revolutions in the 1850's. Mazzini created revolutionary movements throughout Europe calling themselves Young Europe, Young Poland, Young Italy (with Garibaldi), Young England (with Disraeli). Mazzini's revolutionaries even defeated the Pope, temporarily. France had returned into the fold of the Catholic Church, and so troops from France, in an effort to save the Pope, put Mazzini on the run. Mazzini fled to London and the Rothschilds, while the Pope confiscated Mazzini's property in Italy. What about the American War of 1861?

Mazzini also founded the Young America organization in 1845. Its leader was Edwin de Leon, of Charleston South Carolina. Remember the two poles of Intrigue surrounding the War of 1861: Charleston South Carolina and Newburyport Massachusetts. Edwin de Leon became an advisor to Jefferson Davis. Mazzini had secret affiliations with persons in high positions within the Confederate Government, but Mazzini played both sides as revealed in his relationship with abolitionists.

William Lloyd Garrison, editor of the chief abolitionist paper the Liberator, was frequently going to Britain to meet with Mazzini. Mazzini and Garrison were both financed by New York millionaire Garrett Smith, the man who financed and armed John Brown. John Brown's goal was to start a war of North verses South. Brown received funds from the wealthy railroad builder John Forbes and was also financed by the Templar Scottish Rite group in Newburyport, Massachusetts. Brown was hanged for treason, but his financiers, called the Secret Six, survived and continued strategies fomenting war.

Several years before he founded the abolitionist Liberator, Garrison received his training in the newspaper profession in Newburyport Massachusetts under Caleb Huse. Caleb Huse later went to Europe acting as the leading arms procurer for the Confederacy. Also coming out of Newburyport, the Northern axis of the war, was Albert Pike, as pre-

viously mentioned, Pike was the Confederate General who led the Indian Nations into the war against the North that gave the "Union" the
much needed "justification" to violate the Indian treaties and steal their
land for the railroads. Albert Pike was also an associate of Mazzini,
and after leaving Arkansas, served as the Grand Commander of the
Southern Scottish Rite in Charleston, South Carolina. Pike was another
conspicuous link of Newburyport to Charleston, where Pike became the
leader of the American Illuminati. Pike was an avid believer in the Kabbalah and the leader of the Ancient and Accepted Scottish Rite.

Also working with William Garrison, while under the tutelage
of Caleb Huse, was Caleb Cushing. It was Caleb Cushing who chaired
the Democratic Party in 1860 (which was headed by Rothschild agent
August Belmont) when the Party spilt. Divide and conquer, whether a
political party or a nation, it is an old strategy, repeated because it works.
This split provided the Presidential victory to Lincoln, which led to the
creation of the Confederacy.

It should be apparent that the political intrigue out of Europe,
using American agents, played both sides of the Mason-Dixon. The international players involved in this were the Illuminati, British Intelligence, under Lord Palmerston, and the Jewish faction of Asiatica
Masonry which at this time was attempting to gain superiority over the
Ancient and Accepted Scottish Rite (33 degree Templar Masonry).
Also included were the American millionaires on the economic front,
such as Garrett Smith who donated more than $8 million in the push
for war. Smith was connected to the Astor's and the East India Company. Garrett Smith also founded the Liberty Party, where Salmon P.
Chase became a leader. The Liberty Party later evolved into a faction
of the Republican Party of Lincoln.

Out of that 1840's nest of German revolutionaries came another
spin-off of the Order of Asiatica, the "Jewish only" Masonic order of
B'nai B'rth. The B'nai B'rth came to America in 1843, their mission
was to gain Masonic supremacy over the Ancient and Accepted Scottish
Rite in America. And so they set up offices in New York, and
Charleston South Carolina. The leader of the Charleston B'nai B'rth
was Edwin de Leon, yes, the co-founder of Mazzini's Young America
movement, and yes, it was de Leon who later became an advisor to President Davis. Members of Edwin de Leon's family were founders of
Charleston's Masonic Lodge of the Scottish Rite. Another of the

founders of the Charleston Lodge, John Mitchell, was tried along with Benedict Arnold for crimes against the Army during the Revolutionary War. Are you beginning to see how the seeds of war were being sown by "ancient forces" whose plans are long term, unlike a two year Congressmen?

Also coming to America out of Europe was the movement known as Reform Judaism. In 1842, Rothschild's Order of Asiatica and the Great Sanhedrin of Paris created a new religion to act as cover for their hidden agenda: Reform Judaism. Moses Hess, associate of Karl Marx and founder of Zionism, wrote in his book *Rome to Jerusalem*, of replacing Rome with a "new historical cult, to this coming cult, Judaism alone holds the key."

Marxism and Reform Judaism came to America in the waves of German immigration in the 1840's and 1850's. The leader of the American Reform movement was Rabbi Isaac Wise, who settled in Cincinnati, Ohio. Rabbi Wise openly supported the South. Also coming out of Cincinnati at that time were the Knights of the Golden Circle, and Salmon P. Chase, the architect of the postwar money system. The Karl Marx affiliate group of (excommunicated Catholic) Fenians held a convention in 1864, in Cincinnati representing 250,000 members. Cincinnati was becoming a Northern staging area for directing a Southern war.

August Belmont, the Rothschild agent in America who was head of the Democratic Party for twenty years also operated within Charleston's B'nai B'rth. By 1860, New York alone had between 50 and 60 synagogues. Memberships nationwide in the B'nai B'rth totalled over 50,000. German Reform Judaism and the B'nai B'rth were in position to influence the occult war of 1861.

Remember Custer's problem concerning General Grant's family and the selling the post-trader contracts? Well, by that time, 1875, Grant was a political crook, but in 1862, though he may have betrayed the laws of State sovereignty, he was still a soldier in the American Army. Early in the war, Grant was a Union General placed in charge of the Department of Tennessee. The Jewish firm of Mack and Brothers made Grant's father a partner in his carpetbag trading company which wanted to operate within Grant's military jurisdiction of Tennessee.

After many complaints against the company and after a thorough investigation, Grant issued General Order #11:

"The Jews as a class violating every regulation of trade established ... are hereby expelled from the department within 24 hours ... and anyone returning will be arrested and held in confinement ... as prisoners."

Lincoln, being politically correct, and dependent on Chase and the New York bankers, reversed the order.

The Grant controversy, was reborn in 1959, when Grant's grandson General U.S. Grant III, approved the release of his grandfather's writings which were to be published in the Military Order of the Loyal Legion (sons of Union veterans). Grant's writings made the charge that the War of 1861 was fomented by international Jewish interests, especially the House of Rothschild and that Grant considered the B'nai B'rth a spy agency.

This political bombshell brought forth a wave of protests from the Anti-Defamation League (ADL). General Grant (the third) like his grandfather, wimped out and refuted his grandfather's statement. If that were an isolated case, or if there were no more related background, the case should be dismissed, but considering Grant's statement in the light of these other evidences, it appears to be just one of many testimonies exposing international banking as a major cause of the War of 1861. If someone else today were to discover the role of the B'nai B'rth in the War of 1861, and publish it, they too would be labeled "anti-Semitic" by the Anti-Defamation League, because what you need to understand is that the ADL which fights "anti-Semitism" and "racism" is an agency created by the B'nai B'rth in 1913. The ADL is simply a political mechanism to control outbursts of truthful history and to incite racial tensions. When you hear accusations of "anti-Semitism" or "racism" it is more often than not a tactic used to malign someone who is getting too close to the truth.

Another proof of related intrigue, would be found in the policework of Washington D.C.'s Chief of Police in 1861, Lafayette Baker, who became head of Lincoln's Secret Service. Baker named the B'nai B'rth as conspirators involved in the assassination of Abraham Lincoln and arrested B'nai B'rth lawyer Simon Wolf, as a conspirator. Wolf had been seen at a bar drinking with John Wilkes Booth on the day of the assassination. Not only was Wolf not convicted, he later became the head of the International Order of B'nai B'rth.

The Rothschilds supported the B'nai B'rth and attempted to use those connections to control the Confederate Government. Judah Benjamin, a member of a Jewish Secret Society in Charleston that predated the B'nai B'rth was operating the Confederate Secret Service. Benjamin was charged with sedition in connection with Lincoln's Assassination but "escaped" to Britain to practice law.

It is always important to remember the British role in the War of 1861. The British were supportive of the South in the beginning of the war. They sold the Confederate Government rifles and ships and offered promises to the Confederacy if the South won. Britain came to the rescue when "their agents" got in trouble. When James Mason and John Slidell, long time confidant to Rothschild agent August Belmont, were taken captive from a British ship by a Union Naval vessel, in December of 1861, the British Government sent 8,000 troops to Canada and gave the White House less than a week to release the Confederates. The White House yielded to the demands. Spies don't kill spies because at the top, they're all working for the same people.

Would Britain acknowledge political recognition to the Confederacy? No. Britain declared its neutrality one month after the Fort Sumter incident. By February 5th, 1863, Queen Victoria refused to mediate between the North and South saying that such matters cannot be "attended with a probability of success." [What did she know?] And by April of 1863, the Illuminati's secret service, in the person of British Prime Minister Palmerston, turned its back on the Confederacy and sealed its fate. President Jefferson Davis, a true Southern patriot, in an attempt to boost the Southern morale, was right up front about the South being abandoned by the powers in Europe, when he said:

"Put not your trust in princes and rest not your hopes in foreign nations. This war is ours; we must fight it out ourselves."

Mazzini, like his compatriots Hess and Marx, had worked the past twenty years fomenting the destruction of the traditional nations and religions of Europe with their creations of the Young Europe movements, communism, and Zionism. At the end of America's War of 1861,

Mazzini praised his American operatives working for the centralization of nations by saying:

"You have done more for us in four years than fifty years of teaching, preaching, and writing by your European brothers have been able to do!"

Karl Marx stated at the conclusion of our War of 1861:

"After the Civil War phase, the United States really is only now entering the revolutionary phase."

Understand what those two sentences mean: The South lost the war; and in the final analysis, the North also lost the war. Well then, who won the war?

The winners are: Karl Marx and his international socialism and the fact that his graduated income tax was adopted by the Lincoln government. Mazzini with the creation of his Young America movement provided the transfer of the Illuminati from Europe to America. The Illuminati, with its partial victory over American Masonry and with Albert Pike's statue still standing in Washington D.C. today. Who won? The British Government because America's revolution of 1776 was finally revoked. The British Rothschilds because, through Salmon Chase, they centralized American banking and converted the currency, by 1900, into a debt-based money supply. Who won? The B'nai B'rth who escaped the candid indictment by General Grant and who, in 1913, set up their ADL as watchdog against accurate history. The list of winners goes on and on but it does not include the average American.

Masonry
The Building Blocks of War

The role of Freemasonry within the intrigue surrounding the War of 1861 becomes awkward to many Americans today because most Americans are related to, the friend of, or know a Mason. This dimension of history is in no way an indictment of the whole of Masonry with its membership of many good and honorable Americans. The Masons, as pointed out previously, were infiltrated by occult elements who sought to use the brotherhood to accomplish strategies toward achieving their goal of global governance, both political and economic. After the turn of the twentieth century, many of these occult elements migrated into semi-secret, or semi-public organizations to achieve their goals; such as the Anti Defamation League, the Federal Reserve Bank, the Carnegie and Rockefeller Foundations, entertainment and news media corporations and after the 1930's, even some departments of the government, Their need to operate within the secrecy of the organizations like the Masons became less strategic.

The concern with Masonry in regard to its participation in the War of 1861, is mostly with the 33rd degree, the "Templar" or "Ancient and Accepted Scottish Rite" Lodges. However, because it isn't common knowledge who among the political leaders of that time were Masons, or how far up the Masonic ladder they were, some examples could be helpful. Example: perhaps the greatest statesman of the War of 1861, Jefferson Davis, was not a Mason; Robert E. Lee was not a Mason; yet the President that tried to save the South from the radical postwar misery, Andrew Johnson, was a Mason.

Andrew Johnson, being a Southerner, wanted to pardon the Southerners after the war, and he did so. There were blanket pardons and special pardons. Certain cases, like Generals who served in the Confederate Army and high ranking public officials required special pardons. President Johnson pardoned General Albert Pike, the 33 degree Mason and leader of the Illuminati. For that, Albert Pike made Johnson a 32 degree Mason. Notice that Pike did not let Johnson inside the Scottish Rite (33rd degree). Why not? Because President Johnson was a patriot of the U.S. Constitution; a document that conflicts with the international agenda of the Illuminati. So here is an example of a 32 degree Mason, who would not sellout his nation or his God, and who sacrificed his political career and reputation to defend the Constitution. Any Mason today who wants to ridicule any criticism of any Mason, is insisting that "all Masons" are above reproach. This reveals a loyalty to the scoundrels who infiltrated their organization to overthrow American Masonry itself and to perpetrate a secret agenda designed to violate the Constitution.   In seeking the truth of the War of 1861, there is no reason to put certain people above suspicion simply because they were Masons.

The specific component of Masonry involved with the anti-American agenda would be the Cabalistic and British controlled Templar faction of European Masonry, also called the Ancient and Accepted Scottish Rite, particularly the Supreme Council of the 33rd Degree. This European faction sent emissaries to the United States in 1790 to establish new supreme lodges over the existing system of American Masonry.

The emissaries went to the two cities that became the political poles of the War of 1861: Newburyport, Massachusetts and Charleston, South Carolina. There they began a quiet attempt to take over the existing American Freemason organization which was referred to as Symbolic Masonry (32 degrees and under). But being a degree higher (a degree they created) did not automatically give the Scottish Rite jurisdiction or supremacy over all American lodges; America lodges resisted. Jurisdiction is very important in Freemasonry, and Masonic jurisdiction in America, up to that time, was State by State - not national. The centralization of the sovereign American States into "one nation under Lincoln" was also the agenda directed against American Masonry by the European Templar lodges, it was the theme of the Illuminati: centralization toward globalism.

In 1826, William Morgan, a Mason, stated his intentions of publishing a book exposing the Templar infiltration that spawned the radical un-American Masonic activities. Morgan was subsequently kidnapped, tortured and murdered. This developed into the biggest Masonic scandal in American history. Three-thousand lodges dissolved in protest. These resignations were unfortunate for American Masonry because thousands of good patriotic Masons resigned, leaving American Masonry in the hands of the European faction which was attempting to take over.

The greatest opposition to Masonry in American history occurred with the formation of the national political party of the Anti-Masons, whose leader was John Quincy Adams, former President of the United States. Adams and his former Attorney General, William Wirt gathered national support to rein in the European spawned Masonic control over American politics. It was Adams and his followers that formed the Anti-Masonic Party that ran William Wirt for President in 1832. The Anti-Masonic Presidential candidate received 20% of the popular vote. Masonic treason (perpetrated by the European faction operating through their American subordinates) was the big controversial issue in the years surrounding the 1832 Presidential race.

The Anti-Masonic Party was a temporary setback for the Masons. The Anti-Masons, which included former "Symbolic Masonry" members evolved into the "Know-nothings." Because of the Morgan scandal in 1826, and the national Anti-Masonic candidacy of 1832, the next major Masonic convention wasn't held until 1843. By 1860, the European influence within Masonry was almost totally swept under the rug, and by the beginning of the War of 1861, there were 500,000 American Masons, and they were not all dominated by the new Templar Intrigue.

Quick review: The all Jewish "Order of Asiatica" Masonry in Frankfurt Germany, in the 1840's sent out its agents. Karl Marx propagated communism, and the Marxist doctrine came to America with the German immigrants in the 1840's and 1850's. Marx's political associate and 33rd degree Illuminati Mason, Giuseppe Mazzini founded the Young America movement in Charleston with his co-founder Edwin de Leon. Edwin de Leon was the leader of the Charleston B'nai B'rth. The B'nai B'rth was sent here from Germany in 1843, to gain Masonic superiority over the Scottish Rite. Then in 1846, Germany sent Reform Judaism to the United States, which was a secret society posing as a Jewish religion. Now we're up to speed.

Killian Van Rensselaer was the grandson of one of the founders of the West India Company, out of Holland. He lived in New York, where in 1830, he was "irregularly knighted" into the Masons by three British soldiers out of Canada. It was this sort of "irregular" indoctrination that previously sanctioned Benedict Arnold and secessionist Aaron Burr. Rensselaer was given the Masonic patent to establish a western headquarters for the Scottish Rite to be located in Cincinnati Ohio, which he did in 1853.

In 1846, Rabbi Isaac Wise brought Reform Judaism to New York from Germany. Wise was the American leader of Reform Judaism and remained so until his death in 1900. In 1854, he too moved from New York to Cincinnati Ohio where he began preaching to his "flock" about how the South was being used by the North, talking in support of secession, implementing the divide and conquer strategy.

In 1854, also in Cincinnati Ohio, the secret organization, The Knights of the Golden Circle was formed. The tactics of these Knights served strategies benefiting the B'nai B'rth, and the western Scottish Rite, and Reform Judaism. Officially the founder of the Knights of the Golden Circle was George Bickley of Virginia, but that is a meaningless diversion. The Knights were controlled by European Masonry. The Knights of the Golden Circle, based in Ohio, operated in the Southern States prior to the war and supplied weapons to the Confederacy and trained approximately 100,000 Southern militia-men. Union General William Sherman said that Cincinnati furnished more goods to the C.S.A. than did Charleston.

General Beauregard, the original highest-ranking General of the Confederacy was a member of the Knights of the Golden Circle. Beauregard commanded the first shot of the war at Fort Sumter. John Wilkes Booth became a member of the Knights of the Golden Circle in 1860. It could be said that the European Masonic controlled Knights of the Golden Circle fired the first and last shots of the war. Never under estimate the intrigue of wars just because the government and media historians leave it out.

Quick review: The 33rd degree Scottish Rite Lodges were established as early as 1790, in Newburyport Massachusetts, and by 1801 in Charleston South Carolina. The Scottish Rite was in America to take control of American Masonry, but failed, and by 1832, with the "Morgan Affair," it failed miserably. The B'nai B'rth's Masonic faction came from Germany in 1843, and the long-abandoned Masonic conventions in America restarted. But the B'nai B'rth wanted to gain dominance over American Masonry on behalf of the German and Jewish-only lodge "Asiatica" by controlling the 33rd degree Scottish Rite, and placing itself on top of the 32 degree pyramid of America's Symbolic Masonry. This developed into an in-house conflict between traditional American Masonry and this newer European "clandestine" Masonry which was attempting to unite all American Masonry under a national Mother

Lodge. Now we're up to speed.

In some respects, the War of 1861, was a war to control American Masonry. One of the first major battles in the Masonic struggle came in 1858, when one of the clandestine international lodges, the St. John's Grand Lodge of New York, united with a State lodge, the Grand Lodge of New York. This would, in effect, put New York's "State" Masonry under control of the international 33rd degree of Templar Masonry. B'nai B'rth's world headquarters was also in New York City. The Grand Lodge of Virginia objected to the takeover. This began a national Masonic feud between New York and Virginia over "State's rights" while State Masonic jurisdictions, North and South, observed.

Virginia Masonry fought against New York's international takeover of American Masonry. And as it happens, the only Masonic Lodge that was taken captive during the War of 1861, by either Union or Confederate forces was the George Washington Lodge in Alexandria Virginia; it was the first political victim of the war. We will never know what "secrets" that lodge contained, but it was ransacked and forced to disband. The Grand Lodge of the District of Columbia replaced the Alexandria Lodge with the "Union Lodge." The Virginia Grand Lodge then forbade its members to recognize any "Union Lodge" people. Washington D.C. joined the clandestine push against Richmond to centralize the sovereign American States and centralize the sovereignty of the independent Masonic lodges.

The Scottish Rite of Charleston extended its organization into Mississippi, where it commissioned the former New Yorker, John Quitman, in 1830, to open and preside over the Scottish Rite for the State of Mississippi. Quitman used his Masonic power in the 1850's to lead the secessionist movement in Mississippi. The Supreme Council of the Southern Jurisdiction ordered that all Consistories, Councils, Chapters and Lodges under the Southern Jurisdiction were to submit to the 33 degree lodge of John Quitman. Remember the scheme: the 33 degree, British and B'nai B'rth influenced, Scottish Rite was attempting to take over all of Masonry. Therefore, after Quitman's appointment to the Templar position in Mississippi, it should be expected that a mechanism to achieve Masonic centralization in the South would likely come out of Mississippi.

Rob Morris had entered Masonry in 1845, through the Oxford Lodge in Mississippi at age 26. Morris accepted a clandestine task. He left Mississippi on a mission to seek out senior Masons throughout the country to learn about the Masons and their lodges and to make the necessary connections to promote the agenda of centralization. He conferred with over 50,000 Masons and visited nearly 2000 lodges, and in those days, that was quite a feat. By 1858, when the Virginia Grand Lodge challenged the illegal "union" of the New York Grand Lodge with the St. John Lodge, Rob Morris had worked his way up to being the Grand Master of Kentucky. Virginia officially objected to the attempted clandestine "national" control by the Scottish Rite over "State" jurisdictions.

After touring thousands of lodges, and gaining his position as Grand Master of Kentucky, Morris gained access to a wealth of "secrets." He then set out to form a group called the "Conservators of Symbolic Masonry" or "The Conservators." Looking back on it, (which is always easy) the title itself reveals his agenda since "Symbolic Masonry" was the existing American form of Masonry, 32 degree and below. Thus, the Symbolic Masonry which the Virginia Grand Lodge feared was being threatened by the New York Lodge was the object of concern for the "Conservators." Was Morris trying to "conserve" the very thing that Virginia was trying to preserve? The first definition of the word "conservator" is; "One that preserves from injury or violation." Or, was Morris implementing the second definition of "conservator": "a person, official or institution designated to take over and protect the interests of an incompetent?"

The proposed Conservator system was designed to be superimposed onto American Masonry, coincidentally, just as the Scottish Rite had tried, but could not prior to 1861. The Morris mechanism to achieve this was to standardize Masonic rituals in all States, with the "keys to the secrets" being in writing instead of being verbal. The Conservator system, if used would nationalize Masonry through uniform laws, which was the goal of the B'nai B'rth. So here we have the New York Grand (St. John) Lodge attempting a takeover Masonry by employing Scottish Rite Masons in Mississippi and Kentucky, using the Conservators as "Yankees in gray clothing."

Within its "twelve points," the Conservator obligations to Masonic Temples would include these organizational tactics: Secrecy; A top to bottom control over members; Be good to each other clauses; Intimidate all opposition found within the ranks and diminish their influence; Submission to all rules; and "seek by every available means to obtain possession of the Grand Lodges (States) so as to compel all lodges to adopt and use the above named system ... and to break down every Lodge that stands in its way." The B'nai B'rth could not have written a more accurate dogma of its intentions.

A particularly instructive coincidence regarding the "Conservators" is in their mission of Masonic centralization, and their years of operation. The Conservators operated from June 1860 to June 1865. It began a year before the war and closed when the war ended. During the same years that the Union Army fought to centralize the American States into one national governance, the Conservators used infiltration and intrigue to centralize State Masonry into one national Masonry.

The Grand Lodges (State lodges) became alarmed at the agenda and speed of Conservator recruiting. During the five years of existence, Morris recruited 3,000 Masons into the Conservators. Remember, the Conservator doctrine requires that all members belonging to a Grand Lodge, were bound by oath to use all of their influence "to break down every Lodge that stands in its way." Conservators targeted the Grand Lodges, and were able to get members into all but four of the Grand Lodges: Virginia; Oregon; Colorado; and D.C. The push to takeover Masonry came during the confusion of the war. Take note that Virginia's Grand Lodge had no Conservators, and Virginia was the foremost opponent to the clandestine "union lodges" that were attempting to conquer State Masonry. That fact, along with the Conservators' 12 points being so anti-Grand Lodge, shows that the Conservators were working toward the same goal as the B'nai B'rth and St. John Lodge using the Ancient and Accepted Scottish Rite.

The Grand Lodge of Michigan declared the Conservator "scheme to be unlawful, unmasonic, and opposed to the real interest of Masonry." Many others spoke out calling its agenda a scheme to infiltrate so-as-to command every Lodge in America. When the smoke cleared, after the war, the Conservators ceased to exist, and Morris was welcomed back into the fold. Although, the new Masonic spin claims that Morris did not get what he wanted, the Masons did unite under the Scottish Rite and Morris did create a national ritual of Masonry, and he is the founder of the Order of the Eastern Star. But Rob Morris is best known in Masonry as its "Poet Laureate," in the ranks of the other Masonic poets (and Illuminists), like Albert Pike and Giuseppe Mazzini.

Another Masonic takeover-mechanism during the war was "attrition." There were 500,000 Masons before the war, that number was reduced during the war to 400,000. When Masons became soldiers they left their State Lodge, so in many cases State (Symbolic) Lodges shut down; but at the same time, newly recruited Masons opened new Lodges in those same cities and towns. Remember the Morris Conservator doctrine was to purge Masonry of the older Masons to make way for the "young" (which was a theme behind the Young Europe, Young America, Young Britain & etc. movements of Mazzini). The war provided the tactical attrition of existing lodges to be replaced by new lodges favorable to the Conservators.

When Masons became soldiers in the War of 1861, they created a new form of lodge: military lodges. It is estimated that 11% of the troops were Masons. The Union Army had 94 military lodges, while the South had 150. These lodges were issued by regiment and State, and so they were under the control of State Grand Lodges. Virginia would grant "dispensations" to Union soldiers on Virginia soil during the war. They believed that the war should not interfere with their brotherhood. After the war, on December 5, 1865, these military lodges were ordered to turn over all of their records to their respective State Grand Lodges. So, during the war years, American Masonry not only had the changing effect of the Conservators, but also the new military lodges.

It is also instructive to notice who was "not" a high ranking Mason. Lincoln was not, yet his three opponents in the election of 1860 were: John C. Breckinridge, John Bell and Stephen Douglas, as well as Lincoln's opponent in the 1864 election General McClellan. Lincoln's Secretary of War, Edwin M. Stanton was a Mason. In 1861, the non-Masonic Abe Lincoln offered the command of the Union troops to the very Masonic Italian Giuseppe Garibaldi, who was living in exile in London and New York. Garibaldi was wanted by the law in Italy for attempting to overthrow the government and the Pope. Garibaldi was a close associate of Mazzini, and the leader of the "Young Italy" group. Garibaldi was a 33 degree Mason and Illuminist who later captured the Pope and defeated the Church's world headquarters in Italy in 1870. What were you thinking Mr. Lincoln?

The Congressman who hated the South vehemently (and the feeling was mutual) was Thaddeus Stevens, an anti-Mason since the days of the Anti-Masonic Party of 1832. General Grant was not a Mason either. This is said to convey the necessary perspective that a politician "being a Mason or not being a Mason" does not equate to him being a traitor or being patriotic.

The Confederacy was officially established under the chair of Howell Cobb, who was the Scottish Rite Supreme Commander. Many leaders of the secessionist movement were Masons: John Slidell, Robert Toombs, and Albert Pike. Slidell, Toombs, Breckinridge, Judah Benjamin and other Masonic leaders retired to Europe after the war in wealth while leaving Davis, Lee and other patriots to suffer the evils of reconstruction. John Slidell requested a pardon from President Johnson and that he be allowed to return to the U.S. Johnson did not reply.

But still, there is no straight line drawn to demarcate the guilt. A great deal of guilt for the war atrocities must fall on the non-Mason Abe Lincoln, and a great deal of guilt for the postwar atrocities must fall on the non-Mason Thaddeus Stevens. But do not make the mistake of thinking that because the Masons were pro-secessionist, that they were all truly pro-Southern.

The Templar Masons who pushed America toward war were controlled through their chain of command, which came from on high (Europe). The non-Masons, like Lincoln were controlled by New York and European bankers and by their greed for political power. The industrialists were controlled by money. And the bankers were controlled by the Rothschilds, and there again, the origins go back to Britain and France.

During the war, there were feeling of brotherhood between Masons serving on both sides. Generals Sherman, Butler and the other savages loosed upon the South murdered, destroyed, and made homeless countless Southerners. Yet, Yankee Masons spared their Southern Masonic brothers such grief and spared their homes. Their intent was to destroy the truth about the South, yet preserve their Masonic Order.

The very week that the war ended, Yankee General Croxton burned down the University of Alabama, and specifically burned down its library. This type of book burning was the norm. Yet, earlier in the war, when the Grand Master of Iowa, a Colonel in the Yankee army, was conquering Arkansas, he saved the Masonic library of Albert Pike from destruction and placed a guard to protect it; quite the double standard.

Mason's who were prisoners of war were offered medical help and even given parole outside of the prison during the nights. Confederates without such "brotherhood" would continue to freeze to death in Elmira.

This situation existed in the North and the South. The Confederate Army destroyed the iron works owned by the anti-Masonic, Thaddeus Stevens in Pennsylvania, but completely spared the Masonic Temple in Vicksburg, which they used as a hospital, and did not remove any of the Masonic Ritual "furniture." And when the Confederates burned to the ground the entire town of Chambersburg Pennsylvania, they left the sacred Masonic Temple untouched.

The night they drove old Dixie down in Richmond, April 4, 1865, Union Major Stevens went straight to the Capitol building to raise the Union Flag. The second thing he did was ride straight to Richmond's Masonic Hall to protect it from rioters or burning. He met with the General Secretary of the Richmond Lodge and placed guards to protect the lodge as well as protecting the homes of other key Masons. Even "Beast" Butler, a Mason, saved a Southern lodge. Butler:

"Whereas the Government of the United States ... is not warring upon charitable benevolent organizations, and certain proper, worthy and responsible persons representing the Masonic Fraternity have requested to be placed in quiet possession, as trustees, of the property of the same in this city; it is ordered."

This was the normal throughout the war. General Sherman was not a Mason, but his junior officers provided Masonic protection to the property of their fellow Masons in the South as they burned their way through Georgia and the Carolinas destroying the homes and property of the non-enlightened.

It seems strange that this war was caused in a large part by Masonic intrigue, yet the Masons avoided being the President of the North or the South, and that neither Lee or Grant were Masons. It is - as if - they wanted to work in the shadows.

The Jesuits
Mystery in the Church of Rome

One might think that this writing, having discussed the Illuminati, German Asiatica, the Templar Scottish Rite, and the Knights of the Golden Circle, would have completed its insight on Intrigue, but their is yet one more loose end. Why drag the Catholic Church or Jesuits into this mix of scoundrels? Because within this catalog of political Intrigue, there was a role played by the Jesuits in the War of 1861, and, if for no other reason, because history begs that the entire question be answered. Politically correct history has chosen to omit certain "uncomfortable" facts, because certain agents of internationalism operated from within publicly popular benevolent organizations. Yet these obscure facts of today were spoken aloud during the tumultuous days of the War of 1861; President Lincoln himself stated:

"This war would never have been possible without the sinister influence of the Jesuits. We owe it to Popery that we now see our land reddened with the blood of her noblest sons."

And on the floor of Congress, Lincoln's assassination was blamed on the "Jesuitical leaders of the rebellion." How can history expunge such statements? Why should history blot out such controversial statements? Is it because such facts make the Catholics, Masons, or Jews of today uncomfortable because those organizations still exist?

Quick review and question: The Masons and the Cabalistic Jews were sworn enemies of the Church of Rome, they fought against each other for centuries, in every country in Europe. Did their conflict spill-over into America and lead to the War of 1861?

The ancient rivalry among the Masons, Cabalistic Jews and the Church of Rome was carried across the Atlantic to America. The Pope had decreed that all of South and Central America belonged to Spain and Portugal. Therefore the first European settlers to North America were brought here as a cooperative effort of the English and the Dutch. Holland prior to 1660, was the financial center of Cabalistic Jewish activity. In the 1660's, those Cabalists backed Oliver Cromwell against

King Charles. Cromwell won that "civil war" and Charles lost his head, after which the Jews, who were banished from England, reentered England and continued as the West India Company and within the Bank of England. The Dutch-English role in transporting settlers to America from Europe was to insure that only Protestants settled the new world of North America, leaving the Bank of England to control America's wealth. Now we're up to speed.

Catholics finally did come to America but were rejected in colony after colony. Finally they were allowed to stay in one colony which was named Mary-land. Then in the 1850's, the Irish Catholics started entering New York. These two "Catholic" enclaves were, in part, responsible for the draft riots of New York and the hindering of Union troops as they moved through Maryland. The man who fired the "first shot" of the war, Beauregard, was a Catholic and the man fired the "last shot," John Wilkes Booth was a Catholic, and both were members of the Knights of the Golden Circle. But it isn't that simple.

Prior to slavery becoming "the" social issue, there was a "tolerance" issue running rampant in the Northern States. There was a cultural rejection against foreigners and Catholics. Just as Cromwell, a devout anti-Catholic Protestant radical, purged England of its Catholics, on behalf of his Cabalist friends in Holland. The "Calvinist styled" American preachers pushed against the Catholics as hard as the Constitution would let them.

Did the Pope make a play to control the United States? How great of a world power was the Pope in 1861? After the French Revolution, the Jewish-Masonic co-op reduced the Church of Rome to almost nothing. After the French Revolution the Masonic leaders of the "New France" sold all of the Catholic property in France and used those receipts as the collateral for the revolution's "new currency." In 1809 the Masonic "Carbonari" set out to unite all of Italy under Masonry, and eliminate Catholicism. In 1827 Mazzini became the leader of the Carbonari and by 1831 had ousted the Pope, but only temporarily, because of pro-Catholic French intervention. It was that year that Mazzini established the "Young Italy" movement. It was in the Carbonari that Mazzini and Garibaldi joined forces. Both Mazzini and Garibaldi were 33 degree Masons.

The Pope retained some power in Italy and in Austria but in 1848, Mazzini and Garibaldi led a revolt and established the Roman

Republic and ousted Pope Pius IX, who fled to Gaete. Austria and France, under Napoleon III, were sympathetic to the Pope and ousted Mazzini's forces, and in 1850, restored the Pope and his Papal States in Rome. Mazzini fled to Britain and back to the Rothschilds. The Papal States remained a temporal power, but very weak.

The Papal States were, for all intents and purposes, a nation with an economy. In 1859, that economy was administered by Cardinal Antonelli. Antonelli had become the controlling power over the aging Pope. Antonelli had built up the power of the Pope, to gain his confidence so that he and his associates could convert the Catholic Church to the agenda of the Illuminati. Antonelli had the appearance of being a Jew, and in his economic administration position, he ran the Papal States heavily into debt to the Rothschild bank. Antonelli was the mouthpiece for the "Black Pope" which is the title given to the General of the Jesuits.

Remember, the Jesuits were an implant into the Catholic Church from the Jewish Templars, back in 1541. They are a militant religious order used to foment religious wars between Catholics and Protestants. In 1763, the Pope banned Masonry in all Catholic countries. In 1773, the Pope abolished the Jesuits. That act cannot be understated. The Pope abolished the Jesuits. It must be surmised that the Pope discovered the 200 year old Masonic-Jesuit connection and banned them both from Catholic nations. Also remember, the founder of the Illuminati in 1776, Adam Weishaupt, was Jesuit trained.

The Templars used the Jesuits to play the "bad guy." Neither the low level Jesuits, nor the low degree Masons typically know this information. Masonry's 30th degree, the Knight Kadosch, has a rank in it for the "Kadosch of the Jesuit." This becomes more clear in our War of 1861, but you must have this background information.

In 1870, the Illuminati, under Garibaldi, the man Lincoln asked to lead the American troops against the South, conquered the Pope and his Papal States. This "strategic opportunity" occurred when Masonic Germany attacked France (Franco-Prussian War) as a diversion, forcing France to remove its troops from Italy which sealed the fate of the Papal States. The Pope did not regain his "temporal power" again until it was returned to him in 1929, by Mussolini.

Today Vatican City is the smallest nation in the world. So in the 1860's, the Papal States were a dying (almost dead) power. It is essential to your understanding that you are able to separate the "Church of Rome" from the "Jesuits." And so when Lincoln or certain Congressmen made statements about the "Jesuits," which suggests that the Jesuits were synonymous with the Pope, they either just didn't know the difference between the two groups or they were being deceptive.

In the War of 1861, Lincoln and other northern politicians were misled into blaming the Church of Rome for the acts of the Jesuits. This tactic allowed the Illuminati to blame the "intrigue" surrounding the war on their historic enemy, and thus escape any blame being placed on themselves. And remember, the Masons and the Jesuits are supposed to be enemies, but to pierce through the veils of intrigue, it must be learned that they were allies.

John Slidell was the leader of the Louisiana secessionist movement. Slidell was trained by Edward Livingston, the Masonic Grand High Priest of New Orleans. John Slidell hired Judah Benjamin into his law office. Judah Benjamin, a member of the Charleston Jewish secret Orphan Society, became the Confederate Secretary of State and was in charge of the Confederate Secret Service. Slidell was the Uncle-in-law and long time confidant of August Belmont, an agent of the British Rothschild Bank. Slidell's brother-in-law was General Beauregard, a professed Roman Catholic from a family of Jesuits, yet Beauregard was a Templar Mason. Beauregard is a good example of an 1861 "player" with Jesuit ties and a Templar Mason.

Beauregard, like his fellow Catholic John Wilkes Booth, was a member of the Knights of the Golden Circle. Was the secret society, "Knights of the Golden Circle" a Catholic organization? No! It was organized by the anti-Catholic Scottish Rite of Cincinnati, (home to Reform Judaism) the sworn enemy of the Pope. A Catholic Bishop in Iowa commanded that all Catholic members of the Knights of the Golden Circle resign from that organization or be excommunicated; meaning that the real Church of Rome was against the Knights, yet the Jesuitical faction of the Knights, like Beauregard and Booth, were not following the agenda of the Pope but were following the occult leadership of the "Black Pope" (Commander of the Jesuits) who was in league with the Scottish Rite and the Illuminati. Also remember that it was Simon Wolf of the B'nai B'rth who met with Booth on the day of Lincoln's assassination. And that it was a 33rd degree Mason who met with Booth earlier in New Orleans, and then in D.C. right before the assassination, and it was he who "identified" Booth's dead body. Booth was twenty-six at the time of the assassination.

Most of the conspirators in the assassination of Lincoln were Catholics, from Mary-land. The alleged co-conspirator who temporarily got away was John H. Surratt. His mother was one of the four conspirators who were illegally tried by a "military court" and hanged. John, 19 years old, made his way to Canada; then by April 23, 1866, to Britain where he enlisted in the Papal Zouaves. He ventured on to the Papal States in Rome where he fell under the control of Cardinal Antonelli, ally of the Black Pope and financial middleman between the Papal debt and the Rothschilds. The U.S. Secretary of State pursued Surratt through official political channels. Antonelli responded by arresting Surratt but he somehow conveniently escaped, after which Surratt fled to Egypt where he was arrested by the American Navy; he was still in his Papal uniform. He was brought back to America, tried in connection of the Lincoln assassination yet found not guilty, and released.

Who wanted Lincoln dead? And who else was targeted to be assassinated that night? Andrew Johnson was on the list to be assassinated, but the assassin got cold feet. Secretary of State Seward was stabbed but didn't die. Grant was on the hit list too, but cancelled his theater reservation. Those targets were the same people in favor of letting the South return into the Union without punishment. Those were the people who were standing in the way of the radical reconstruction plans of the fanatic Republicans. Was Abraham Lincoln's assassination revenge from the South or from the Catholics or was it simply the necessary phase two of the American Transfer of Power, a transition from war to oppression; a transition from martial law (wartime) to martial law rule (the claim of unconstitutional powers during peacetime)?

The Papal States never really recovered from the Illuminati's power-play with Garibaldi, but the power of the Jesuits lived on. Today there are 25,000 Jesuits worldwide, with 4,500 in the United States, and today's Masons are filling Catholic Churches as laymen and Priests. Listen carefully: Today's anti-Catholic movement comes from within the Catholic Church and is run by the Illuminati. However, the Jesuits are always a "wildcard" and their stronghold is now South America; they backed the communist takeover of Nicaragua in the 1980's. Keep an eye on South America.

So there you have the international intrigue behind the war, Judaistic, Masonic and Catholic; make your own judgements. The reason you don't hear about such "taboo" subjects in the media or in text books, is because those "occult" forces are still around today and number in the millions. The higher levels of these networks are remaining hidden behind their "cover" vehicle. And whenever a small amount of truth slips out, as was the case with General Grant III releasing his grandfather's candid opinions, the network's anti-defamation defense mechanism will accuse such persons or groups of being "anti-Semitic," which has been very effective in sweeping the nuggets of history back under the rug. And books such as this one are just ignored by the establishment; what else can they do. They wouldn't dare get on live T.V. and debate anyone who understands the shadows of history. The media makes the loudest claim that they believe in freedom of speech, but they jealously guard access to the microphone.

It would be presumptuous for an outsider to pretend to know the absolute "capstone" of their plans, after all, they operate in secret, or now in semi-secret, but it is obvious that they have worked long and hard toward their ancient goal of global governance, both political and economic (centralization). Today they are safely entrenched behind religious and racial politics. They have made "Race" and "Religion" very effective defense mechanisms in which to hide their global agenda. And when, or if, their agenda is challenged, their corporate media would step in and label the challenger as a religious bigot or racist who would therefore be discounted by the well-groomed politically correct public. Very cleaver, very effective. But what happens when hundreds of thousands, or millions of people wake up? How long before the cries of "anti-Semitism" or "racist" are overplayed and the public smells a rat? And when global governance establishes its infrastructure and tax systems within national borders, will the public see beyond the tactical rhetoric of social quilt assignments?

The powerful forces of intrigue are determined to rule over America by deceit or by force, but there will always be those who pledge their allegiance to the truth, just for the sake of truth. Hopefully there will always be people who oppose the intrigue and delusions of a proposed global harmony that can only be realized at the expense of national sovereignty. Truth may not always be comfortable, and may not always make us feel "happy," therefore, the weak among us have turned away, but without truth, our liberty will finally and forever pass away.

Our own U.S. Government continues to be directed by a global agenda, therefore, that government cannot provide us with the liberty we must have. The War of 1861 was not just about "State's rights" or "slavery" or the "right to secede" or a war to "preserve the union," those were merely the rhetorical excuses needed to satisfy both sides of a divided uninformed public. The War of 1861 was a Transfer of Power: the national government destroyed its own Constitution and the Constitutions of the separate sovereign States and consolidated them into one "union." This centralization of America, was followed a hundred years later by the centralization of the Europe into one "European Union," which will likely be followed by the American nations being united into one "continental union," and an Arabian-Persian Union, and an Asian Union, and a new Soviet Union. Then all such "unions" will be centralized into one global government. Looking back (which is easy) on the 1865 words of Karl Marx, and considering these previous statements, and considering that it was Marx who first proposed a "United States of Europe," his words today reveal his deeper reality; Marx:

"After the Civil War phase, the United States really is only now entering the revolutionary phase."

Chapter 6

The Confederate States of America

After Lincoln was elected in November of 1860, but before he took office, (in those days) on March 4th, 1861, seven of the Southern States seceded. These secessions were a direct response to the Republican Party getting in the White House, although Republicans did not control Congress, and neither did they control the Supreme Court. The remaining four States, of those who would eventually join the Confederacy, stayed in the Union until after Lincoln called-up the military to subdue the "insurrection" in South Carolina.

The international intrigue deployed out of Europe to separate the American States, North from South, had worked, however, that does not mean that all of the contentious issues surrounding secession were false. The Northern powers, whether Radical Republicans, industrialists, or bankers, were forcing the South into an agenda of division that the occult Southern secessionists had made ready to accommodate. But without the general public knowing of the occult politics at work, there was no way for them to avert the well-scripted "irrepressible conflict."

The plan was to create a war between the States that would change America forever. Pardon the metaphor but, it was like taking 34 individual eggs and mixing them in a pan, creating a "union" impossible to unscramble. In this political strategy to scramble "the law of the land" the agents had to alter the Constitution in such a way that America could never return to its original purity or regain State sovereignty.

Lincoln was elected in November 1860. South Carolina, the leader of the secessionists, along with Mississippi, seceded on December 20th; Florida, December 22nd; Alabama, December 24th; Georgia, January 2nd; Louisiana, January 7th; and Texas seceded on February 23rd.

On February 4th the initial meeting of the Confederate Provisional Congress was held. On February 8th, 1861 the seven State Confederate Provisional Government was established. And on March 11, they adopted the Confederate Constitution unanimously. On March

16th, the U.S. Territory of Arizona voted to leave the Union and applied to be a Territory of the Confederacy, which was granted in August of 1861.

Other Southern States, Virginia, North Carolina, Tennessee and Arkansas held individual State conventions and voted against secession. On February 9th, the Confederate Government chose Jefferson Davis as President; Davis was not seeking that position.

Jefferson Davis was the best Constitutional mind in the country. He opposed the secession. He toured the North before the war speaking out to avoid secession and spoke-out to avoid a regional war by expounding the legitimate grievances that the South had against the unconstitutional encroachments of the national government into the States' jurisdictions. The well funded and established occult secession machine needed to legitimize their power play yet conceal themselves and so chose a true American statesman, Jefferson Davis, to lead their new nation.

Jefferson Davis accepted the position of President of the Confederate States of America, and from day one, he carried a tremendous burden. The day after his inauguration, Union forces captured Nashville, the Tennessee Democrat, and future President Andrew Johnson was made Military Governor. It may seem like a contradiction that perhaps the two greatest Statesmen of this era, Davis and Johnson, were serving on opposite sides. This is not a contradiction at all because both men worked to serve truth and both sought justice for the much-abused Southern States, during or after the war.

Andrew Johnson was the only Southern Senator, to keep his seat in the U.S. Senate after all of the Southern States, including his own State of Tennessee seceded (June 8th, 1861). Virginia had Senators in Congress during the War but they were unlawful Senators from a bogus Pierpont Virginia government. Andrew Johnson became Lincoln's military Governor of Tennessee, and in 1864, was elected Lincoln's Vice President. When Lincoln was murdered, Andrew Johnson became President. Lincoln died six days after Robert E. Lee surrendered his army, yet before the Confederate Government was captured; the Confederate Government never surrendered. Lincoln died before President Davis was captured. President Johnson offered a $100,000 reward for the capture of President Davis.

Jefferson Davis had a great legal and ethical mind before, during and after the war. Andrew Johnson, did not become a great patriot until after the war, when he fought against the Congressional usurpation of power called "reconstruction."

Once Davis (not a Mason) became President, the Templar-Scottish Rite conspirators turned against him. Those who served the cause of Europe fled to Europe after the war, these were the critics of Davis during the war. Davis' own Vice President, Alexander Stephens, hated Davis and abandoned his post. Robert Barnwell Rhett, mouthpiece of Charleston, attempted to depose Davis. Even Generals like the pro-Jesuit Templar Beauregard worked against Davis. Confederate President Davis vetoed 38 bills passed by the Confederate Congress, all but one passed over his veto. Davis represented the best of the Confederacy but he was confined within a political structure designed in the secret conclaves of Charleston, Newburyport, London and Frankfurt.

Davis knew that as bad as things were in the war-torn South, there was no political hope to be found in the North. Even as late as April 23rd, 1865, Davis told his wife Varina that if the States returned to the Union it would be the subjugation of the South. Was he right? Yes he was right!

Davis was a statesman in the truest sense of the word, not a political puppet nor a two faced lawyer for hire. Davis' request to the North was simple: "All we want is to be let alone." He spent the night before his inauguration on his knees in prayer. He personally observed the first major battle of the war at Bull Run. In February 1862, Davis called upon the Confederacy to observe a day of fasting and prayer. The White House of the Confederacy was in Richmond Virginia. On Sunday, On April 2, 1865, Davis was in St. Paul's Church when the message reached him that Richmond would fall to the Union Army. President Davis was forced to leave Richmond on April 2, and by April 4th, Abraham Lincoln himself was standing in Richmond, at which time he said "Dixie is federal property." Spin-historians say he was referring to the song "Dixie."

After Richmond fell, April 4, 1865, Davis, a military graduate of West Point, said the war was entering into a new phase. He moved the Capital of the Confederacy to Danville, Virginia, then to Greensboro, North Carolina, and finally to Charlotte, North Carolina. He received requests to keep fighting; General Hampton suggested that they continue the war west of the Mississippi, but his Cabinet suggested surrender. Davis preferred that the South never surrender. For the cause of American liberty, Davis was willing to transform the thus-far conventional war into partisan warfare. Davis issued a defiant order to fight.

Even General Lee, after his own surrender, advised Davis on April 20th, to give up and not pursue this struggle into a guerilla war. Only after seeing the evils of Reconstruction did Robert E. Lee realized the wisdom of Jefferson Davis' defiant order for the South to resort to guerilla warfare; upon seeing the radical "Construction" of the "New America," Lee said:

"Had I foreseen these results of subjugation, I would have preferred to die at Appomattox with my brave men, my sword in this right hand."

The President of the Confederacy was captured in Georgia on May 10, 1865. He had been able to send his children to Canada to be with their grandmother. He was put in chains in the Army prison at Fortress Monroe on May 22, 1865. Davis was denied all communication, grossly mistreated, and became very ill. He was finally allowed a visitor, his wife Varina. She was shocked into outrage at his condition. She let the world know the condition of her husband's health which brought public pressure to bare from around the country and around the world. European newspapers insisted on Davis receiving humane treatment, to prevent his death. Finally, after two years of imprisonment, Davis was to stand trial for treason in Richmond, Virginia. The jury picked in the Davis trial was to be the first Negro jury in American history.

According to R.G. Horton's 1868 - Youth's History of the Civil War: Davis' legal counsel demanded a speedy trial; but the Federal Government had postponed the trial for three years. When the lower court finally called the case to trial, Supreme Court Chief Justice Chase interceded with an order of certiorari and changed the proceedings venue from the docket of the lower court in Richmond to the docket of the Supreme Court. Davis was released on bond on May 13th, 1867, his case remained on the docket but was tactfully never heard. Chief Justice Chase stated:

"If you bring these leaders to trial, it will condemn the North, for by the Constitution, secession is not a rebellion. His (Jefferson Davis) capture was a mistake. His trial will be a greater one. We cannot convict him of treason."

Salmon P. Chase advised that the Court avoid hearing the case because there was too great a possibility that the Constitutional genius of Jefferson Davis would prove, in the highest court in the land, that secession was legal. Such a trial could result in the legal reestablishment the Confederacy, after Lincoln and his New America caused 600,000 deaths and wasted billions of dollars of resources. The charge remained against Davis but never called to court. Friends and international media asked Davis to apply for a pardon and reenter political life to which Davis replied:

"It has been said that I should apply to the United States for a pardon; but repentance must precede the right of a pardon, and I have not repented. Remembering, as I must, all which has been suffered, all which has been lost, disappointed hopes, and crushed aspirations, yet I deliberately say, if it were to do all over again, I would do just as I did in 1861."

In one of Andrew Johnson's last acts as President (1868) he pardoned all Southerners which included Jefferson Davis; whether the Radical Republicans obeyed that is another matter. Jefferson Davis may be the source of the old prediction: "The South will rise again," but to put it in his exact words:

"The principal for which we contended is bound to reassert itself, though it may be at another time and in another form."

How prophetic; that time is now upon us, but in what form will it ultimately reassert itself? The answer is to be found among the individuals and groups of today, that is, those who know the specifics of the Transfer of Power from the War of 1861. The answer will come from those who can clearly see that the "New America" born in 1861 became the center of operations to implement global centralization, both political and economic, with its United Nations headquartered in New

York and its World Bank headquartered in Washington D.C.

After the complete take over of the Original United States by the treason of 1861-65, the new government required Southerners to swear allegiance to the "New America" before they could be granted citizenship. Jefferson Davis never applied for the new citizenship, he preferred "True America" to "New America."

The Confederate Constitution was almost identical to the U.S. Constitution. There were no freedoms that existed under the U.S. Constitution that did not exist under the Confederate Constitution. In fact, on February 9th, the day after the Confederacy was formed, they adopted all of the existing laws of the U.S. excepting any that were in conflict with the additional provisions of the Confederate Constitution, (such as tariffs).

The Confederate Constitution was more specific concerning States Rights, as expressed in its opening words:

"We, the people of the Confederate States, each State acting in its sovereign and independent character..."

There was no "Supreme" court to rule over the States. There would be no tariffs, a result of the previous government's abuse of Southern taxation to fund the primarily Northern "internal improvements." No tariffs also reflected the unfortunate presence of the international "free trade" influence of Britain's laissez-faire, and also Confederate "federal" judges could be impeached. The "Bill of Rights" clauses of the 1789 compact were incorporated into Section Nine of the Confederate Constitution; the right to bear arms, freedom of speech, press and religion etc. The Confederate Constitution outlawed "The importation of Negroes of the African race" but did not interfere with such trade between States.

At this point in time (1861) there were really 3 regions of the United States: The solid North; the solid 7 State Confederate South; and the "middle" States. Those middle States were New Jersey, Delaware, Maryland, Virginia, North Carolina, Kentucky, Tennessee, Missouri, and Arkansas. Its a shame that these States couldn't knock some sense into the North and South which might have resulted in either a peaceful separation of States, or a "Union" that wouldn't destroy the Original Constitution. These three political regions are best observed in the results of three Presidential elections: 1856, 1860, and 1864.

In the Election of 1856, there were three parties: the Republicans, the Democrats, and the American "Know Nothing" Whig party. The Know Nothings were the remnants of the Anti-Masonic Party. In the 1856 election, the Know Nothings received 22% of the popular vote, but only 3% of the Electoral votes. They only carried one State, Maryland, (the Catholic anti-Masonic feud spill-over from Europe). The Republican Party took Iowa, Wisconsin, Michigan, Ohio, New York, Vermont, New Hampshire, Maine, Massachusetts, Rhode Island and Connecticut: the 11 most Northern contiguous States. The other 19 States, including all Southern States went Democratic. This revealed that America had two philosophical regions: the North, and everything else, which included the South and the middle States.

The Election of 1860, had four parties: The Republicans, the Northern Democrats, the Southern Democrats, and the National Constitutional Union Party. The Republican Party (Lincoln) was the anti-Southern pro-banking, pro-industrialist party.

The Democratic party held their 1860 convention and could not reach a two-thirds agreement on candidates and adjourned without candidates. The Masonic elements within the Democratic Party created that split and walked out of the national convention. The split resulted in two separate Democratic conventions, Baltimore and Charleston, creating two separate parties, the Northern Democrats and Southern Democrats.

Caleb Cushing presided over the Charleston convention. Cushing had previously worked in the newspaper offices of Caleb Huse in Massachusetts. It was Huse who later went to Europe to procure weapons for the Confederacy. Also working in the newspaper offices of Caleb Huse was William Lloyd Garrison the leader of the abolitionists. Isn't that ironic, Confederates working with abolitionists for the same Massachusetts news media? No, not when you observe the big picture.

The new National Constitutional Union Party was created for the 1860 election, it hoped to salvage the Union and prevent the war, without burning the Constitution. This was a compromise party out of the middle States which included many older Whig Party members.

The 1860 national election results differed greatly between popular votes and electoral votes:

Party	Popular Vote	Electoral Vote
Republican	40%	59%
N. Democrats	29%	4%
S. Democrats	13%	24%
Const. Union	13%	13%

The States carried by the Constitutional Union Party were Virginia, Kentucky and Tennessee. The States carried by the Northern Democrats were Missouri, and New Jersey. The Republican Party carried the Northern States, and the Southern Democrats took the nine most-Southern contiguous States and Maryland and Delaware (slave States). The Constitutional Union Party of the middle States separated the two political poles.

In the election of 1864, there were only two parties: the Republicans and the Democrats; the South was considered out of the Union. It was Republican Lincoln against Democrat (Union General) McClellan, the General who was deposed by Lincoln sometime earlier. With the South not voting, the Republicans carried every State except Kentucky, Delaware and New Jersey. The Republican Party got 91% of the electoral vote, but the popular vote gives a better reflection of Northern sentiment: Republican 55%, Democratic 45%.

The Republican Party had actually downplayed the name Republican during the election because it was known as the "war party," they took on a new name, the National Union Party. In the Republican's attempt to show moderation, they nominated Andrew Johnson, a Southerner and a Democrat to be their Vice Presidential candidate. A choice they would live to regret.

Before the secession, the United States was politically three regions, North, South and middle. The North wanted the middle States and the South wanted the middle States. Those middle States would be divided up between North and South after Fort Sumter.

When the Union Fort Sumter was fired upon by Confederate forces on April 12th, 1861, the alignment of the middle States began. The North had already used force to take Nashville, Tennessee. Lincoln placed troops in Kentucky, declared martial law over Maryland, sent troops to secure Missouri, and supported a coup in western Virginia.

Even Kansas, which became a State on January 29, 1861, was placed under hostile Union control. During the war, the Union Army depopulated three entire counties in ~~Kansas~~ which became known as the Burnt District. So, the Northern method of "preserving the Union" was at the point of a bayonet.

However, the Confederate Government was not recruiting by bayonet, in fact it offered all who entered their Confederation of States, a Constitution almost identical to the Original U.S. Constitution, and actually spelled out State's Rights. As a result of the difference between the Northern tactics for "recruiting" loyalty and the Southern offers of voluntary Constitutional unity, no middle States "joined" the Union, in fact the middle States who remained in the Union were forced to do so by military might. In contrast, after Fort Sumter, Virginia, Tennessee, North Carolina and Arkansas voluntarily joined the Confederacy. More middle States (perhaps all) would have joined the Confederacy if not for the Federal Government's maxim that "might makes right."

It is generally accepted that there were only eleven Confederate States, however, there were others to consider. Arizona became a Confederate Territory in August of 1861. The Confederate government had treaties with five Indian Nations who are referred to as "Little Dixie." In response to requests from representatives from other border States, on November 28th of 1861, the Confederate Congress formally admitted Missouri into the Confederacy, and on December 10th formally admitted Kentucky into the Confederate States of America. These two States were unfortunately under Lincoln's military fist, yet when the ad hoc Provisional Confederate government ended and the official Confederate Congress convened, Missouri and Kentucky took their seats with full power. They were the 12th and 13th Stars on the Confederate Battle Flag.

The legitimacy of the Confederate States is based upon whether American States have a "Right to Secede" as found in the Original compacts among the States when they United. After the war, Salmon P. Chase, as Supreme Court Chief Justice, avoided a "head to head" challenge with Jefferson Davis on this issue; but after the Supreme Court became just another department of federal treason, Chase and the Court declared that secession was not legal. Chase, along with his "stacked Supreme Court" were altering jurisprudence to conceal the new usurpations. The Court did not give a fair and impartial hearing of that historic

Constitutional issue. Chase and his kangaroos chose to turn a blind eye to secession, but here are some facts for those who have eyes to see. The Executive Branch was no better, if fact it must be said that America's greatest usurpation of Constitutional law began at the White House. On March 4th, 1861, on his first day in office, President Lincoln stated in his inaugural address:

"No State, on its own mere action, can get out of the Union."

The Right to Secede

There is no doubt that "opinion" and "interpretation" are societies' greatest source of legal and social unrest, and the use of opinion or interpretation is always invoked when discussing the subject of the legality of secession. The best American minds during that era, or today, find it difficult to separate their beliefs from their bias. The truth of the legality of secession requires an objectivity to weigh the question simply in the context of the Constitution, without whistling Dixie or singing John Brown's body lies a moulding in the grave.

It is necessary to remove the opinions and interpretations supplied by the men of that era who worked for the agenda of Intrigue; both North and South. Judgement in this matter will not have the luxury of an authoritative document written in the precise language needed, such does not exist, and so, to some degree, any determination may appear to resort to opinion or interpretation. The best opinions and interpretations are to be found somewhere in the credible middle ground, not a middle ground of bias or agenda, and not in a middle ground of compromise or consensus, but in a determination based upon the most correct foundation of legal intention. All credible answers must be decided based upon the principles in the Founding Documents of this Nation. Before presenting the germane stipulations of those Founding Documents, it is necessary to review some lesser yet credible sources that help corroborate the original intention.

Some observations toward discerning the truth of this matter can be made by noting certain contemporary traditions that were based upon an obvious accepted truth. One example would be that in the United States Military Institute of West Point, prior to the War of 1861, the right of a State to secede from the Union was taught as fact. So, the Union and future Confederate officers who fought against each other in a war over secession, were taught at West Point that secession was legal as stated in their text book "View of the Constitution" by William Rawle, Chancellor of the Law Association of Philadelphia and author of the Code of Pennsylvania, the text stated: "It will depend upon the State itself whether it will continue a member of the Union." The book further stated: "If the States are interfered with they may wholly withdraw from the Union."

Another example of a contemporary truth is revealed in the "sought-after legislation" as proposed in the U.S. Congress. After the first seven States seceded, and formed the Confederate States of America, James Doolittle, an anti-secessionist, on March 2, 1861, proposed a Constitutional Amendment which read:

"No State or any part thereof, heretofore to be admitted into the Union, shall have power to withdraw from the jurisdiction of the United States."

This example shows, by an attempted amendment to the Constitution, that the anti-secessionist conceded that it must be legal for existing States to secede, because Doolittle was attempting to prohibit any future States from having that right.

Former President John Tyler, led a Peace Delegation to Washington prior to the conflict at Fort Sumter. This and other peace attempts were rejected by Washington D.C., and so after Lincoln incited the conflict at Fort Sumter, John Tyler voted for Virginia to secede. The contemporary truth here is that a former President of the United States believed that the State of Virginia had a right to secede.

Lincoln's predecessor, President Buchanan stated that he did not think that States could legally secede, but saw no Constitutional authority to stop them with guns of war. As President Buchanan put it in his message on December 3, 1860:

"Congress may possess many means of preserving the Union by conciliation, but the sword was not placed in its hand to preserve it by force."

That puts a spin on the secession question. "Whether or not it was legal to secede" may not be the only question to ask; but whether Lincoln could Constitutionally invade South Carolina, and eventually invade all of the Southern States. And when considered in the light of this clause in the U.S. Constitution that defines treason as: "Treason against the United States shall consist only in levying war against them..." (Art. 3, Sec. 3, clause 1). Treason is to make war against the States.

John C. Breckinridge, Vice President of the United States in the Buchanan Administration (1857-1861), and Democrat Presidential candidate for President in 1860, expressed his belief that secession was legal by serving as a Major General in the Confederate Army and was later appointed by Jefferson Davis to be the Confederate Secretary of War. [Jefferson Davis served as the U.S. Secretary of War in the Pierce Administration.]

When the question of secession is considered in reverse, that is, to question an abuse of federal power, the admonition against such coming from two of America's most qualified Presidents should bear considerable weight. Thomas Jefferson, author of the Declaration of Independence, and James Madison author of the U.S. Constitution both faced the assumption of undelegated powers by the Federal Government of their time. They voiced their opposition in the form of two declarations representing the General Assemblies of two States.

Most power plays by the Federal Government have been based on so-called "national threats." This was the case with Lincoln, Wilson, and Roosevelt, all three damaged the U.S. Constitution. But perhaps the first conspicuous attempt by the Federal Government to use a "national threat" as an excuse for a power-grab was during the days of Jefferson and Madison.

The conflict was brought on by the Alien and Sedition Acts of Congress, along with other supportive legislation. In response to Congress creating new undelegated powers, Madison wrote the Virginia Resolutions and Jefferson wrote the Kentucky Resolutions addressing the Constitutionality of the Federal Government's self-empowerment. The Resolutions were passed by the Virginia General Assembly and likewise in Kentucky. In these writings Madison and Jefferson stated that it is the State's duty to "interpose" for the citizens by restraining the unconstitutional powers adopted by the Federal Government. Some call this the Doctrine of Interposition, which clearly places the final legal judgement of federal abuses or assumptions of powers to be determined by the States.

In the Virginia Resolutions, passed by the Virginia General Assembly in December of 1798, James Madison wrote:

" ... this Assembly doth explicitly ... declare that it views the powers of the federal government ... as limited by the plain sense intention of the instrument constituting the compact ... and that in case of a deliberate ... and dangerous exercise of other powers ... the States ... are in duty bound, to interpose for arresting the progress of the evil ... That the General Assembly doth also express its deep regret, that a spirit ... has been manifested by the federal government to enlarge its powers ... so as to consolidate the States by degrees, into one sovereignty, the obvious tendency and inevitable consequence of which would be to transform the present republican system of the United States, into an absolute, or at best a mixed monarchy."
(James Madison, Father of the U.S. Constitution.)

In the Kentucky Resolutions written by Thomas Jefferson and passed by the Kentucky General Assembly, it states:

"Resolved, That the several States composing the United States of America, are not united on the principle of unlimited submission to their general government ... and whensoever the general government assumes undelegated powers, its acts are unauthoritative, void, and of no force ... that the government created by this compact was not made the exclusive or final judge of the extent of the powers delegated to itself; because that would have made its discretion, not the Constitution, the measure of its powers ... each party has an equal right to judge for itself..."
(Thomas Jefferson, author of the Declaration of Independence.)

Despite this "historic testimony" by the two most prolific Founding Fathers, the anti-secessionist forces in the North knew that they had to sell the War of 1861 as being Constitutional, and so architects of deception carefully changed the issue from being a "legal question" of secession, into the South committing an "illegal action." In their politically correct rhetoric, they stopped using the word "secession" and started using "insurrection." This provided the much-needed constitutional claim to their otherwise treasonous invasion of South Carolina and the South. Their claim was based on federal powers derived from Article I, Section 8, (clause 15) of the U.S. Constitution:

"To provide for calling forth the militia to execute the laws of the Union, suppress insurrections and repel invasions."

The Northern war machine also turned against its own people in the border States by placing "home-grown" terrorism under the boot of martial law. Instead of Northern politicians calling Southerners "Confederates," they disciplined themselves to label them "rebels" to portray the conflict as an insurrection providing themselves with the constitutional mandate. This "rebel" word game, like that of "insurrection" also provided the Lincoln regime with powers to be used against citizens in the North. Lincoln invoked martial law throughout the North based upon his "constitutional spin" of Article I, Section 9, (clause 2) of the Constitution:

"The privilege of the writ of habeas corpus shall not be suspended, unless when in cases of rebellion or invasion the public safety may require it."

That is why they called Southerners "rebels," so they could declare martial law in the "north." Martial law also excused their printing the "funny money" and all of those wartime deals with the railroads and industrialists and bankers. The Federal Government's official name for the War of 1861 was "War of the Rebellion." Yes, it was a word game.

The Washington D.C. government chose their words well. They had to sell the American people on the "rebellion and insurrection" clauses of the Constitution to preclude any and all legal challenges, because an honest legal decision would likely not be in their favor. Cooler heads in the North suggested to "let the South go, in a few years, those States would come back, one by one." But cooler heads did not prevail. The North would never consider the legality of secession; yet the South was risking everything on the legality of secession.

The Southern States that did secede, based their Right of Secession on the Constitution of the United States and on their State Constitutions. Secession was the question, not rebellion or insurrection. Why did the North refuse to take the case before Congress or the Supreme Court? Consider, there were forces in the South that wanted not just secession but war, and, there were forces in the North that wanted war, not to preserve the Constitution but to rewrite it. The reason the legal question of secession never had its day in court was because war was the intended agenda. The case for the Right to Secede was not complicated, it was simple; yet the issue was laced heavily with "opinion" or "interpretation" concerning the relative facts. No matter how solid a legal argument may be, the loyal opposition will deny its validity. Nonetheless, these facts, as presented, favor a legal existence of the Right to Secede.

All of the former 13 British colonies that declared their independence became sovereign individual nations. They joined together in a confederacy, uniting with each other under the Articles of Confederation, and later under the conditions of the U.S. Constitution. Consider Virginia as one example.

On May 15, 1776, the 5th Virginia Convention declared Virginia to be a free and independent nation. Virginia ceased to be a colony of Britain. On June 12, 1776, the Virginia Constitutional Convention approved the Virginia Constitution and the Virginia Bill of Rights (sometimes called the Declaration of Rights). From that day forward, those Documents were the Law of the Land, and excepting that if we were conquered by a foreign power, or suffered an internal revolution, or lawfully ceded those laws and rights to another governance, the Virginia Constitution and the Declaration of Rights should still be Virginia's Law of the Land.

On July 4th, 1776, the Declaration of Independence boldly stated: "... these United Colonies are, and of right ought to be, FREE AND INDEPENDENT STATES; ..."

In the Treaty of Paris with Britain after the Revolutionary War, each State was treated separately, because they were separate, independent nations. Later, those States entered into a Constitutional compact that stipulated specific areas of sovereignty were ceded to their mutual "federal" government of the States united. A true "federal" government (federation) is composed of sovereign nations, sovereign in all things except specific areas as stipulated in their mutual constitution. This maxim is summed up in the Original U.S. Constitution's concluding 10th Amendment:

"The powers not delegated to the United States, nor prohibited by it to the States, are reserved to the States respectively, or to the people."

This Amendment delegated limited sovereignty to both the State governments and the national government as determined by the wording of the U.S. Constitution. And so the legality of secession must be found from within our Original Founding Documents: the States' Constitutions, the Declaration of Independence, the United States Constitution and Bill of Rights.

In the Virginia Bill of Rights, the very first Right listed says:

"That all men are by nature equally free and independent, and have certain inherent rights, of which, when they enter into a state of society, they cannot, by any compact, deprive or divest their posterity; namely, the enjoyment of life and liberty..."

So, from that moment on, Virginia could not enter into any compact which would deprive its posterity of the liberty that they had in 1776, that means any compact, including the U.S. Constitution. There are 16 Rights listed in the Virginia Bill of Rights. Right 15 states:

"That no free government, or the blessing of liberty, can be preserved to any people but by a firm adherence to **justice, moderation, temperance, frugality and virtue**, and by a frequent recurrence of fundamental principles."

Can the Right to Secede be found in Virginia's State Constitution? Well, Virginia cannot enter into any compact that divests its posterity of liberty. If there was no loss of liberty for Virginians when Virginia entered into the U.S. Compact, then it was lawful at that time. Question: What validity would that compact have if years later, the "federal" partner acted to "divest the posterity of its liberty?" Surely if the "federal" partner violated the compact, after the fact, the compact would be rendered void by Virginia's Law of the Land, the Virginia Bill of

Rights. Did the "federal" partner actually violate the compact? Yes! Then, specifically, what part of the compact was violated? The federal partner cannot divest the people of Virginia of their liberty. Was liberty divested. The Virginia Constitution did something very important: it defined Liberty. Right 15 states that the blessing of liberty requires a "firm adherence to justice, moderation, temperance, frugality and virtue," and any "compact" or partner of that compact who does not maintain "a firm adherence" to these prerequisites of liberty renders the compact null and void.

Did the State of Virginia, in April 1861 have the Right to Secede from the Federal Compact? The answer would be based on whether or not the Federal Government had a "firm adherence" to Virginia's Constitutional prerequisites of liberty and governance as stipulated:

Justice: The Federal Government refused to provide a legal decision on the question of secession and invoked martial law on the entire nation, North and South.

Moderation: The Federal Government passed "internal improvement" legislation which favored the North and hindered the South.

Temperance: Lincoln called on the States to provide 75,000 troops, to march across Virginia to attack South Carolina even though the Union Fort Sumter suffered no deaths and all Union soldiers were allowed to leave by ship.

Frugality: The Federal Government was bankrupt in 1860 and at the end of the war was 2.6 billion dollars in debt and had issued 500 million dollars in fiat money.

Virtue: The Federal Government had been bought out by special interest groups: industrialists, railroads, and bankers and had stolen one billion acres from the Indian Nations.

When the U.S. national government of 1861, performed its Transfer of Power, it became the Federal Government that we know today. If you can judge a treason by its roots (1861) maybe you can also judge it by its branches today. Fast forward to check the record of today's Federal Government concerning Virginia's measurement of Justice, Moderation, Temperance, Frugality, and Virtue. We can judge this tree by its roots, and we can we judge this tree today by its branches. If there weren't enough causes for Virginia to secede in 1861, there surely there would be today. There was indeed enough legal cause for secession in 1861, based solely upon the Virginia Constitution. The Southerners of 1861 perceived the threat of America's Transfer of Power because they understood the nation's foundational laws.

Can the Right to Secede be found in the Declaration of Independence? Consider the case as based on the first and second paragraphs.

"When in the course of human events, it becomes necessary for one people to dissolve the political bands which have connected them with another..."

So, it can be proper "to dissolve the political bands" if it becomes "necessary." When Jefferson Davis gave his farewell message to the Senate on behalf of his seceding State of Mississippi, he said: "I concur in the action of the people of Mississippi believing it to be necessary and proper." Necessary? What did the Declaration of Independence say would make such a political separation necessary? Paragraph two:

"We hold these truths to be self-evident, that all men are created equal, that they are endowed by their creator with certain unalienable rights, that among these are Life, Liberty and the Pursuit of Happiness .... That whenever any form of government becomes destructive of these ends, it is the right of the people to alter or abolish it, and to institute a new Government..."

So, according to the Declaration of Independence, it is proper to "dissolve the political bands" and the people have the Right to "alter or abolish" any government when it is destructive to liberty. Was secession a legal mechanism to "dissolve the political bands" "and alter" the Federal Compact, and even "institute a new government" (or Confederacy) because the Federal Government was guilty of violating the definition of liberty? Considering Virginia's definition of Liberty, yes.

Now consider the legal case for secession as found in the third Original Document of this nation, the United States Constitution; it too is germane to the Right of Secession. The Articles of Confederation are not considered here because they were superseded by the U.S Constitution, except to say that in that document the States united was called a "Confederacy." The Bill of Rights is an inseparable part of the Constitution. The original Bill of Rights contained 10 Amendments, those are sacrosanct, however, any Amendments beyond those are only lawful if they were Constitutionally approved and if they do not violate the U.S. Constitution or the Constitutions of the States. There are only two Amendments beyond the original 10, that are Constitutional: the 11th and 12th Amendments. The rest of the Amendments were passed by the unconstitutional post-1861 Federal Government.

Because most of the Constitution is devoted to the workings of the governmental structure and operations and not related directly to "liberty" or "rights," it is most prudent to go straight to the Tenth Amendment which is the Right most often used by Southerners to support a Constitutional Right of Secession.

"The powers not delegated to the United States by the Constitution, nor prohibited by it to the States, are reserved to the States respectively, or to the people."

When opponents deny that States have a "right" or "power" to secede, they are admitting that secession is a "right" or "power." Obviously, secession is a power, the power of a sovereign member of a federation to leave the voluntary union. Does the Constitution say that the "power" of secession is "prohibited ... to the States?" Or, was the power to deny or confirm the secession of a State specifically "delegated to the United States?" The "power" to control the secession of a State was not delegated to the national government nor was such a power denied the States, therefore, as stipulated in the Tenth Amendment, secession is a power that is "reserved to the States respectively, or to the People."

And second, if the U.S. national government passes an unconstitutional amendment or law and it proved to be destructive of liberty, then it is void and of no effect. If such legislation were forced upon the States, the compact between State and national governments is voided.

We the People were never to be held captive to laws proscribed by a majority vote nationally (or even by State) if the preexisting liberties are not preserved.

Opposition to this "interpretation" will point out Article 5 of the Constitution states that when an Amendment is passed by the prescribed method, it "shall be valid ... as part of this Constitution..." In other words, if there was a Constitutional Amendment passed that said every first-born male child will be sacrificed to Baal, would such an atrocity beome law? There is no difference. Lawful amendments to the Constitution of the United States must preserve the liberties of each State as spelled out in the Declaration of Independence and in every State Constitution.

In the third consideration, there is another group of documents in addition to the Declaration of Independence, State Constitutions, and the U.S. Constitution which also comprise a lawful part of the National Compact. Each State had to ratify the U.S. Constitution. Those State Ratifications are an essential component of the National Compact, without the accepted State Ratifications, there is no Compact. Consider the words of Daniel Webster spoken in 1851:

"The Union is a Union of States founded upon Compact. How is it to be supposed that when different parties enter into a compact for certain purposes either can disregard one provision of it and expect others to observe the rest"

The stipulations written into each State's ratification is as binding a part of the National Compact as the Constitution itself. The ratifications do not impose restrictions on other States, but only between the national government and each individual State. These are the conditions that bind the compact, and without these agreed upon stipulations, the State would not have joined the Union. Virginia's Act of Ratification to the U. S. Constitution includes these protections for the People of Virginia:

"We, the delegates of the people of Virginia, duly elected ... in behalf of the People of Virginia, declare and make known, that the powers granted under the Constitution, being derived from the people of the United States, may be resumed by them, whensoever the same shall be

perverted to their injury or oppression; and that every power not granted
thereby, remains with them and at their will: that, therefore, no right, of
any denomination, can be cancelled, abridged, restrained, or modified."

The People of Virginia may resume all powers yielded in the
National Compact if and when the national government perverts its
power to the "injury or oppression" of the State of Virginia or the People
of Virginia, thus, no right can be cancelled, abridged, restrained or modified. Therefore, Virginia's Ratification refutes the liberal interpretation
of Article 5, that all national amendments are the law of the land. Instead, all amendments are subject to the proviso that such amendments
are not "perverted to their injury or oppression" and that "no right, of
any denomination, can be cancelled, abridged, restrained, or modified."
If the People of Virginia determine that they have suffered such violations, they may withdraw from the federation and resume all powers
previously ceded in said compact. That is the Right to Secede.

Review the following documental excerpts from these in a perspective of confirming a State's Right of Secession:

"That all men are by nature equally free and independent, and
have certain inherent rights, of which, when they enter into a state of
society, they cannot, by any compact, deprive or divest their posterity;
namely, the enjoyment of life and liberty..."

"That no free government, or the blessing of liberty, can be preserved to any people but by a firm adherence to justice, moderation,
temperance, frugality and virtue, and by a frequent recurrence of fundamental principles."

"When in the course of human events, it becomes necessary for
one people to dissolve the political bands which have connected them
with another..."

"We hold these truths to be self-evident, that all men are created
equal, that they are endowed by their creator with certain unalienable
rights, that among these are Life, Liberty and the Pursuit of Happiness
.... That whenever any form of government becomes destructive of

these ends, it is the right of the people to alter or abolish it, and to insti-tute a new Government…"

"The powers not delegated to the United States by the Consti-tution, nor prohibited by it to the States, are reserved to the States re-spectively, or to the people."

"We, the delegates of the people of Virginia, duly elected …in behalf of the people of Virginia, declare and make known, that the pow-ers granted under the Constitution, being derived from the people of the United States, may be resumed by them, whensoever the same shall be perverted to their injury or oppression;…"

How can Americans in States, other than Virginia, compare their own State privileges to the privileges of Virginians? Obtain a fa-vorable "interpretation" to the U.S. Constitution's Article 5, Section 2: "The citizens of each State shall be entitled to all privileges and immu-nities of citizens in the several States." And consider the words of Daniel Webster as spoken in 1833:

"If the Union was formed by the accession of States then the Union may be dissolved by the secession of States."

Proving the legality of secession does not undo the Treason of 1861. Today, the rights of the posterity of Virginia have been lost in countless ways. Where are the Sovereign States? Where are the liber-ties Virginia was so surely guaranteed? Where is the original national government? There is a body politic calling itself the State of Virginia; and there is a body politic calling itself the United States, but they fail to provide the abundance of liberties as guaranteed in 1776 or 1789. This unconstitutional body politic, by its abuse of "emergency powers" and legislative malfeasance, has grossly constrained our liberties and thus has proved itself to be a "Pretender to the Throne."

If the loss of liberty came by war, please provide the name of the victor; but the victor claims to be the "United States!" And if liberty was defeated by war then surely there would be a treaty, the legal and civilized ending of wars; where is the treaty? So if liberty was lost at war, yet there was no treaty, then provide that truth in history so that

"We the People" may now treat with the victor for our lawful standing. But if there is no "victor," but instead, a Pretender to the Throne, then surely America's loss of liberty came not by war but by "legislation."

If the loss of liberty came by "law" then provide "We the People" with those specific laws, because both governments, the United States and the State of Virginia guaranteed liberty and held liberty inviolate and perpetual, and carefully defined it as a government of Justice, Moderation, Temperance, Frugality and Virtue. The absence of these conditions within the current governments is self-evident. So this "Pretender to the Throne" cannot be the Original Virginia or the Original United States. The loss of liberty cannot have come by "law" because no law is allowed to place itself above liberty.

America's loss of liberty did not come by "war" and neither did it come by "law," therefore, with those options eliminated, it is determined that America's loss of Liberty came by Treason; yes Treason, ascending in war and calling itself "law."

This unfortunate situation calls upon Americans to invent a new word to describe themselves. When a citizen is kicked out of his country, he is called an "expatriate." But because the defenders of Constitutional law, previously called "rebels," have not actually been kicked out of our country, they cannot rightfully be called "expatriates." Yet, as Constitutionalists still living upon the same geography that our Founding Fathers claimed for us in perpetuity, it must be stated that an evil group of powerful men have used the stealth of legal fictions to pull our Nation from under our feet and replaced it with their "New America." Yet they tell us nothing has changed, and that their "New America" is our original and beloved America. We have not left our Nation, but our Nation has been stolen from us. We are not expatriates, we are "dispatriates." We have been "dispatriated."

So, if American liberty has not been subverted, and the land of our forefathers is still beneath our feet, and we have not been defeated in war, and no law is allowed to be placed above our Liberty, then we owe it to our ancestors and posterity to challenge this pretense of law that has destroyed our People, our liberty, and our land. We must make a stand for liberty now, or forget it forever.

Chapter 7

Fort Sumter
and the
Treason of 1861

The treason surrounding the War of 1861 can be traced further back in time than 1861, it goes back into the hidden chambers of Newburyport, Charleston, New Orleans, Britain and even Frankfort, Germany. But the treasons hatched in these occult conclaves did not come to fruition until 1861 when they gained control of the United States Government.

Should the beginning of "governmental" treason be considered at the State level in 1860, when the first Southern States seceded? As Chief Justice Chase said, secession is not rebellion, and so the technical answer is no. There is no treason in secession when measured by the Constitution which qualifies treason as in making war against the States. Or can it be claimed that after secession, and upon the first conflict at Fort Sumter, that South Carolina, and those States comprising the Confederate Army committed treason by firing upon the military forces representing the United States in South Carolina? If secession was legal, as explained earlier, then the sovereign State of South Carolina voided the Federation Compact and reasserted total sovereignty within the State and thus had the natural right to defend itself against invaders and trespassers; there is no treason in self defense.

If the intent of the occult forces operating within the Southern States was to create a war, then yes those persons would be guilty of treason. If one, some, or all of the Southern Sates invaded the Northern States or Washington D.C., there would be grounds for treason against those instigating such an invasion, but technically treason is a crime against one's own government, and if the States in question lawfully seceded, it is not treason, it is an international war. The same could be said for the occult forces operating in the North who were instigating a war against the South. The war began with planning and pre-war preparations and instigations. Those persons, North or South, could likely be guilty of treason for activities taken before the secession.

As mentioned earlier members of the Ohio based Knights of

the Golden Circle fired the first shots of the war (General Beauregard at Fort Sumter) and the last shot of the war (John Wilkes Booth at Ford's Theater). That is a generalization based closely upon the official dates of the war. The last battle of the war was fought in Texas on May 12th and 13th 1865, almost a month after Booth shot Lincoln. And the first deliberate, instigated conflict of the war could be placed at Harpers Ferry, on October 16, 1859.

John Brown was financially supported by a group called the "Secret Six" in New England. Brown was raised on farm owned by the radical New York millionaire Garrett Smith. Brown and his men received training from a British mercenary named Hugh Forbes who had served under Giuseppe Garibaldi, the European military leader that conquered the Papal States, who Lincoln later asked to lead the Union Army. John Brown was a political extremist trained by associates of the European Illuminati and controlled by Thomas Higginson of the Newburyport Massachusetts nest of Templars.

Brown's wife, six first-cousins and two children were pronounced medically insane; Brown proved to be just what the Northern instigators wanted. Prior to Brown's showdown in Virginia, he massacred innocent farm families in Kansas. But, Kansas not being a Southern State, and because the slave owning Kansas families he murdered were not a "government," those shots cannot be considered the first shots of the war.

John Brown was a White man who led thirteen White men and five Negroes to attack a federal arsenal in Harpers Ferry, Virginia. The New England war-mongers used him in their attempt to instigate a slave rebellion in Virginia. Brown's intent was to set up his own territory in western Virginia as a base of operations where all escaped slaves could go and join in his rebellion.

Certain American statesmen pondered the deeper tactical intent of Brown's actions as stated by Senator Andrew Johnson after Brown's capture but before any secessions:

"John Brown stands before the country as a murder ... The time has arrived when these things ought to be stopped; when encroachments on the institutions of the South ought to cease ... when the Southern States ... should be let alone ... when you must either preserve the Constitution or you must destroy this Union."

John Brown captured the Harpers Ferry armory to acquire more weapons for his future army of runaway slaves. The local militia responded, a fight ensued and men died on both sides. Among the Virginians killed by Brown's insurgents was a free Negro of Harpers Ferry. Colonel Robert E. Lee was sent from Washington D.C. on the 17th of October, with 100 U. S. Marines to end the siege. Brown refused to surrender. Lee's men broke through the arsenal doors, entered into close quarters combat and when the smoke cleared Brown had lost ten men. John Brown survived and was tried for treason, found guilty and hanged on December 2nd, 1859.

Brown's raid is instructive toward the clarification of two contentious points that usually surround the War of 1861.

Point One: The U.S. Constitution, Article 3, Section 3, (clause 1) defines treason: "Treason against the United States shall consist only in levying war against them...." Notice the plural "them" that is, the State or States. Federal troops from Washington D.C., under the command of Colonel Robert E. Lee stopped the insurrection in Virginia. Treason is a crime against a "nation." John Brown was found guilty of treason against the "Commonwealth of Virginia" and not treason against the United States. Thus the federal government, under President Buchanan, admitted that Virginia was a sovereign nation, and thus under the Constitution (Art.1, Sec. 8, clause 15), the federal government called out the militia to suppress a true insurrection.

Point Two: There are certain uninformed persons who contend that Robert E. Lee committed treason when he resigned from the U.S. Army on April 20th, 1861, to eventually lead an army in defense of his home State of Virginia. The federal government had, two years earlier, admitted that John Brown committed treason against the Commonwealth of Virginia by raising arms against that State. From that, it can only be concluded that if Lee had remained in the federal army, and employed in the raising of arms against the Commonwealth of Virginia, he too would have been guilty of treason against his nation. Lee was forced to abandon his home, which was confiscated by the Union Army and made into Arlington National Cemetery. Lee sacrificed all; the charges against him (by idiots) will not stand.

As the Southern States started to secede, beginning on December 20th 1860, they reclaimed their Sovereign Rights even before they entered into the Confederacy on February 8, 1861. When they reclaimed their sovereignty, they also reclaimed the "U.S." Forts that were located within their respective States. Radicals North and South were looking for an excuse to start a war; and forcing jurisdiction over these forts could be that excuse.

South Carolina send a delegation to Washington D.C. to negotiate with President Buchanan for the equitable exchange of federal property located within South Carolina, which included Fort Sumter. Buchanan refused to see them saying that it was up to Congress. By January 1st 1861, all of America was taking the Southern State secessions very seriously.

On January 2, the Commanding General of United States forces, Winfield Scott, advised that a non-naval vessel be used to resupply the troops at Fort Sumter. Scott went to President Buchanan and persuaded him to allow a civilian ship, Star of the West, to secretly carry 200 to 250 troops and ammunition to Sumter, however the South had allies (and ears) within the U.S. government. The pro-Southern U.S. Secretary of War had already made a secret agreement with the State of South Carolina to supply them with 10,000 U.S. Rifles. And remember, Buchanan did not believe that the U.S. had any right to use force against a seceded State. The details of General Scott's plan leaked out, but the plan continued.

The intentions of the Federal Army seemed ominous. Other Southern States, having other Union forts in them, struggled with the same situation. On January 5th the Sovereign State of Alabama seized Fort Morgan and Fort Gaines. Florida had seceded on December 22nd and began repossessing the Union forts within its borders. On January 6th, Florida seized the Federal Arsenal at Apalachicola. On January 7th, they seized Fort Marion and St. Augustine. Many of these forts were empty, after all, the entire U.S. Army in 1860 consisted of only 16,400 men. However, the Union troops at Fort Barrancas did resist the Florida State troops at Pensacola and on January 8th, 1861, Union troops fired the first shots of the war against the State of Florida. Remember, at that time there was no Confederate government, only seceded Sovereign States. The Union Army fired on the Nation of Florida. There were no deaths.

In 1861, army forts were changing hands throughout the South and the federal government was letting them go. That's when the Commanding General of the Union forces decided to secretly load a civilian ship, Star of the West, with soldiers and munitions and send them to the South's foremost fire-eating secessionist city of Charleston, South Carolina.

The Star of the West reached Charleston Harbor on January 9th 1861, but word that it contained troops and munitions had gotten there first. The South Carolina State Troops (no Confederacy yet existed) opened fire on the ship, put a dent in its hull and the Star of the West returned to New York. (This incident was not the famous first shot on Fort Sumter that is to have started the war; that shot came three months later after Lincoln took office.) The next day, orders arrived by telegraph from Washington D.C. to the Commander of Fort Sumter, Major Anderson, directing him to take a defensive position.

All across the South, States were responding to the political and military escalation. On January 10th, the Union Troops at Fort Barrancas, Florida withdrew to Fort Pickens. The State of Louisiana, which seceded on January 7th, took control of Fort Jackson, Fort St. Phillip and the arsenal at Baton Rouge. January 20th, Mississippi Troops took control of Fort Massachusetts, (in Mississippi). January 24th, Georgia State Troops took control of the federal arsenal in Augusta and two days later took Fort Jackson in Savannah. On January 31st, Louisiana forces seized the U.S mint in New Orleans.

All of these seizures were actions of individual States against the federal government after Lincoln was elected but before he took office. States were reclaiming their sovereign property after being denied a political or judicial hearing in Washington D.C., yet still, there was no Confederacy.

On February 8th, 1861, the Confederate States of America was created by the seven seceded Southern States. Individual Southern States continued to reclaim U.S. forts within their jurisdictions. An odd note: On February 12th, Arkansas took the U.S. munitions stored at Napoleon Arkansas even though Arkansas had not yet seceded.

Lincoln took office on March 4th 1861 to become the 16th and last President of the United States. General Winfield Scott sent a letter to the incoming Secretary of State, William Seward, stating that the relief of Fort Sumter is no longer practical. One day prior to Lincoln taking office, Confederate General Beauregard took command of the forces at Charleston South Carolina. Supreme commander of the Union Army,

General Winfield Scott met with Lincoln on March 11th, and told him that the Army could not handle the Fort Sumter crisis and that he could not be responsible for the hostile consequences that would likely follow any more attempted reinforcements. Scott, a military tactician was only being practical considering the Star of the West incident, and the fact that there were more Confederate troops in Charleston than there were Union troops in the whole country.

On March 13th, Confederate envoys were in Washington D.C. trying to get an audience with the President, or Secretary of State or any influential persons. The federal government refused to give them a hearing because the Republicans would not recognize the Confederacy. A matter of principle? No, because Lincoln himself met with Confederate officials toward the end of the war in Virginia. Why couldn't Lincoln meet with Confederate representatives at the beginning of the war, when he could have averted the subsequent 600,000 deaths? Was it ego, agenda, politics, or treason, or all of the above?

Stephen Douglas, Northern Democratic candidate for President against Lincoln in the 1860 election, spoke out against Lincoln's war tactics:

"Lincoln is trying to plunge the country into a cruel war as the surest means of destroying the Union..."

On March 29th, against the advice of the Commanding General of the Army, and against the advice of most of his own Cabinet, the Commander-in-Chief, Abraham Lincoln announced his plan for Sumter. He prepared to send a military force to South Carolina escorted with a fleet of naval vessels including warships.

Charleston South Carolina had become the political focal point for both sides. General Scott had attempted a covert military action against Charleston in January with the Star of the West but failed. When the Confederacy was organized, and with the help of his brother-in-law John Slidell, Pierre Beauregard, member of the Knights of the Golden Circle, assumed the position of the Confederacy's highest ranking general and was given the command at Charleston over an estimated 20,000 troops.

The Union Major Anderson had been allowed by South Carolina and the Confederacy to maintain constant communication with his superiors in Washington D.C., by way of Charleston. There have been books written claiming that Anderson's garrison was being starved out, however, the Governor of South Carolina was if fact allowing the garrison to buy fresh meat, vegetables and groceries. As late as March 17th, Anderson wrote the Governor's representative about the Governor's policy and stated:

"... I did not solicit any modification of his original permission about receiving supplies of fresh vegetables. I am satisfied with the existing arrangement..."

On April First, Secretary of State Seward suggested that Lincoln open negotiations with the Confederate Commissioners in Washington, However, Lincoln ordered Secretary Seward not to receive any Confederate Commissioners. Seward had convinced Lincoln to send the Powhatan Warship to Florida to help hold on to the strategic Fort Pickens, leaving Lincoln's planned Charleston expedition less powerful, perhaps thinking that Lincoln may cancel the plan. But not so, Lincoln resumed his plan which was to instigate a fight. To test the waters in Charleston, on April 3rd, a federal schooner entered the Harbor; it was fired upon and so retreated back to sea.

On April 4th, a Union fleet of war ships carrying soldiers set sail for Charleston. Lincoln ordered his Secretary of War, Simon Cameron, to send a confidential letter to Major Anderson at Fort Sumter telling him that "the expedition will go forward." Lincoln gave Anderson freedom to respond to any Confederate aggression as he deemed necessary (permission to use deadly force). That same day, April 4th, Lincoln ordered Secretary of State Seward to recall the diverted Warship Powhatan back to Fort Sumter; he did, but it would arrive too late.

There was no war; Lincoln was not acting on behalf of the American people; Lincoln was not acting on behalf of Congress; Lincoln was not acting within the law. The question of Fort Sumter was a question of law which could have been addressed in Congress or the Supreme Court if allowed by Lincoln. Lincoln was deliberately trying to start a war with a seceded State. Five days before the Fort Sumter conflict, the New York Hearld reported on April 7th 1861:

"Unless Mr. Lincoln's administration makes the first demonstration and attack, President Davis says there will be no bloodshed. With Mr. Lincoln's administration, therefore, rests the responsibility of precipitating a collision, and the fearful evils of protracted war."

Major Anderson responded to Lincoln's "expedition will go forward" letter of April 4th. Major Anderson's letter of April 7th to Washington stated:

"I ought to have been informed that the expedition was to come .... We shall strive to do our duty, though I frankly say that my heart is not in the war which I see is thus to be commenced."

Helpful note: Major Anderson was the senior Union officer at Sumter, and General Beauregard was the senior Confederate officer at Charleston. Major Anderson was an instructor at West Point, Beauregard was one of his favorite students and friend. They were both brothers in Masonry. Beauregard was asked by Anderson at West Point to be his assistant instructor, which he accepted, but the secessions occurred and Beauregard left West Point.

Beauregard allowed Anderson and his garrison to have access to Charleston for supplies and to communicate with Washington. But on April 6th, Lincoln and his "War Department" sent a telegram to the Governor of South Carolina declaring that the naval fleet was on its way to resupply Fort Sumter; yet everyone in Charleston knew that they were actually warships carrying troops.

General Beauregard responded to Lincoln's telegram by ending Anderson's access to Charleston and disallowed further communications with Washington. However, Beauregard allowed Anderson to send his "my heart is not in the war" letter to Washington on April 7th.

After the firing on the Star of the West, loaded with troops and munitions, in January, and after firing on the federal schooner four days earlier, it was clearly understood that attempts to reinforce Fort Sumter would be challenged by the State of South Carolina, and now also challenged by the Confederate Army. Major Anderson knew that Lincoln's expedition would spark a war. And remember, the General of the Army and most of Lincoln's Cabinet advised him not to reinforce Fort Sumter. Consider how many forts were already in the hands of the Southern States, without the loss of a single life.

Lincoln also sent a telegram to the Confederate government in Montgomery Alabama, notifying them of his intent to reinforce Fort Sumter. Lincoln was stirring up as many hornets as possible. So on April 10, the Confederate War Secretary, Walker, ordered Beauregard to require the surrender of Anderson (before it could be reinforced).

The next day, April 11th, the Confederate Commissioners left Washington in a failed peace effort that lasted months. The State Department refused to see them. Who ordered Seward not to receive the Confederate peace Commissioners; thus who was the obstacle to peace? Who ordered warships, soldiers, and munitions to a Union Fort that was not in danger? Who knew how South Carolina would respond? Who sent lying telegrams to the leaders of the State of South Carolina and the Confederacy, claiming there were no military reinforcements when everyone knew there were? Who conspired with the Navy to insight a war? Who? The less than honest, Abe Lincoln.

Lincoln's Secretary of War, Gideon Welles wrote:

"It was very important that the Rebels strike the first blow in the conflict."

Yet War Secretary Welles also confessed:

"There was not a man in the Cabinet that did not know that an attempt to reinforce Sumter would be the first blow of the war."

That statement is confirmed in words by Lincoln's Secretary of State William Seward:

"Even preparation to reinforce will precipitate war."

The squadron of warships that was sent to Fort Sumter was suggested to Lincoln by Captain G.V. Fox. And so Lincoln placed Fox in charge of the fleet to Charleston. How is it that tyrants can always find volunteers to kill innocent people and start wars?

Captain Fox provided Lincoln with his plan to insight the Confederates to fire first shot:

"I simply propose three tugs convoyed by light-draft men of war … the first tug to lead in empty, to open their fire."

This was the man Lincoln chose to put in charge of the Fort Sumter "provision" fleet. Placing this man Fox in charge, and approving Fox's plan to draw their fire revealed Lincoln's true intent: to start a war by inciting the politically necessary first shot to be fired by the Confederacy. But, that particular plan to instigate the war did not take place, because the Confederate forces decided to fire on Fort Sumter prior to the entry of the Union fleet into the Harbor. When Lincoln's warships came in sight of Charleston Harbor, while still out at sea, Fort Sumter was fired upon with artillery.

Captain Fox was saddened that he was not able to perform his tasks, to resupply Fort Sumter and instigate a war. Lincoln consoled Fox on his annoyance of his failure. Lincoln let Fox know that their desired result, instigate a war (by ships and telegrams) was obtained. In his letter to Fox dated May First, 1861, Lincoln wrote:

"I sincerely regret that the failure of the attempt to provision Fort Sumter should be the source of annoyance to you … You and I both anticipated that the cause of the country would be advanced by making the attempt to provision Fort Sumter, even if it should fail; and it is no small consolation now to feel that our anticipation is justified by the result."

Lincoln's great "anticipation" was not to get provisions to Fort Sumter, but that the so called "cause of the country" would be "advanced" even if the false attempt to resupply had failed; because it was "no small consolation" that they forced the South to fire the first shot! In other words, what happened is exactly what Lincoln wanted to happen. International law recognizes that it is not the nation who fires the first shot that is responsible for starting a war, it is the nation that causes the first shot to be fired: United States via President Lincoln and the United States Navy!

But even then, on April 12th, after 3,341 artillery shells were fired at Fort Sumter, and with Sumter returning equal fire, no one was killed by enemy actions. The federal troops under Union Major Anderson, were ferried by Confederate forces out to the Union ships waiting at the mouth of the Harbor and were allowed to sail away alive and free. There was still a chance for peace, except Lincoln's "anticipation [was to be] justified by the result." Two days later Lincoln called for 75,000 troops to march against South Carolina to destroy the Confederacy.

Where is Lincoln's Constitutional Treason? This is an odd twist. If such treason "shall consist only in levying war against them" ("them" meaning the United States, singular or plural) and if South Carolina was lawfully seceded from that Union, where is Mr. Lincoln's treason? South Carolina, having seceded, cannot claim treason against South Carolina. Mr. Lincoln, who claimed that there was no lawful secession, is guilty of treason by his own admission.

The odd twist continues. Did Mr. Lincoln's actions cause a war by Confederate States to be levied against the United States? Yes. Now reread the Constitution's definition of treason keeping that in mind; "Treason against the United States shall consist only in levying war against them…" ("them" being the United States). This definition includes "giving them aid…." Lincoln "aided" the "enemies" into levying war against the United States; he planned it, instigated it with telegrams and ships and soldiers, and then called for 75,000 troops from the States he had entrapped into war; thus again levying those States into war. What was the fate of the States that refused to enter the war, such as Virginia? They were also invaded by Lincoln's Army. As mentioned earlier, Lincoln would attempt to justify his treason by interpreting the "insurrection" clause of the Constitution in his favor. The instigation of the war is of great importance for many reasons, and that episode cannot be resolved without settling the legal question of secession (previous chapter).

A review of the events that took place at Fort Sumter, which preempted the plans of Captain Fox, will provide some beneficial insight.

On April 7th, after Lincoln threatened to send ships to Charleston Harbor, Confederate General Beauregard confined Anderson's garrison to the island of Fort Sumter. Anderson said that he would not fire the first shot (of course) but does tell Beauregard: "If you do not batter us to pieces, we will be starved out in a few days." Beauregard, conveys that message to the Confederate Secretary of War, Walker, who had revoked an earlier order to fire on Anderson:

"If Major Anderson will state the time at which he will evacuate ... you are authorized thus to avoid the effusion of blood."

On the night of April 11th, Beauregard sent representatives to Fort Sumter, an island fort, to give Union Major Anderson the offer to avoid bloodshed. They spoke for hours, but by 3:30 A.M. on the morning of the 12th, the negotiations ended. Anderson's reply stated he would be out of food and would surrender at 12 P.M. April 15, unless he received "prior to that time controlling instructions from my Government." April 15th was over three days away. Anderson's reply sounded reasonable, it met Walker's requirement of an exact time of evacuation. History shows this to be the last thread holding the peace. Question: Why wouldn't this work?

Answer: The last letter Anderson received from Washington contained Lincoln's instructions, via the War Department, on the 4th of April? The letter provided Anderson with Lincoln's timeframe via the War Department directive:

"On the information of Captain Fox, he [Lincoln] had supposed you could hold out till the 15th ... and had prepared an expedition to relieve you before that period."

So, Anderson had instructions to hold out until the 15th. And notice Anderson said he would surrender at 12 P.M. on the 15th, to perform, to the letter, his part in the Lincoln - Fox scheme. Also notice that Anderson left the "honorable" door open not to surrender, by saying that he would surrender unless he received "prior to that time controlling instructions from my Government," orders which he had already received. Anderson was the bait in Lincoln's trap.

The Confederates knew that by the 15th, the warships would enter Charleston Harbor; they knew because Lincoln told them in his telegram to the Confederate Capital and to South Carolina. So when Anderson provided his "story" about the 15th, the negotiations ended at 3:30 A.M. on that morning of the 12th, and sealed the fate of both sides. Beauregard's representatives gave Anderson written notice that the Confederate Army would open fire in one hour.

Given the fact that Beauregard was a Knights Templar in the Knights of the Golden Circle, and that the Knights wanted war, Fort

Sumter was Beauregard's opportunity to serve the European agents who had infiltrated the Southern States and brought them to this brink of war. Beauregard may have wanted war, but without Lincoln, there could be no war. This tragedy belongs to Lincoln.

At 4:30 A.M. on the morning of April 12th, 1861, some say, Edmund Ruffin, from Hanover, Virginia, under the orders of a Confederate Officer named Chestnut, acting under the command of General Beauregard, fired the first cannon at Fort Sumter, as the U.S. warships were positioned at the entrance to the harbor. The first shots being fired by the South, relieved Captain Fox of the need to send out his "planned targets" which were to draw fire from the Confederate positions.

By 7:30 A.M, the Confederate shelling had caught a barracks at Fort Sumter on fire. Beauregard later described his response to this fire: "Apprehending some terrible calamity to the garrison, I immediately dispatched an offer of assistance to Major Anderson."

Beauregard sent a fire engine over to Fort Sumter on a steamer, but by that time, the fire had almost died out. Beauregard's men returned unharmed and reported:

"We again asked if he (Major Anderson) did not think it best to use the engine which accompanied us on the steamer. He replied no, that he thought that everything had been consumed that could burn ... He asked us to thank General Beauregard for his kindness; and on leaving, the Major accompanied us himself as far as our small boat."

The bombardment of Fort Sumter lasted 34 hours. Southern forces captured Fort Sumter, but allowed Anderson to march his troops out with banners flying and drums beating Yankee Doodle. Beauregard provided a steamer to transport Anderson and his men to the Union fleet which was anchored outside the harbor. Beauregard's report concluded:

"When, on the 15th instant, he left the harbor on the steamer Isabel, the soldiers of the batteries on Cummings point lined the beach, silent, and with heads uncovered, while Anderson and his men passed before them."

Had the South really crossed the line; crossed that point of no return? No one had been killed in the opposing bombardments. Two men died in accidents, not during hostilities and not from enemy fire. Fort Sumter, at that point was just another one of the many Southern repossessed Forts. Lincoln did not react to the dozens of other repossessions, why not leave "secession" to be settled as a legal question? Peace was still possible even on the 15th of April, when Anderson's men were given safe passage to the Union fleet. Peace, Mister Lincoln? No! Mr. Lincoln had already called for 75,000 troops on the 14th. And when Congress reconvened in July because of these events, Lincoln had the hypocrisy to say that the South was to blame and that the North did everything in its power to preserve peace.

Some statesmen in the North asked what good is a Union if it must be held together at the point of a bayonet. A few months before the Sumter incident of April 1861, back in December, January, and February, Southern States were seceding, but not Virginia. The Virginia Legislature held a special session in January to discuss the situation and passed this Resolution.

"Resolved by the General Assembly of Virginia, that the Union being formed by the assent of the sovereign States respectively, and being consistent only with freedom and the republican institutions guaranteed to each, cannot and ought not to be maintained by force.

"That the government of the Union has no power to declare or make war against any of the States which have been its constituent members.

"Resolved, that when any one or more of the States has determined, or shall determine, under existing circumstances, to withdraw from the Union, we are unalterably opposed to any attempt on the part of the federal government to coerce the same into reunion or submission, and that we will resist the same by all the means in our power."

That was in January; Virginia was still in the Union during the Fort Sumter incident. There was a Peace Delegation led by John Tyler in February of 1861 composed of 133 delegates appointed by the Legislatures of 21 non-seceded States, but that grand attempt to preserve the peace had been unfruitful in the war-hungry atmosphere of Washington D.C. The South Carolina Delegation which had also gone to Washington in an attempt to preserve the peace was denied a hearing. The Confederate Commissioners sent to Washington were not even received, so they left Washington the day before the bombardment of Sumter. Even peace attempts by individual Northern States to avoid the war went unheeded. All of these cries for peace went unheard by the national government. No one was killed at Fort Sumter, but the U.S. Commander-in-Chief Lincoln demanded the States provide 75,000 troops to march across Virginia and North Carolina (non-seceded States) to make war on South Carolina.

The Virginia Legislature had already stated in January that it would resist by all the means in her power, any attempt by the national government to coerce any State into submission. On April 17th, three days after Lincoln called for troops, the Virginia General Assembly declared:

"That said Constitution of the United States of America is no longer binding on any citizen of this State."

On the 21st of April, Virginia joined the Confederacy and on that same day, Richmond, Virginia was made the Capital of the Confederacy. The secession was confirmed by a popular vote on the 23rd: 128,884 in favor, 32,134 opposed. It was at this moment in history that Virginia declared its lawful duty to its citizens was to give priority to the original compact of its people: the Virginia Constitution which includes the Virginia Declaration of Rights. The Federal Government, or really at this point Abraham Lincoln, Chief Executive Officer of the United States, had violated the Virginia Constitution. His violation of that compact is treason. Virginia's Constitutional duty to preserve Liberty and Justice mandated that Virginia withdraw from the new, war-hungry rogue U.S.S. (Union of Subordinate States).

Two days later, Lincoln's "New America" killed 12 civilians in Baltimore and lost five soldiers. These were the first deaths of the war, not in a Southern State, and not killed by the Confederate Army, but it was Lincoln's troops from Massachusetts killing freedom loving civilians in the Union State of Maryland. Lincoln's New America was consecrated in the blood of Northern resistance.

The "New National Government" had a big mouth, but very little muscle, and so it had to convince the Northern States to supply the necessary warm bodies, which, as pointed out previously, was met with great resistance in the North. But time has proved that when the New

National Government used the Northern States against Southern States, all of the States lost, and the new unconstitutional national government acquired more and more power with each passing year.

The new centralized national government continues to call itself the "federal" government, but a true "federal" government is composed of sovereign States; that ceased to be after the Transfer of Power in 1861. The present day so-called Federal Government has a multitude of its own armies of occupation: the FBI, CIA, IRS, NSA, FEMA, U.S. Marshals, EPA, Forestry Service, and countless more. The United "States" of America, changed into a "Federal Government" of America, but because they conquered by stealth, there was no change of official letterhead. Even today, the Pretender to the Throne still claims to be the United States of America.

Lincoln, without Congress, without the Supreme Court, and without the States, assumed new unconstitutional powers, the authority of which was based on his personal "interpretations." America was to be a republican form of government, and the republican form of government was designed to prevent governance by one man (or one man's interpretation).

Lincoln had to exonerate his constitutional sins in political double-speak. He called for Congress (and his Republican allies) to come into an emergency session on July 4th, 1861. Choosing July 4th to reconvene was a political ploy to wrap his ascension to the throne in Red, White and Blue. July 4th 1776 was America's collective Declaration of Independence; July 4th 1861 was the Congressional confirmation of Lincoln's new regime. Eighty-five years of liberty ended.

Up until the last year of the war, 1865, Lincoln played politics as well as any politician today. He played on the heart-strings of everything patriotic and moral; but that was only politics, only an act, as revealed in his statement to Congress when he claimed that the North (meaning himself) had done everything possible to avoid war, when the non-political reality was that he sent warships to force the Confederates to fire the first shot.

Recapturing Fort Sumter became an obsession of Lincoln's ego. From August 12, 1863, until February 18, 1865, when the Union finally regained it, they bombarded the Fort with over seven million pounds of iron contained in over 44,000 shells. When the Confederates took Fort Sumter from Anderson, the walls were still standing. But the new Federal Government leveled it, leaving Fort Sumter as it appears to tourists today: a pile of rubble. General Lee surrendered his forces on April 9th, 1865, five days later, on April 14th, four years to the day when Lincoln called for troops, Major Anderson, now a General in Army recruiting, took the same flag Beauregard had him lower, and raised it over Fort Sumter. This act represented the future arrogance of a new Federal Government. Later, on that Good Friday evening, Lincoln completed his destiny by attending a comedy at the Ford Theater.

The Transfer of Power is not about the military campaigns of the War of 1861, it is about a treason that began in 1861, but it must be said that this war was the greatest slaughter in American history. It is common knowledge that the South was defeated by the North simply by population numbers. The North enlisted thousands of the 764,000 war-time immigrants as replacements for their embattled army. More Union troops died in combat than Southern troops but with the Northern population almost four times that of the South, victory was in the simple math of attrition. And to that end, the Union genocide of the South showed no mercy. Consider the words of General Grant toward the end of the war:

"The rebels have now in their ranks their last man. They have robbed the cradle and the grave."

If that conflict from 1861 to 1865 was not a "war" as claimed the victor, and with no "treaty" (which there wasn't) then there can be no claim that any such military victory could have altered the preexisting "Law of the Land." Therefore the only justification for the obvious changes in our State and national governments, must be changes made properly under the "Rule of Law."

The validity of a New America cannot be based upon a victory at war, yet neither can the New America be based upon the Original Law of the Land, it is instead based upon the unconstitutional creation of a "New Law." These new laws are enforced as if they were created through the lawful process but they were not, in legal parlance these new laws are referred to as "Legal Fictions." In becomes necessary to dismantle the Legal Fictions that have become the new foundation of power for the Pretender to the Throne, that is, the new so-called "Federal Government." The method to prove that Lincoln's New America is legally fraudulent and morally bankrupt is to compare its legal fictions to the Original Law of the Land.

Chapter 8

The Original States "United"

When the national government (a.k.a. Federal Government) deceived the Northern States into entering a war against the Southern States, it was a violation of the Original Compact between the States. The subsequent unconstitutional use of force to constrain the States as "United" was treason because it violated the Constitutions of those States, and violated the national compact with those States. The lawful balance between the national government and the many State governments could only be maintained if the State Constitutions remained unaltered by the national government and that the national government did not expand its powers beyond its Constitutional limits. Any violation of the State Constitutions by the national government would be treason against the State governments as well as treason to the national Federation of States.

If the 1861 violations of the National and State Constitutions were only a temporary measure, the Federal Government might argue that the nation's self-preservation justified the action; yet, without the Constitutional prerequisite of an "insurrection or rebellion," it would be an unlawful expansion of federal powers. Even if such an assessment overlooked the lack of an insurrection, the "emergency powers" invoked by the Federal Government continued its use of force after the "conflict" toward the end of establishing an unconstitutional, legally fictitious, control over all 36 States, North, South, East and West. This extension of "martial law" into a postwar "martial law rule" violated the Original State Constitutions, and remains in place to this day. In the years since 1861, the Federal Government has had ample opportunity to prove its loyalty to, and obedience of the Lawful Constitution by repairing the treason of 1861, but it has chosen to retain its unlawful powers.

The military victory is without question: the South was destroyed. However, because the new political creature called the Federal Government has never claimed that their "police actions" against the South were a "real war" and thus, have not provided the vanquished Southern States with a treaty; which is the official and civilized end to wars; that is, letting the vanquished know their legal rights and station within the New Nation, one can only conclude that the so-called "civil war" of 1861 was itself unconstitutional and was the military imposition of a new form of law unauthorized by We the People.

It is important to remember that it was the Federal Government that won the "conflict" and chose not to treat for peace because it claims that its emergency action was not a "war." Yet, as a result of the conflict, Federal and State Constitutions were permanently altered while the nation was under the Federal martial law. Therefore, without a treaty to justify its new postwar laws and powers, the victor must be able to prove that their new "Federal Government" is based entirely on properly proposed and adopted laws, and not on war or emergency powers.

The new Federal Government cannot claim to be a Constitutional government if it was founded on the destruction of State Constitutions, yet it was. All of the Southern States had to rewrite their Constitutions as a prerequisite to get from under the fist of martial law (which existed until 1877). The mandatory alteration of State Constitutions proves the Federal Government to be guilty of the usurpation of the Law of the Land, usurpations of the United States Constitution and the many State Constitutions. This usurpation is not found in only a single act, there are many violations of law in this Transfer of Power. Many of these violations are in the form of "legal fictions." Certain of these legal fictions will now be reviewed to reveal the Federal Government's obvious and intentional methods used to destroy the sovereign States and establish the Federal Government as America's supreme central power, as per the European plan.

The Federal Government would have been better off if it had claimed a military victory in 1865, admitting that they overthrew the United States. Such a confession would have provided some pathetic treaty, after which, "We the People" would have had to "revolt" or become "We the Subjects." The Federal Government's victory, if viewed as a victory over all 36 States, would not have been tolerated by the Northern States because it would have exposed their "Save the Union" rhetoric as being fraudulent. The commanders of the Federal Government (Radical Republicans) chose not to make their insurrection known; although the treason was obvious to Americans living in the South. If a wrong is never made right, it remains wrong. The Federal Government of 1865 chose to deal with the legal "damage control" later; and although later has been a slow burn, it is nigh at the door; and the reckoning will choose one generation! The time has come for the dispossessed posterity of the Founding Fathers to make the long-overdue lawful challenge, using whatever methods or deeds are required to restore liberty.

Without the lawful adherence to the U.S. Constitution, there is no United States; without the restoration of State Constitutions, there are no States. If those persons commanding the Federal Government today continue to disallow the restoration of the true Law of the Land, they are nothing more than a collective of tyrants lording over both the National and State governments. From a Southern perspective, this "war" is often described as a war where the Federal Government conquered the State governments, but the War of 1861 was actually a war instigated by just a few power-hungry individuals (some within the Federal Government) who caused the destruction of the State governments, and caused the destruction of the Original Federation Government. Those persons eliminated Constitutional Law with the creation of their new "Federal Government." Those at the helm of this usurpation knew exactly what they were doing. Lincoln himself stated that the "Old Union" cannot be saved and that a "New Union" must be established in its place. Mr. Lincoln betrayed America.

Attempts to justify these usurpations of law echo through the media today. One such statement is that the Constitution is an "evolving" document. That may be said of the new Federal Government's "mood-swing constitution" but may not be said of America's perpetual Original National or State Constitutions. By the Constitution, liberty cannot "evolve" into being less liberty. Constitutional liberty is defined and perpetual.

There have been more recent "stealth attempts" to remedy the Treason of 1861, attempts to provide the usurpers with some legal footing. There have been subtle suggestions by some of our Federal Princes calling for a Constitutional Convention to rewrite the entire Original Compact. Even good patriotic Americans have been coaxed into supporting this action as a means to contain the Federal Government's abuses of power. They have been deceived to expect real change, yet they will sacrifice the only lawful claim "We the People" have remaining: The Original Compacts. A lawful Constitutional Convention cannot convene because there are no representatives of the Original governments, State or national! The New Union has painted itself into a corner, with no lawful way out; it is forced to continue in fraud until the existing government yields to the ultimate centralization: global governance.

The most probable way for today's "Federal rulers" to get out of the Constitutional legal dilemma is for them is to simply turn "We the People" over to an even larger legal fiction: World Government.

The Federal usurpation must be measured by the Original Constitutions; which are not "evolving" documents. Early in America's legal history, 1803, the Supreme Court confirmed the limitation on the power of Congress "men" to pass any law simply because they believed it was a good law, when Chief Justice John Marshall said in the case of Marbury verses Madison:

"Ours is a government of Laws, not of men."

Liberals interpret the "law" of the Constitution as being "evolving" yet when there are attempts to reverse their agenda-based legislation, they invoke Marbury verses Madison: "Ours is a nation of Laws, not of men." Yet they avoid asking themselves: "by what lawful authority does the post-1861 Federal Government operate?" If America is a government of laws, then certainly included among those laws would be the Original Law of the Land, the one promised in perpetuity! And if that Original Law is not included within today's jurisprudence, then surely the government in power must provide a Constitutional explanation for the elimination of the original guaranteed liberties. But Washington D.C. and its State tributaries are silent on this question; instead, they claim authority from the post-1861 Amendments and statutes of their new Federal Government.

The usurpations of law, unlike international intrigue, must be performed in the light of day, in venues open to the public. The concealment of legislative motives and intents requires persons with a deliberate talent toward a "legal" slight-of-hand to perform within legislatures and courtrooms. The lawyers providing such "legalese" to support the assumption of unconstitutional powers in 1861 and beyond, seem to have performed well enough to obtain the public's confidence, yet anyone who earnestly seeks the truth is able to uncover the conspicuous step-by-step construction of the system of law that replaced the Original Constitution. The Transfer of Power of 1861 and beyond is somewhat complex, but when their actions are unravelled and described in plain English, usurpation by usurpation, their expertize fails to win a constitutional verdict in their favor. The following chapters will unravel the entire fabric of the kings' legal clothing and find that such attire is better suited for the climate of a banana republic.

Chapter 9

Martial Law

On April 14th, 1861, Abraham Lincoln, having been the President of the United States for only 41 days, responded to the bloodless eviction of Federal troops from Fort Sumter South Carolina by calling for State Militias to supply a total of 75,000 soldiers to march against the Southern States. He claimed his action was authorized in the Militia Act of 1795. But there was no "insurrection" or "rebellion" therefore that claim was not valid. An insurrection or rebellion or "civil war" would have the purpose of overthrowing the existing government. That was not the case. What did occur was the lawful (and bloodless) withdrawal from the Union by certain Southern States and the People thereof. There was no attempt on the part of these States to threaten or attack Washington D.C. or any other State, there were no acts of insurrection or rebellion.

There is another Constitutional option for calling out the militia, as stated in the Constitution (Art. 1, Sec. 8, clause 15): "to execute the laws of the Union...." Such laws would be null and void on States that have seceded from the Union, which again brings the legal question of secession to the forefront, the question that multiple peace delegations from the South and North sought answers to but were turned away by the national government in Washington D.C.

Secondly, the authority of a President to call out State Militias was limited to a maximum service time of three months. Remember, Congress was not in session in April, so Lincoln called for Congress to reconvene on July 4th. If the militias were called on April 14th, then the three month limit would expire on July 14th. So Lincoln, on his own authority, on May 3rd, before Congress could reconvene, called upon the States to supply 40 regiments of volunteers to be directly under United States control, not militia. Lincoln raised a national "standing army" under his personal control to be used within the borders of the States; without an act of war, and without Congress. What law is this? The so-called law from which Lincoln claimed his authority is called "martial law."

"Martial law" is a term which originates from the Roman god

of war: Mars. Martial law is a historically vague "right" of a government to break its own laws in order to preserve itself or protect its people. In the American model under Art. 1, Sec. 8, (clause 15) the use of "militias" (martial law) requires the prerequisite of insurrections, invasions, or for executing the laws of the Union. These "martial law" prerequisites are also addressed in Art. 1, Sec. 9 (clause 2) which says:

"The privilege of the writ of habeas corpus shall not be suspended, unless when in cases of rebellion or invasion the public safety may require it."

Habeas corpus (hold a body) is the legal term that a person cannot be held for a crime without an arraignment. In this Constitutional clause, the prerequisites for invoking extra-constitutional powers is toward insuring the public's safety during a rebellion or invasion.

Combine the two clauses and you still only have rebellions, invasions, and the execution of the laws of the Union. Mr. Lincoln and the Republican Congress must claim their extra-constitutional powers from these prerequisites.

It becomes an "interpretation" as to what was the legal standing of the seceded States. Were they still States? Was there one big rebellion, or was each State a separate rebellion? Was there one rebellion or seven; one for each of the original seven seceded States? Or, were there eleven rebellions, the final number of Confederate States; or were there thirteen, when counting Kentucky and Missouri who were under Lincoln's martial law because they would join the Confederacy if able? Or, were there thirty-four rebellions considering that Mr. Lincoln declared martial law in the North and South? Does the U.S. Constitution apply to secessions? The assumption of power and the permanent usurpation of the Constitution became more obvious when Congress joined Lincoln's power-grab in July of 1861.

America's official Transfer of Power began in April of that fateful year 1861, Lincoln first used Army troops to kill Marylanders, and then on April 27th, suspended the writ of habeas corpus from Philadelphia to Washington D.C. Upon suspension of the writ of habeas corpus, Lincoln declared martial law and abused his position as Commander-in-Chief of the U.S. Army. He also, at that same time, extended the naval blockade of the Confederate States to include the non-seceded states of Virginia and North Carolina. Look at the unconstitutional power that this one man had assumed. It is important to notice that Washington D.C. itself was placed under martial law. The seat of Lincoln's new "Federal Government" was born outside of the Constitution, the post-1861 Federal Government of today was created out of martial law.

Lincoln later expressed his "interpretation" of Constitutional laws that justified his war measures; he claimed that his actions were required as a "public necessity" and to "preserve the Union" and "whether strictly legal or not" they "superseded Constitutional niceties." Constitutional niceties? Is that all the Constitution was to Lincoln: some sort of ladies' club nicety! Martial law began in April 1861, under Mr. Lincoln, and ended in 1877, under President Hayes. The Original America was buried in an unmarked grave!

Lincoln's suspension of the writ of habeas corpus was challenged out of court by the Supreme Court Justices. Lincoln's response to the Justices reveals an implied admission of his violation of the Constitution, as stated in his defense:

"Are all the laws but one to go unexecuted and the government itself to go to pieces lest that one be violated?"

There are several inaccuracies with Mr. Lincoln's rationale. The writ of habeas corpus was not the only law "to go unexecuted." He violated any law that got in his way. When a nation lets a tyrant break one law, the tyrant will break two, then three, until finally one day that nation will wake up in chains. Secondly, if a tyrant needed to choose which law to break to achieve the most power; the writ of habeas corpus is that law. Suspending the writ reverses the great American maxim that "This is a nation of laws, not men," therefore, under Lincoln's leadership, we have become a nation of men, not laws. And third, his statement contains the fundamental error that his unconstitutional actions prevented "the government itself to go to pieces" when actually Lincoln's abuse of the Constitution destroyed the Original States United. Mr. Lincoln and the Radical Republicans used every legal fiction they could muster to excuse their power-grab and in doing so, today's Federal Government has no lawful, legitimate basis for its existence. In his political theater of not allowing "the government itself to go to pieces"

Mr. Lincoln destroyed America itself. Mr. Lincoln did more to destroy America than did any other President in history.

Mr. Lincoln called Congress to join him in his usurpation of power, to reconvene on July 4th, 1861. Congress had adjourned in March, in a state of confusion. The confusion stemmed from how to count "States" with regard to the passage of laws; if States cannot secede, are they to be figured in the congressional numbers. It raised several questions. What was a quorum? And to override a veto, what number of State representatives equals a two-thirds vote? Congress adjourned without a date to reconvene, which meant they would convene on the traditional date in December.

The Commander-in-Chief of the "Federal Government" called Congress to reconvene under his order, under his new unsanctioned powers of martial law. Also, when Congress reconvened it would be within the martial law boundaries of the District of Columbia, which they did on July 4th, 1861.

Upon that date "They the Politicians" created a new nation, in order to form an irrevocable union, to secure the blessings of martial law rule onto their posterity. The birthday of the New America, the Federal Government we know today, is the same as its predecessor July 4th, perhaps to allow the fireworks celebration to conceal the Transfer of Power. When the Federal Government today celebrates the 4th of July, it celebrates the "second birth," the birth of the Pretender to the Throne. Lincoln called upon Congress to handle the legislative aspects of the war measures; Congress accepted their expansion of power. And on August 6th, Congress empowered Mr. Lincoln to take whatever actions he deemed necessary concerning the military. Congress and the President now shared in the power, and shared in the guilt.

Lincoln declared martial law in April 1861; called Congress into session in July and asked them to share in the new power, Congress accepted and in return, attempted to "legalize" Lincoln's usurpation of power. The Congress reconvened in December of 1861; the Senate and House voted to set up a joint committee to run the war. The Legislative and Executive branches of the new Federal Government created the most powerful army on the face of the Earth to be used against fellow Americans, against anyone who questioned or defied them, North or South. When the martial law powers were used against the South, it was done to fight what Congress labeled the "insurrection" or "rebellion," but when the U.S. Army was used against civilians in the North, during the war, or even in the South after the war, the legal justification was that the abuses were performed because the "public safety may require it." They were careful to choose Constitutional language.

Lincoln and Congress avoided the use of the term "martial law" because they were uncertain as to its Constitutionality, but eventually their usurpation rested squarely on the principle of martial law. Congress formally "legalized" martial law in March of 1863. Prior to that, Lincoln needed a "legal claim" to exercise police powers over the citizens of the North. Lincoln crafted a declaration that would make any individual in America an "insurrectionist." Lincoln's proclamation of September 1862:

"That during the existing insurrection and as a necessary measure for suppressing the same, all rebels and insurgents, their aiders and abettors within the United States, and all persons discouraging volunteer enlistments, resisting militia drafts, or guilty of any disloyal practice, affording aid and comfort to rebels against the authority of the United States, shall be subject to martial law and liable to trial and punishment by courts-martial or military commissions."

That Presidential edict imposed martial law over any person within any part of the U.S. who was suspected of disloyalty to the new Federal Government. After the war, that presumptuous "junta" was struck down by the Supreme Court. During the war, Commander-in-Chief Lincoln "suppressed" every pen or printing press that dared commit word crimes against the new regime.

Baltimore felt the tyranny first. The Mayor was imprisoned for one year for exercising his Freedom of Speech. A Maryland Court Judge who proposed inquiring into the legality of the Federal Government's military control over the State of Maryland was beaten at his bench and dragged bleeding out of his courtroom and imprisoned for six months. One Baltimore citizen, John Merryman, was arrested by Union General Cadwallader and imprisoned at Fort McHenry. While awaiting military trial, Merryman appealed to Supreme Court Justice Roger Taney for a writ of habeas corpus. General Cadwallader refused to honor the writ. Chief Justice Taney protested to Lincoln saying that only Congress could suspend the writ of habeas corpus. Justice Taney:

"... I can only say that if the authority which the Constitution has confided to the judiciary department and judicial officers, may ... be usurped by the military power at its discretion, the people of the United States are no longer living under a government of laws, but ... at the will and pleasure of the army officer in whose district he may happen to be found."

Lincoln issued a warrant for Taney's arrest. Taney was threatened with imprisonment and expected himself to be placed captive in Fort McHenry. Lincoln chose not to push his power that far, he never confined Chief Justice Taney. Taney died in 1864. Lincoln continued suspending the writ of habeas corpus, person by person without any Congressional consent; there were over 40,000 cases.

On the first day of the "insurrection" Lincoln assumed control of all Northern railroads, seized all telegraph stations, and placed military Generals in control over newspaper editors. These Generals had the final say on all the news that was fit to print, and had the final say on editorials. The Army decided how much "Freedom of the Press" would be "permitted." On August 16, 1861, the newspapers "Brooklyn Eagle," "New York Daily News" and the "New York Journal of Commerce" were put on trial for the crime of having "Confederate leanings." These restrictions, loss of rights and subsequent punishments existed all across America.

Finally, on March 3, 1863, Congress "legalized" the national suspension of the writ of habeas corpus. This action was coordinated with the passage of the National Currency Act because martial law was the only way to make the Federal Government's "paper money" legal tender. On that very same day, with Congressionally sanctioned martial law over the entire North, Union troops ransacked the Columbus Ohio Newspaper "Crisis" for having so-called anti-Union sentiment. In May 1863, Union troops wrecked the office of the Richmond, Indiana newspaper the "Jeffersonian" for its anti-Union sentiment. Freedom of the Press was dead and it was Lincoln and Congress that killed it!

Congress joined in Lincoln's power grab when they sanctioned the suspension of the writ of habeas corpus, which is martial law. Even though Congress legitimized an expansion of unconstitutional power, these new "laws" still hung by a thread. Without a sanction of these new powers by the Supreme Court, the President decided to buttress his position with a new law of his own. In April, under General Order number 100, Lincoln commissioned the "Lieber Instructions" which became a quasi legal code to justify his acts of martial law. The code was in no way Constitutional, but Lincoln's Federal Government desperately needed a legal standing among the other nations of the world and so the Lieber Code was presented as a law which explained America's Transfer of Power. Section I, Article I of the Lieber Code states:

"A place, district, or country occupied by an enemy stands, in consequence of the occupation, under the martial law of the invading army, whether any proclamation declaring martial law, or any public warning to the inhabitants has been issued or not. Martial law is the immediate and direct effect and consequence of occupation or conquest."

Plain English: This country is under the martial law of an unconstitutional occupation army, even if they never explained that fact to the citizens. Martial law is the direct effect of the Federal Government's usurpation of the Constitution. Article 10 of the Lieber Code states:

"Martial law affects chiefly the police and collection of public revenue and taxes whether imposed by the expelled government or by the invader, and refers mainly to the support and efficiency of the army, its safety, and the safety of its operations."

Plain English: Martial law is a police state using the IRS, imposed by the invader, to pay for the efficiency of the oppressor and to protect itself from We the People. Section II, Article 31 of the Lieber Code states:

"A victorious army appropriates all public money, seizes all public movable property until further direction by its government, and sequesters for its own benefit or that of its government all revenues of real property belonging to the hostile government or nation. The title to such real property remains in abeyance during military occupation and until the conquest is made complete."

Plain English: We win, you lose; winner take all. Winner keeps all powers until "conquest is complete." Therein lies the problem, the "war" had no treaty and as long as "they" claim the conquest is not complete, the unconstitutional powers remain; though they are cleverly disguised.

Opposition to Lincoln was growing but could not be printed in the North without military reprisals. Finally on August 30th, in the Presidential election of 1864, the (Northern) Democratic Platform, at risk of being arrested, complained about Lincoln's:

"Usurpation of extraordinary and dangerous powers not granted by the Constitution" stating that "the aim of the Democratic Party is to preserve the Federal Union and the rights of the States unimpaired."

Northern States represented at the Democratic National Convention had come up-to-speed regarding the violation of States' Rights. It proved to be too little, too late. By the end of the war, there were over 40,000 political prisoners in the North.

It goes without saying that after the war, the South, while under military occupation until 1877, had no "Freedom of the Press." Southerners were prohibited from writing about the war or the causes and effects of the war. The Union Army was burning books and universities all across the South. This was an attempt by the Federal Government to erase the truth about its rise to power. Today's Southern school children are taught to hate the Confederacy.

The Federal Government, which destroyed the States, had to create a legal venue in which to litigate the interpretations of its use of martial law and extra-constitutional powers. The Lieber Code was used to justify the Transfer of Power within the international community, but New America needed a controlled venue to use within the States. It decided to conceal its new powers within corporate law, and then take American citizens out of their "We the People" legal standing and use deceit to bring them "voluntarily" under their new venue of corporate law.

The transition went this way. Under the Constitution, the power to control Washington D.C. belonged to Congress. In 1861, under martial law, Lincoln took that power from Congress. Then Congress wanted to share in the expanded powers with Lincoln and so joined with him.

In 1863, one month before Congress "legalized" the suspension of the writ of habeas corpus (martial law), Washington D.C. was reestablished as the military "Department of Washington." Nine years later, under President Grant, in 1872, Washington D.C. became a corporation, and in U.S. titles and codes, this new "corporation" called Washington D.C. can legally be called "The United States." They created a "New District of Columbia" to pose as the Original "Washington D.C."

In a similar manner, every State in the Union was legally reconstructed after the War of 1861 into franchisees of that Federal Corporation. This was the stealth system of governance that replaced the sovereign States after they lost the war and lost their sovereignty. The new system of States is centered in the District of Columbia, the district that can "legally" use the name the "United States." The New States were placed under the control of the corporation of Washington D.C., a.k.a the United States and thus placed the States under corporate law. Citizens may have other options if they know an individual convoluted legal trail out of the maze and have not personally entered into a corporate jurisdiction.

These type of history nuggets are not to be found in public schools or on public T.V., because the Lieber Code still allows for the enforcement of secrecy. But the treason did not go unnoticed. After the War of 1861, the London "Telegraph" reported that Washington's postwar control over the South showed that the U.S. "may be a republic in name, but some 8 million of its people are subjects not citizens." President Andrew Johnson fought against the radical elimination of States' Rights and warned America:

"Your States are sinking into mere petty corporations ... mere satellites of an inferior character, revolving around the great central power here in Washington. There is where your danger is."

President Johnson also called a spade a spade when he called reconstruction "the legislative machinery of martial law." President Johnson knew that "reconstruction" was the Congressional conversion of war-time military "martial law" to a peace-time legislative "martial law rule."

The Congressional assumption of undelegated powers transferred the United States of America into an unconstitutional legal structure which could not be undone. This legal quagmire was the foundation of the New America. Congress made sure that they had changed the Original government in such a way that it could never change back. The two primary political tools that the Federal Government used to achieve this were: forcing States to rewrite their Constitutions; and granting Negroes citizenship and the vote. Once Negroes voted, all elections were Constitutionally void, without question. It wasn't about "freedom and equality and justice," it was a legal maneuver to create and irreversible, permanent rogue government to rule over the People of the United States using an extra-constitutional body of law.

Martial law destroyed many freedoms and laws, and it created many legal fictions and abuses. Perhaps one of the most conspicuous abuses was in its division of the State of Virginia with the martial law establishment of the State of West Virginia.

The Bogus State of West Virginia

The following questions of law are in no way to be construed as an insult to persons born or living in West Virginia, they are great people living in a beautiful environment.

Is it Virginia, or West Virginia, or were there three Virginias? After the conflict at Fort Sumter on April 12, 1861, and after President Lincoln called for troops to move against South Carolina on April 14th, Virginia held a convention to consider secession on April 17th. After the Virginia convention voted 85 to 55 to secede, representatives from the western counties of Virginia went back to Clarksburg (in what is now West Virginia) and called for a convention in Wheeling. Wheeling (in what is now West Virginia) is located in the utmost northern panhandle wedged between the two powerful Union States of Pennsylvania and Ohio, a position which guaranteed "Union" protection for the creation of a Union-loyal Virginia government, which also guaranteed Union influence in the convention and any subsequent legislation.

The western Virginians were split on which course of action to take, either seceding from Virginia to create a new State of Kanawha or assuming the status of the State of Virginia itself.   Lincoln needed an immediate and loyal Virginia to endorse his legislations and amendments, and waiting for the formation of a new (and dubious) State of Kanawha was a luxury not afforded. The convention met on May 13th, 1861 to establish operational procedures and propose a public vote on secession of the western counties from the State of Virginia. They agreed to convene a second convention on June 11th if the people voted in favor of secession. On May 23, 1861, the people voted (with some irregularities) for secession.

The legal question: Can counties secede from a State? Answer: No. The U.S. Constitution clearly states in Article IV, Section 3, "no new State shall be formed or erected within the jurisdiction of any other State ... without the consent of the Legislatures of the States concerned..." Western Virginia could not secede, however if it received permission from the Virginia Legislature it could form a new State. First the problem, then the solution.

In the second convention, with Arthur Boreman presiding, Francis H. Pierpont, acting on the best interests of the Lincoln government, motioned to pronounce the State of Virginia in Richmond to be a nonfunctioning government and that the "constitutional convention" in Wheeling could establish a "restored government" of Virginia. The June convention declared the Richmond-based Virginia secession from the Union to be null and void. On June 19th, the convention organized a new "restored government" of Virginia, complete with Legislature, and authorized Francis Pierpont to be Governor. The June convention created a "restored" Virginia, thus the Legislature of the restored Virginia could then grant western Virginia statehood.

This "New Virginia" Legislature met for the first time in Wheeling on July 1st, 1861, it hired State officers and sent two U.S. Senators to Washington. Congressmen were not allowed to be seated in the House of Representatives because the number of Congressmen is based on population, and who would be counted among the population of this new "State of Virginia?" The "restored government" would be allowed to ratify (as the State of Virginia) any amendments to the Constitution that came from Congress. This created two Virginias, neither of which was "West" Virginia. There existed a Governor of Virginia in Richmond, John Letcher; and a Governor of "restored" Virginia in Wheeling, Francis Pierpont.

The Constitutional Convention of the western Virginians continued through July; it was this convention that authorized another convention in August to work out the details for the creation of their proposed State of Kanawha, which they now called West Virginia. The August convention decided to put the question to a vote of the people on October 24th 1861. The people voted (with some irregularities) in favor of Statehood (according to a pole taken by the Union Army). The affirmative results of the pole called for another convention in November 1861 to form a State of West Virginia. The tone had changed from secession, deemed not legal by Lincoln, to Statehood because Pierpont's "New Virginia" Legislature would likely "consent" the creation of this State from within a State as provided in the Constitution; and Lincoln could always use more Republican Congressmen and another State to ratify any expedient Constitutional Amendments needed to overthrow the Constitution of 1789.

The November convention assembled the framework for a new government complete with a State Constitution; they sent the motion to be voted on by the people who (with some irregularities) ratified the conditions of Statehood on April 11, 1862. On May 13th, the Pierpont Legislature (acting as the State of Virginia) approved the formation of the State of West Virginia from within the boundaries of Virginia and sent the motion to Congress. On July 14th, the U.S. Senate passed a bill to create the State of West Virginia. On December 10th, the House passed a bill to create the State of West Virginia. On December 31st, 1862, President Lincoln signed into law the creation of the State of West Virginia, but with a proviso that the slave State make an allowance for the eventual abolition of slavery in that State.

Lincoln acted contrary to his own beliefs as stated in his inaugural address:

"I have no purpose directly or indirectly to interfere with the institution of slavery in the States where it exists. I believe I have no lawful right to do so, and I have no inclination to do so."

The day after signing the legislation, Lincoln gave his Emancipation Proclamation; and in doing so, Lincoln, after twenty months of a war against secession, disguised his war against the Original Constitution as a war to provide social justice. This was the beginning of America's race war, instigated for the purpose of disguising tyranny; a race war still in operation today to preserve the tyranny of 1861.

Another convention was held in Wheeling on February 12th 1863, and adopted Lincoln's changes to the proposed Constitution on March 26th. From a legal perspective, Lincoln's "condition" for acceptance in the Union altered the Congressional legislation thus voiding the Act; but who's counting. All of this effort to create the State of West Virginia, the conventions, the Pierpont legislation, the U.S. Senate and House legislations, and the President's signature, could all be undone when the war ended because there were so many deviations from the rule of law.

Lincoln's December 1862 proviso on West Virginia was to buy time. Lincoln had given himself martial law powers over the entire country in September of 1862, but those powers were brought into question by Supreme Court Chief Justice Taney. As commented by B.T. Benjamin:

"During the whole war the Lincoln government ... was unanimously impeded by the decisions of the Supreme Court, so that President Lincoln was obliged to suspend the Writ of Habeas Corpus [invoke martial law] in order to relieve himself from the rulings of the Court."

But one day the war would end, and where would Lincoln's "New America" be then? So to insure his plans for new States, new laws, new powers, and a new national currency, Lincoln awaited Congressional recognition of his assumed martial law powers. On March 3rd 1863, Congress confirmed Lincoln's total power over the country. The convention in Wheeling approved Lincoln's constitutional changes on March 26th. On April 20th, 1863, Lincoln, using Congressionally backed martial powers, issued a Proclamation of Statehood to begin on June 20th 1863, with Arthur Boreman as Governor. Boreman had presided over the conventions and worked with Pierpont. Meanwhile, the "Union-loyal" Pierpont Virginia government moved from Wheeling to Alexandria Virginia to assume its function as Lincoln's Virginia under the protection of the Union Army. The bogus Virginia would be called upon by Lincoln to ratify (on behalf of the State of Virginia during the war) any politically expedient constitutional amendments needed to undergird the "legal standings" of Lincoln's New America, such as the Thirteenth Amendment.

On June 20th 1863, Lincoln's martial law powers proclaimed

that West Virginia was, in his words "the 35th State." Well, if as Lincoln proclaimed, there were now, in June of 1863, thirty-five States, then Virginia, had not seceded, therefore how could Lincoln and his Congress violate Article IV Section 3, of the Constitution? They had to claim that the Pierpont government was legitimate. If the Pierpont government was legitimate, why use a martial law proclamation to create West Virginia? After Lincoln's declaration of statehood, West Virginia entered Congress, and assumed operations of its own General Assembly where it too could be called upon by Lincoln to ratify any politically expedient constitutional amendments needed to undergird the "legal standings" of Lincoln's New America, such as the Thirteenth Amendment.

After the war, on May 9, 1865, Pierpont was sent by the national government to unseat Virginia's Governor William Smith. Pierpont attempted to support the postwar policies of Democrat President Johnson, showing mercy to the South. Pierpont's term ended as it began, at the behest of the Federal Government's military regime. He was succeeded as Governor by Union General Henry Wells in April 1868 under orders from Union General John Schofield who commanded the "Military Department of Virginia." The South had been divided into military districts with no district having its pre-war State boundaries.

West Virginia became a State by the strangest quasi-legal mechanism ever devised: legal fiction. Concerning the formation of the State of West Virginia, Colliers Encyclopedia states:

"By the legal fiction of the consent of a Virginia-loyal government, the western counties secured admission to the Federal Union as a new State."

So, West Virginia became a State by the "legal fictions" as reviewed herein. Black's Law Dictionary defines legal fiction this way:

"Fiction of Law: Something known to be false is assumed to be true."

Black's Law Dictionary defines "Fiction" as:

"An assumption or supposition of law that something is or may be false is true, or that a state of facts exists which has never really taken place."

"An assumption for purposes of justice, of a fact that does not or may not exist." "A rule of law which assumes as true, and will not allow to be disproved."

In 1866, the Virginia General Assembly, in Richmond, repealed the tranfer of certain counties ceded to West Virginia (counties loyal to Virginia) which challenged the very Statehood of West Virginia requiring Congress to pass an act to settle the particulars of the illegality (with more illegality). The case led to an 1871 Supreme Court challenge (Virginia vs West Virginia). Supreme Court Chief Justice, Salmon P. Chase and the other "Lincoln stacked" justices found in favor of West Virginia and set the precedent in favor of legal fiction (thus "will not allow to be disproved"). However, in 1872, the Constitution of West Virginia was found to be unlawful and required a rewrite.

Plain English: The all-powerful Federal Government is just as bogus as the State of West Virginia, they are based on a lie being the truth, and the United States of Washington D.C. created a new court system that will not allow its legal fictions to be disproved. What does that mean? The Lieber Code allows martial law to govern America in secret and is not obligated to tell anyone what they are doing. And when some crackerjack law-patriot challenges the authority of this bogus "Pretender to the Throne" and backs the judge into a corner, the case is dismissed or never even heard; because legal fictions are lies, not laws, lies that the Federal Government "will not allow to be disproved."

Martial law; the Lieber Code; legal fiction; does that sound like America? Does that sound like liberty or justice, or any of the guaranteed Constitutional freedoms? The hypocritical effrontery of this systemic Pretender to the Throne, that came out of the War of 1861, is witnessed in his claim that the "New America" is the same America created in 1789! Sorry, not even close!

Chapter 10

Legislative-Executive
Power-Struggle

Congress Attacks Lincoln

Lincoln and Congress had made a working agreement in July of 1861 to share in the federal expansion of power that was created out of Lincoln's emergency powers. Lincoln and Congress enjoyed three years of agreement co-usurping the Constitution, but something happened to Lincoln by December of 1863. As it became more obvious that the Federal Army would defeat the Confederate Army, he looked beyond the war; he also looked at the destruction that he wrought; his guilt had aged his face twenty years. Lincoln had a change of heart, he wanted to end the destruction of the South the moment they surrendered, and neither did he want to punish the South after the war. With over a year remaining in the war, Lincoln was ready to make peace with the Confederate States, and welcome them back into the Union, not that the Southern States were seeking to be welcomed back into the corrupted Union; the South had a less favorable opinion of Washington D.C. in December of 1863 than they did in 1861.

As early as 1861, Lincoln had stated that the postwar status of the South was the responsibility of the Executive Branch. That was an academic issue in 1861, but by December 8, 1863, that issue became strategically important. Lincoln, in his annual message to Congress, gave an Executive Proclamation of Amnesty regarding the postwar status of the South which included a full pardon to all Confederates except high ranking officers, government officials, officers who resigned from the U.S. Army to join the Confederate Army, and those who mistreated prisoners of war.

These Executive pardons were dependent upon recipients taking a loyalty oath, after which, all property except slaves would be restored. Statehood, back into the Union, would be recognized when one-tenth of each State's citizens had taken an oath of loyalty to the Union and had renounced slavery.

Lincoln's proclamation sent shock waves through the Radical

Republican members of Congress. Did Lincoln grow a heart that day? Or was his proclamation an expression of guilt for his part in causing the ever-growing numbers of dead Americans; all because he had to prove a point at Fort Sumter? No one can know, but as for Congress, they didn't care. The next month, January 1864, Lincoln even approved a plan whereas after the war, the freed slaves could go back to work for their former masters for wages. Also in January of 1864, he loosened the amnesty requirements to allow Southerners living in areas that had already been conquered to receive citizenship based on the approval of the governing generals of those areas.

On February 22, 1864, after Lincoln eased the amnesty policy, the Radical Republicans turned against him forever, except for issuing forth some crocodile tears upon his assassination. They launched a campaign against his reconstruction policy. New York publisher (of Karl Marx articles) Horace Greeley called for a new Presidential Candidate for the 1864 elections. In Cleveland, the Radical Republicans nominated General Fremont for President, but in Baltimore, the Republican "Union" Party nominated Lincoln. Salmon P. Chase had tried several times to resign from Lincoln's Cabinet, in 1864, he was secretly organizing support for his own Presidential campaign. After Lincoln heard that, the next time Chase offered to resign, Lincoln accepted saying: "You and I have reached a point of mutual embarrassment."

Horace Greeley decided to back Benjamin Butler for President instead of Chase. Butler was to become a major player in the next few years.

Benjamin Butler was a Massachusetts Lawyer, who was appointed a General in the U.S. Army for political reasons. It was Butler, in May of 1861, after the Baltimore riots against the Massachusetts troops, who illegally, with no higher authorization, occupied Maryland under his own martial law. It was General Butler who became known as "Beast" Butler because during his occupation of New Orleans he ordered his men to mistreat the Southern women who showed any disrespect to Union troops. Confederate President Jefferson Davis responded by calling Butler a felon and an enemy of mankind, and suggested his execution if caught. Butler had voted for Jefferson Davis to be the Democratic Party's Presidential candidate in the 1860 Convention, but that was just part of the occult attempt to split the Democratic Party. After the war, Benjamin Butler advocated hanging Robert E. Lee and Jefferson Davis. Even the English Parliament called for "Beast" Butler's resignation.

Butler was also called "Spoons" because of his repeated thefts of Southern silverware, as did so many other "Union" troops. Some Union soldiers even exhumed the dead looking for jewelry to rob. Butler is also the General who coined the term "contraband" when referring to freed slaves, putting them into work camps, incurring the wrath of the famous Black orator Fredrick Douglas. Yet when Butler ran for Congress in 1865, as one of the first politicians to use the race-card to his advantage, he invented the first commendation metal for Negro soldiers. General Grant, in December of 1864, called for Butlers dismissal; Lincoln obliged on January 7th 1865. All of these sordid qualifications made Benjamin Butler an ideal associate the Radical Republicans. But Butler's Presidential hopes in 1864 were short lived.

In June of 1864, the Radical Republicans were able to get the Wade-Davis reconstruction bill through Congress, but Lincoln gave it a pocket-veto on July 4th. The Radical Republicans who opposed Lincoln were referred to as the "Black Republicans." They were outraged at Lincoln. Senator Wade, namesake for the harsh reconstruction bill, was also running for President in opposition to Lincoln. Senator Wade and Congressman Davis issued the Wade-Davis Manifesto on August 5th, proclaiming that it was: "their right and duty to check the encroachment of the Executive on the authority of Congress." (This means political war.)

In the elections of 1864, the Republicans tried to distance themselves from the popular label of being the "war party," and ran under the name of the "National Union Party."

The November 8th, 1864 election provided Congress with a Union (Republican) majority, there would be no stopping their radical plans for reconstruction, except that it takes a two-thirds majority to override a Presidential veto. President Lincoln was reelected by less than a half of a million votes. In these earlier times, the post-election "lame duck" Congress still had an entire session ahead of them, from December until March 4th. The President would begin his term of office on the same day that Congress adjourned for the year. The new Congress, elected in November of 1864, would not take their seats until December of 1865. So, after of the election in November of 1864, Lincoln and the more moderate Congress had 13 months to bring the Southern States back into the Union under Lincoln's more benevolent conditions before submitting the South to the vulgar reconstruction plans of the Congressional-elect Radical Republicans.

On February 3rd, 1865, Lincoln and his Secretary of State William Seward met with Confederate Vice President Stephens on a ship offshore of Hampton, Virginia to discuss terms of peace. Remember, Lincoln, in 1861 ordered Seward not to speak or acknowledge any representatives of the Confederacy. Why couldn't Mr. Lincoln have done that 600,000 lives ago? After all it was Seward who stated before Lincoln took office:

"I do not know what the Union would be worth if saved by the use of the sword."

How prophetic! But Lincoln at that time was not yet guilt-ridden with the deaths of hundreds of thousands of Americans. It was only one day before Seward's statement that Lincoln made his own statement as expressed in his letter to James Hale of Pennsylvania concerning allowing the Southern States to secede; Lincoln:

"If we surrender, it is the end of us, and of the government."

Lincoln began appointing civil Governors in the defeated Southern States even during the war. In March of 1865, in Louisiana, Lincoln transferred the governing power from the military back to civilian control. Under Lincoln, Tennessee and Arkansas held Constitutional Conventions and rewrote their State Constitutions, as required for Lincoln Statehood. The mandatory rewriting of State Constitutions is tantamount to treason, yet the Radical Republicans even considered Lincoln's elements of treason as uncalled for generosity.

Lincoln met with Generals Sherman and Grant on March 27th, 1865, and told them that as soon as the Southerners laid down their arms he was willing to grant them full citizenship. As April and the last days of the war approached, Congress had already adjourned until December, so the Radical Republicans of the next (39th) Congress demanded that Lincoln call for an extra session of Congress to handle the reconstruction issues. Lincoln refused. By the end of March 1865, the Legislative-Executive power-struggle was dangerously over-heating.

General Lee was not given command of the entire Confederate Army until February 4th, 1865. On April 2, 1865, Lincoln declared that the insurrection was at an end. Lee surrendered on April 8th, 1865. Lincoln called for the Virginia Legislature to reconvene to assemble their postwar government. He was going to appoint (the Virginia turncoat) Francis Pierpont as Governor of the real State of Virginia. The Original State of Virginia already had a Governor, William Smith. Pierpont was Lincoln's puppet Governor who had been acting out the role of Governor of the "Virginia Loyal" government operating in occupied Northern Virginia. After the war, Pierpont was "provisional governor" from 1865 to 1868; followed by Governor and Union General, Henry Wells.

Lincoln, finding the taste of victory sour because of his legacy of deceit, was attempting to spare the South of a radical reconstruction that came to be America's greatest shame, yes even worse that slavery: reconstruction. Because of Lincoln's change of heart and his actions to readmit the South on equal footing, he was walking on very dangerous ground. His Republican enemies were desperate to stop him because he might reverse the Congressional plans for a "New America" with its all powerful Federal Government. Lincoln's abandonment of his fellow usurpers came much too late for the South, yet he was beginning to sound the alarm. Lincoln, with no more to gain in life, saw the big picture and started to expose the occult forces behind the war, that is, the marriage of corporations and politicians, men who were looking to manipulate and acquire America's wealth and men who were setting up a venue of racial politics. Lincoln warned America:

"I see in the near future a crisis approaching that unnerves me and causes me to tremble for the safety of my country; corporations have been enthroned, an era of corruption in high places will follow, and the money powers of the country will endeavor to prolong its reign by working upon the prejudices of the people, until the wealth is aggregated in a few hands and the Republic destroyed."

Lincoln told Secretary of the Navy, Gideon Welles, the day before his assassination, that it would be best to have the Southern State governments already in operation before the 39th Congress reconvened in December. Welles was also an opponent of radical reconstruction.

But Lincoln, age 56, was shot on April 14th, and his plan for recon-struction died with him on April 15th. Official history tends to down-play the events surrounding Lincoln's assassination. Lincoln was not the only target that night and Booth was not the only assassin.

Four men were to die in the assassination attempts on that April 14th: Lincoln, Vice President Johnson, Secretary of State Seward, and General Grant. Grant had a fortuitous change of plans that night, and was a no-show at the theater. Seward, one of the men who advised Lin-coln against the Fort Sumter instigation, was stabbed but lived. Vice President Andrew Johnson's assassin backed out, but was later caught and confessed to his part in the conspiracy. If the intended victims had been killed with Lincoln as planned, the radical Congress would have gained the opportunity to choose their own President, who very likely would have been Ohio Senator Benjamin Wade, co-author of the radical "Wade-Davis" reconstruction plan. However, as fate would have it, An-drew Johnson was not murdered that night, and the Radical Republicans lived to regret it.

The power-struggle between the Legislative and the Lincoln executive ended with murder, but because Vice President Andrew John-son survived, the Legislative power-struggle against the Executive Branch became a war of Radical Republicans against the new Democrat President Andrew Johnson. A philosophical distinction between the Presidency of Andrew Johnson and the Presidency of Abraham Lincoln is that Johnson inherited an existing unconstitutional Federal Govern-ment, he did not create it.

Andrew Johnson

Andrew Johnson was born in North Carolina, but moved to Tennessee. He was a Southerner, and even owned a slave once. He was a Jacksonian Democrat, nominated at the "National Union Party" (Republican) Convention to be Lincoln's Vice Presidential candidate in the 1864 election. Johnson was chosen to secure the moderate vote. Johnson ran on the "National Union" (Republican) ticket but was no Republican. Johnson was a Democrat and voted Democrat. In his po-litical career he had been an Alderman, a State Legislator, a Representa-tive in the U.S. House, the Governor of Tennessee, and a U.S. Senator representing Tennessee. Johnson kept his Senate seat even after secession; and at Lincoln's request, became Military Governor of Tennessee in February of 1862. He was elected Vice President of the United States in 1864, and upon the death of Lincoln, and after only 42 days as Vice President, on April 15th 1865, became President of the United States.

Johnson was a "poor man's" candidate who came to be known as the "Old Commoner." He did not like the "rich" Southern aristocracy nor the corrupt Northern money powers. He had been a tailor by trade, and made his own clothes, even while in the White House. His honesty was apparent during his time as military Governor of Tennessee. In the other occupied Southern States, embezzlement and fraud by military governors was the normal, whereas Johnson left his office as Military Governor poorer than when he entered. As President, he usually worked until midnight. Andrew Johnson had two passions: the Union and the Constitution. So after the South lost the war, his concerns changed from preserving the "Union" to restoring and preserving the Constitution.

Legislative-Executive
Power-Struggle

Congress Attacks Johnson

President Johnson made the Radical Republicans wish that Lincoln was alive and well. Lincoln never had the ability or backbone to brandish Constitutional Law against his Republican enemies; Johnson had the ability and the backbone. Johnson knew of Lincoln's plan to get the Southern States organized and ready to take their seats in Congress before the 39th Congress convened. As a Southerner, he agreed with Lincoln's plan and continued toward that goal.

President Johnson appointed Governors in the six States where Lincoln could not because of the war. Johnson first fully restored his own State of Tennessee back into the Union. On May 10th, 1865, Johnson stated that the armed insurrection should be considered "virtually at an end." On May 27th, Johnson ordered the release of all persons held in military prisons, with some special exceptions. On May 29th, he issued a proclamation of amnesty to all non-supporters of the Confederacy. Johnson was trying to mend the nation while Congress was in adjournment. He established his own conditions for Statehood, after which, the radicals called the hopeful returning Southern States the "Johnson States."

Johnson called upon every Southern governor to hold a Constitutional Convention in order to save the States from the Republicans. Johnson's requirements for delegates to the Constitutional Conventions were that they had to be eligible to vote in 1860; they had to take the oath of allegiance to the national government (whatever it may be); they could not have been a Confederate official or served in the Confederate Army as an officer; or have a net worth of over $20,000. Any person not meeting these delegate qualifications, could apply to Johnson for individual consideration for citizenship, Johnson was very liberal in granting such. Each State would be required to rescind its Ordinance of Secession; repudiate the State war debts; abolish slavery and amend their constitutions. Johnson may have been trying to save the South, but in the letter of the law, it was still treason against the Original Constitutions of the Southern States. Most of Johnson's actions were later reversed by the Radical Republican Congress.

On July 1st, 1865, President Johnson, by Executive decree opened all Southern Ports that had been closed by Lincoln. On August 20th, 1865, Johnson declared that the insurrection was at an end. In October of 1865, Johnson lifted martial law off of Kentucky. On December 1st, only days before the radical Congress was to convene, Johnson restored the writ of habeas corpus throughout the entire nation. (By January 1866, civil administrations were functioning in every Southern State except Texas.)

Before the 39th Congress could convene, President Johnson had done an admirable job of getting the nation back together (all things considered). All of the Southern States, except Texas, were ready to enter the Union with newly elected Congressmen and Senators ready to take their seats when the 39th Congress convened on December 4th, 1865,

Nice try by President Johnson, very efficient, very patriotic; but if his actions were allowed to stand, it would create a huge political problem for the Radical Republicans who had worked so hard to rewrite American law. If Southern Senators and Representatives were allowed to take their seats, Congress would not have a Republican majority. Backed into a corner by the surviving remnants of the Original America, the Republicans had to pull a procedural coup in order to perpetuate their newly acquired unconstitutional powers. The Republican coup was achieved through several pieces of legislation. But before reviewing that legislation, it is instructive to ascertain the mood of the radicals in Congress as they struggled to retain their ill-gotten powers from the attempted reforms of President Johnson.

Charles Sumner was the leader of the Senate in the Republican Party, he was the Senator with the most hate for the South. Thaddeus Stevens was the leader of the House and hated the South more than Sumner. It was these two radicals that convinced the two Houses of Congress to destroy President Johnson and subjugate the South. They were also assisted by Horace Greeley, Secretary of War Edwin Stanton, Salmon P. Chase, Senator Benjamin Wade, and of course Benjamin (Spoons) Butler. The Republican attack on President Johnson spanned his entire time in office.

In the first days of Johnson's Presidency, Sumner and Chase lobbied Johnson to grant Negro suffrage in the South. This was not an expression of egalitarian altruism, but a political ploy to get the much needed (hopefully Republican) Negro vote to offset the returning Southern Democrats. Sumner and Stanton financed a newspaperman named Schurz to tour the South and send back false stories of Southern racial atrocities, many of which are now considered facts because it is written on paper a hundred and fifty years old, most were fabricated political lies to achieve political gains. Senator Sumner based his actions on his belief that the Southern States committed "State suicide." Sumner also said:

"I insist that the rebel States not come back except ... with all persons equal before the law."

He had no concern about "all persons equal before the law" in the Northern States where there was no Negro suffrage; his concern was only for the four hundred thousand potential Republican Negro votes in the South.

Thaddeus Stevens wrote to Charles Sumner:

"Get the rebel States into a territorial condition and [Negro suffrage] can easily be dealt with, that should be our great aim."

Stevens also said that the restoration of the States can only come when the Constitution has been amended:

"...as to secure the perpetual ascendancy of the Party of the Union." "The Republican Party alone can save the Union."

So, Senator Charles Sumner devised a plan to put the South under a martial law rule: the Reconstruction Acts.

Candid comments by Thaddeus Stevens include:

"The future condition of the conquered powers depends on the conqueror."

"We shall treat the South as a defeated enemy."

"They must come in as New States or come in as conquered provinces." (New States for their New America)

"Hang the leaders, crush the South, arm the Negroes, confiscate the land..."

One Alabama newspaper editor challenged the Republicans to show the Constitutional basis for their plan to oppress the South, to which Thaddeus Stevens replied:

"The Constitution ... has nothing to do with it, I propose to deal with you entirely by the laws of war."

(War, what war? The insurrection?)

House Leader, Thaddeus Stevens called the Constitution a "Scrap of Parchment." Is it any wonder that the First Amendment was not allowed in the postwar South. Former U.S. President, Franklin Pierce, turned against Lincoln because of his use of martial law in the North, and denounced the 1865 Radical Republican's new "theories outside the Constitution."

President Johnson was going to fight for the South, and for the Constitution. He objected to the term "reconstruction" being used for a process he termed "restoration" and the difference in those two words represents the contrary philosophy of governance held by the new Federal Government toward the Constitution. It was Johnson, back when he was in the Senate, that introduced the Senate version of the Crittenden Resolution, which declared that the purpose of the war was not for the conquest or subjugation of the South nor to interfere in the rights or established customs of the States. Johnson knew that the Republicans were attempting to gain total power over the South. That was why on May 10th, 1865 Johnson declared that the insurrection was at a virtual end, some historians reference that day as the official end of the war.

The 39th Congress convened in December of 1865. In the months that followed volumes of anti-Southern legislation was introduced. Johnson realized that the radical Congress based their legislation on the assumption that the Southern States were still in insurrection. So again, in April of 1866, as he had done months earlier, Johnson stated:

"the insurrection which heretofore existed … is at an end and is henceforth to be so regarded."

But, because Congress attempted more and more legislation directed against the South, in August of 1866, Johnson stated it once again, this time more plainly:

"I do further proclaim that the said insurrection is at an end and that peace, order and tranquillity, and civil authority now exist in and throughout the whole of the United States."

This proclamation is why August 1866 is considered by some historians as the "other" official end of the War of 1861. But the Republicans could not let it end. They needed to insure the perpetuation of the Party of the Union and the "enthroned corporations" that Lincoln warned against.

Johnson also revised legislation passed by Congress which confiscated Southerners' property. Johnson's Attorney General ruled that wartime had become peacetime and so the Executive altered the Congressional "confiscation" of Southerners' property to only be "sequestration" of property until citizenship could be reestablished.

It was Thaddeus Stevens who said just three days before Lincoln's death that he would dispossess the rebels of "every foot of ground they pretend to own." Stevens' plan was simple. Confiscate 394 million of the 465 million acres in the South. Give 40 acres and a mule to every Negro (future Republican voters), sell the rest and pay toward the national debt. There was only one man in the way of the Republicans subjugation of the South: Andrew Johnson. They needed to end Johnson's Presidency, not in assassination (too obvious) but by impeachment.

Impeachment

The term "impeachment" does not mean "kicked out of office." It means a public official is accused of one or more high crimes or misdemeanors, and the House of Representatives, in a majority vote compels the President to face a competent tribunal in the Senate, which if decided by a two-thirds vote to be guilty, the President would then be kicked out of office.

The Radical Republicans Thaddeus Stevens, Charles Sumner, Benjamin Butler, Benjamin Wade, Salmon P. Chase, Edwin Stanton, and late arrival Ulysses S. Grant combined to make a rogues' gallery calling for the impeachment of President Andrew Johnson. Grant's motivation was to replace Johnson as President, which he did at the next election. The Radical Republicans knew they had to stop Johnson's agenda of "forgiveness" for the South.

The legality of Congressional emergency powers to install a martial law rule over the South was based on their manipulation of specific Constitutional words which grant extra-constitutional powers; words like "public safety," "tranquillity," and "civil authority." Johnson knew of their reliance on these words and so was careful to use those same words to declare that the insurrection was over. Johnson wanted to end the insurrection officially and end the power-grab to control the internal affairs of the Southern States. Johnson intended to undo the Transfer of Power that began under Lincoln yet now continued after his death with the legislation of the Radical Republicans. For the Transfer of Power to remain in Washington, the Radical Republicans had to unseat a President who would veto their every usurpation.

One of the first attempts to unseat Johnson was by Benjamin "the spoon collector" Butler. Butler introduced a resolution to investigate Johnson for the murder of Lincoln. Butler had fabricated an elaborate conspiracy theory which implied that Johnson was behind the plot to kill Lincoln. Butler even went to the extreme of making an offer to a man in prison to supply a fabricated testimony. This prisoner, named Durham, had already perjured himself in an earlier scheme to falsely testify against certain Confederate leaders in a failed attempt to convict and hang them. Using the same strategy against Johnson, Butler scripted the testimony of Durham, to meet his needs. The witness was to testify that he had seen Johnson with Booth on several occasions, and that Atzerodt, the man sent to Johnson's hotel to kill the Vice President but backed out, was actually sent there to disarm any suspicion of Johnson's involvement.

But the "would-be witness" Durham, insisted that Butler give him a pardon in advance, or he would not testify; Butler could not, and the hoax fell apart. There was another accomplice in the Butler-Durham attempted perjury, a Congressman named James Ashley of Ohio. The impeachment attempt accusing President Johnson of involvement in the assassination of Lincoln, offered by Congressman Ashley, was voted down 108 to 57. This scandal was made public and quickly swept under the rug. This first attempt failed but others would follow.

History note: Of course there was never any Congressional investigation of the Dahlgren Papers which were taken off of the body of Union Colonel Ulric Dahlgren after he was killed leading his Cavalry into Richmond in 1864. The papers revealed he was part of a Union plan to assassinate President Jefferson Davis and his entire Cabinet.

There were also less-than-legal attempts to silence President Johnson: threats on his life. Thaddeus Stevens spoke out that King Charles had lost his head for less cause than the sins of Johnson. Johnson responded to this and other threats on his life by not flinching in his efforts to restore the Original Constitution:

"[The Republicans'] intention was to incite assassination: to remove this obstacle to their seizure of place and power. Do they want more blood? If my blood is to be shed because I vindicate the Union and the preservation of this government in its original purity and character, let it be shed."

The next "at law" attempt to get rid of Johnson came from Lincoln and Johnson's Secretary of War, Edwin M. Stanton. Andrew Johnson, upon filling Lincoln's vacancy, kept Lincoln's Cabinet (big mistake). Up until one month prior to his own impeachment, Johnson had been deceived into thinking that Secretary Stanton supported him.

Stanton, a nationally known trial lawyer, was appointed as Lincoln's Secretary of War, replacing Simon Cameron in January 1862. In this position, Stanton controlled all Union Generals, but it was common knowledge that almost every officer in the Army hated him. Although originally a Democrat, as was Grant, he became an operative of the Radical Republicans.

The Democrats controlled the White House before Lincoln. Stanton, then a Democrat, had access to high ranking Democrats including President Buchanan. Stanton spied on Buchanan for the future Secretary of State, William Seward. After Stanton became Lincoln's Secretary of War, he spied on Lincoln for the previous President, James Buchanan. During the war, he spied on his own Generals. He hired Charles Dana, who later became editor of the New York Sun, to spy on General Grant. By the end of the war, he had a network of spies everywhere. It is therefore not surprising that during the Johnson Administration, Stanton was supplying confidential White House Cabinet secrets to the Congressional Radical Republicans. During the Johnson impeachment hearings, the District of Columbia was crawling with Stanton's spies.

When Lincoln was shot, Secretary of War Stanton placed Washington under his military fist. He was at Lincoln's bedside when the President drew his last breath. Stanton, never known to show emotion, sobbed like a baby (or crocodile?). Lincoln had called Stanton the "original gorilla." It was Stanton who proposed combining Virginia and North Carolina into one military district (which did not happen).

The conflict between Johnson and Congress regarding the reconstruction of the South became desperate. By 1867, Congress had passed the Reconstruction Acts which placed the South under military control. Stanton had said that there ought to be a way to deprive the President of his duties as Commander-in-Chief. Stanton cleverly had a "rider" placed on an appropriations bill to require that the President go through the Secretary of War (himself) or the General of the Army

(Grant) before giving any orders to the Army. This would remove the martial law application of reconstruction out of the hands of Johnson and into the hands of the Radical Republicans. With his manipulation of the appropriations bill, Stanton revealed his true loyalties; he was a spy for the radicals.

The Legislative-Executive power-struggle expanded with the passage of this appropriations act, Congress had usurped the President's position as Commander-in-Chief. They also passed an act which said "No military commander is bound by any civil leader" which was to head off any legal moves by Johnson's Attorney General. (This "law" was later proved unconstitutional.)

The Radical Republican's removal of any Executive control over the military was done in part to continue military control over the South after the war had ended. Johnson's Attorney General had stated earlier that "war-time" had become "peace-time" which meant the Congressional "confiscation" of land in the South would be reversed back to Johnson's temporary "sequestration" of Southern land. But after the unconstitutional "rider" that removed Johnson as Commander-in-Chief, the military control over the South would be executed by either Secretary of War Stanton or General of the Army Grant, both in league with the Radical Republicans.

When Johnson realized that Stanton, a member of his own Cabinet, was a spy acting against him, he asked him to resign or get fired. Congress responded with the "Tenure in Office Act" (also later proved unconstitutional). This "law" required that the Senate must approve all Cabinet member removals. This was a trap to have Johnson break the "law."

First, the Reconstruction Acts put the South under military control. A member of Johnson's Cabinet (Stanton) devised legislation giving himself control over the military Department of the South, deposing the President of his Constitutional duties. Second, Congress passed an unconstitutional law preventing Johnson from removing Stanton from his Cabinet.

So, if Johnson did nothing, the Radical Republicans would control the "reconstruction" of the South, through their Secretary of War, Edwin Stanton and General of the Army, Ulysses S. Grant. Or, if Johnson, as Commander-in-Chief, broke the law stating that "No military commander is bound by any civil leader" and usurped both Stanton and

Grant, he would have committed a "high crime or misdemeanor." Or, if Johnson fired Stanton from his Cabinet, in violation of the "Tenure in Office Act," he would have committed a "high crime or misdemeanor."

The Radical Republicans had President Johnson in political checkmate. Any action, or even a lack of action, would result in dire consequences, either for Johnson or for the South. Let Congress rule the South; or get impeached! A "politician" would have sacrificed the South, but this President of the United States, Andrew Johnson, proved to be a statesman. He chose to defend the South and preserve the Constitution while placing his position and reputation at risk. And for that, President Johnson was impeached.

The play-by-play of the impeachment is worthy and lengthy enough to warrant an entire book of its own; but this writing will only provide a thumbnail sketch.

The Tenure in Office Act was passed in March of 1867. In August of 1867, President Johnson asked for Stanton's resignation. Stanton refused. Johnson appointed a replacement, and sent a guard to evict Stanton. Stanton locked himself in the office, but that did not last long. The deed was done, the trap was sprung, all that was needed was for Congress to reconvene.

Thaddeus Stevens drafted the impeachment resolution and offered it before Congress on February 22nd of 1868. There were eleven charges; nine charges related to Stanton, one charge of Johnson defaming Congress in a speech; and the last was a catch-all article of impeachment written by Stevens, of which Stevens said:

"If my article is added, what chance has Andrew Johnson to escape? … Unfortunate man, thus surrounded, hampered, tangled in the meshes of his own wickedness - unfortunate, unhappy man, behold your doom."

The House of Representatives voted to impeach. Johnson's portrait was removed from the House. The Senate convened its impeachment trail on March 13th. Presiding over the trial was Salmon P. Chase, the same Chief Justice that had sworn Johnson into office the day of Lincoln's death. Most reports credit Chase as attempting to provide a fair hearing (yet, he was running for President again). The prosecution was headed by both Ben Butler and Thaddeus Stevens.

A pre-vote survey in the Senate showed that the vote would be very, very close. In some earlier testimony before the Senate, Johnson's defense revealed that Grant had not kept an agreement with Johnson, implying that Grant was not a man of his word. Secretary Welles had warned Johnson that "Grant is going over" to the radicals. Grant was also running for President at that time. From that day forward, Grant, who up to that time, had been a "closet radical," finally publicly turned against Johnson. Privately, Grant tried to sway a Senator to vote in favor of impeachment.

If Johnson were removed, Congress surely would have appointed Benjamin Wade as President. Wade was the co-author of the infamous Wade-Davis Manifesto that proclaimed that it was: "their right and duty to check the encroachment of the Executive on the authority of Congress." The Manifesto was even used against Lincoln when he pocket-vetoed the Wade-Davis reconstruction bill. Politics is fickle. It was Grant who insisted that Lincoln relieve "Spoons" Butler of his command, and now he and "Spoons" were working together to relieve Johnson of his command.

"Spoons" Butler was lobbying Senators to vote to impeach Johnson, offering them private bank accounts at Jay Cooke's bank. He sent word to a Senator through a middleman "that if he wants money, there is a bushel of it to be had." Needless to say that the media was in a feeding-frenzy for Johnson's blood. Stanton's spies were everywhere. The Senate hearings voted on March 16th: Andrew Johnson remained President by one vote.

Thaddeus Stevens, being the oldest and most powerful man in the House, too old to walk, was carried out of the Senate Chamber by his "Negro boys" like a sultan, saying "The country is going to the devil." Stevens was taken back to his home where he lived with a mulatto woman who was the widow of his former grounds keeper. He died that August, God rust his sole. And upon his request, Thaddeus Stevens was buried in a Negro cemetery.

The year was 1868, General Grant, financed by Jay Cooke and the railroads won the Presidential election against Seymour to become Johnson's successor. Johnson, as a political "lame duck" in December of that year issued a proclamation which pardoned all Southerners except for 300 high Confederate leaders. Andrew Johnson returned to

Washington as Tennessee's U.S. Senator in 1875, to continue fighting for the restoration of the Constitution. Senator Johnson was struck down by a mysterious paralysis in July of that same year and died.

Who won the Legislative-Executive power-struggle? Lincoln was dead, Johnson was impeached yet Legislative martial law over the South remained in effect. In fact, when Grant left office, eight years after Johnson, Legislative martial law remained in effect. Lincoln had recruited the Legislative Branch into his usurpation. The two branches shared the power until Lincoln had a change of heart and attempted to reclaim his power, the struggle returned. Lincoln was assassinated and the Legislature held the power. Vice President Johnson entered the Executive Branch back into the power-struggle and would not yield to the Legislature and stopped the Congressional expansion of power.

The 39th Congress had expanded their months of operation. The traditional allotted time for legislation was from December to March 4th. However in their attempt to preclude any further Executive advantages, they set the time for the 40th Congress to convene on the same day that the 39th Congress was to adjourn, March 4th. This power-struggle gave America a "perpetual" Congress to bring forth endless corruption.

Johnson was impeached, but they failed to remove him from office. Grant became President under the tutelage of the radical Legislative Branch. Who won? The Legislative won, and with Grant as President, Congress recruited the Executive Branch back into the Treason of 1861. By 1869, the Transfer of Power had transferred power away from the Constitution and into the hands of the Legislative and Executive Branches who now serve a perpetual unconstitutional, all powerful Federal Government.

Chapter 11

Legislative-Judicial
Power-Struggle

Congress Attacks the Supreme Court

Congress opted to support the treason and usurpation of power created by the Executive Branch in the War of 1861. Then Congress legally out maneuvered the Executive Branch to become the Supreme Branch of the "New America" government. Even during the war, Congress used its weaker Executive partner to achieve a military victory over the South. However, if Congress were to continue to reign supreme after the war, they had to provide a credible Constitutional interpretation of their new powers, which ultimately meant a confrontation between the Radical Republican Congress and the Supreme Court.

Supreme Court Chief Justice Roger Taney, of the famous Dred Scott decision was a strict interpreter of the Constitution. Early in the war, he verbally challenged Lincoln's use of martial law, specifically concerning the arrest and confinement of a fellow Maryland citizen named John Merryman. Lincoln, the Executive Branch, issued a warrant for the arrest of Roger Taney, the Judicial Branch (the warrant never was enforced).

Taney had replaced John Marshall as Chief Justice of the Supreme Court in 1836. Marshall had been Chief Justice since 1801. Taney was appointed to the Supreme Court by Andrew Jackson. Prior to Jackson's appointment of Roger Taney to the Supreme Court, he appointed Taney as Secretary of the Treasury in 1833, replacing William Duane during the critical Bank of the United States monetary crisis. Duane refused to obey Jackson's order to remove the U.S. securities from the private, internationally controlled, second Bank of the United States. Taney agreed with Jackson that the central bank had too much financial control over America's economy. Having fought the bankers while serving under President Andrew Jackson, Chief Justice Taney stood in defense of the Constitution, and against the international bankers during the Lincoln years.

How apropos in this Transfer of Power, that when Chief Justice Taney died in 1864, Lincoln replaced him with his former secretary of the Treasury, Salmon P. Chase. Taney worked to preserve Original Constitutional law and Constitutional money; Chase represented the usurpation of those traditional philosophies and replaced them with a new law and new money. As Lincoln's Secretary of the Treasury, Salmon Chase authored America's unconstitutional National Banking System and replaced America's Constitutional commodity-based currency with a debt-based monetary system. Chief Justice, Chase irreversibly altered Constitutional law as much as Treasury Secretary Chase irreversibly altered American monetary policy.

In order for Congress to increase the power of the Legislative Branch, relative to the power of the Judicial Branch, it had to carefully craft legislation whose "legal interpretation" would transfer new authority to Congress, and Congressional agencies. Congress crafted favorable interpretations of the Constitution to justify their new laws. The President and the Senate could also conquer the Judicial Branch by political appointments to the court.

The following itemized review of the particular articles, sections, and clauses of the U.S. Constitution on which Congress erroneously based their so-called "new authority" will expose their new system of laws and justice to be carefully crafted legal fictions and self-empowered judicial malfeasance.

Article VI, (clause 2)
"This Constitution, and the laws of the United States which shall be made in pursuance thereof; ... shall be the supreme law of the land;"

Meaning: Any law that Congress makes, if not in pursuance of the Constitution within its stipulated powers, is not the law of the land. This clause is the "legal technicality" that requires Congress to write legislation that conforms to the Constitution. Our founding fathers deliberately constrained Congress within the powers stipulated in the Constitution so that no branch of the government could ever expand its powers to rise above the Rights of the Citizens or eliminate existing freedoms.

Article II , Section 2, (clause 2)
[The President] "shall have power ... and he shall nominate ... and with the advice and consent of the Senate ... appoint ... Judges of the Supreme Court..."

The Senate could abuse its Constitutional separation of powers, that is, to keep Supreme Court decisions independent, by attempting to control the Supreme Court itself through politically bias Justice appointments. The Constitution meant to appoint the best legal minds who would be loyal to a strict interpretation of the Constitution, but the Senate misused its power and attempted to control the Supreme Court by appointing men of the same political persuasion, who served the same political agenda. This violated the intended separation of powers and compromised the independence of the Judicial Branch.

Article I, Section 8, (clause 9)
"The Congress shall have the Power: To constitute tribunals inferior to the Supreme Court..."

Meaning: This is the basis of the much-abused "Article One" Courts. The Articles of the Constitution, in part, divided the three branches of the national government. Article One covered the Legislative Branch; Article Two covered the Executive Branch; Article Three covered the Judicial Branch. The Article mentioned above implies Congress (Article One) has some tribunal power.
Article One courts were originally designed to serve interstate or international business needs like Customs Courts and Patent Courts. Article One courts were intended to serve the peculiar needs of business. Article One was never intended to create a criminal court for citizens.

Article III, Section 1
"The judicial power of the United States shall be vested in one Supreme Court, and in such inferior courts as the Congress may from time to time ordain and establish."

Meaning: This gave Congress power to create new federal courts as needed to serve the growing population or to serve other interstate business needs. The Original Judiciary consisted of One

Supreme Court and thirteen District Courts. These courts are considered Article Three courts and are Constitutional. The Congressionally created inferior courts were supposed to remain within the control of the Judicial Branch, but instead, Congress created Legislative courts to intervene between the citizens and their Judicial Branch Article Three courts.

The Legislative Branch expanded its power as certain postwar legislation took effect. Congress could pass a law and then use its Article One courts to sit in judgement of that law. Unchallenged by the prostrated States, Congress made itself two branches of the national government. Citizens seeking to appeal from an Article One court up to an Article Three court were regularly denied a hearing because those citizens didn't appeal correctly, dotting every "i" and crossing every "t" and thus few could ever navigate through the maze of legislative courts to receive a hearing in a judicial court meant for the citizens.

Article III, Section 1 (clause 2)

[In court cases authorized by the Constitution] "the Supreme Court shall have appellate jurisdiction, both as to law and fact, with such exceptions, and under such regulations as the Congress shall make."

Meaning: In order to drive a legal wedge between citizens and their Constitutional Law, Congressional legislation created a new court designed to reduce and control all legal appeals to the Article Three Courts. In 1891, Congress created and instituted the United States Court of Appeals, and placed it between the existing "District Courts" and the "Supreme Court." This new appellate court decided which cases were appealed to the Supreme Court. The Supreme Court still retains the "writ of certiorari" which is their power to reach down into a lower court and choose to hear a case, but for most cases it is the U.S. Court of Appeals.

Article IV, Section 3 (clause 2)

"The Congress shall have Power to dispose of and make all needful rules and regulations respecting the Territory or other property belonging to the United States..."

Meaning: Using martial law slight-of-hand Congress could change the defeated Southern States into a "Territory" and rule them unhindered by the Supreme Court. Remember the words of House Majority leader Thaddeus Stevens:

"Get the rebel States into a territorial condition, and it [Negro suffrage] can be easily dealt with. That, I think, is our great aim."

[They knew exactly what they were doing.]

The Constitution gave Congress exclusive sovereignty over the District of Columbia. Years after the 1861 Transfer of Power, Congress created "The Courts of the District of Columbia." Within their Congressional Territory of D.C., Congress created its own Article I "District Court" as well as its own "United States Court of Appeals." These Legislative courts were created to judge violations of the laws that were carefully worded to disallow Article Three court jurisdiction. Violations of certain laws were prosecuted by the Legislative courts of federal agencies, such as the IRS. This is the Congressional long arm of the law. The people who write the laws, now prosecute the laws.

That is the legal framework within which Congress acted out, (and continues to act out) its role as "Pretender to the Throne." Meanwhile "We the People" remain dispatriated! Those are the specific Articles of the Constitution, upon which, Congress built its road to treason and separated We the People from our Constitution. It is vitally important that "We the People" know exactly how "they the politicians" committed their usurpation of power, so that we can discuss it with authority. Sometimes the subject of "law" might seem dry and boring, but the vigilance required to regain those lost liberties insists that this lesson be learned, and learned well. So if you must reread this explanation several times until the pieces fit, please do so because YOU can be part of Liberty Restored.

It is not difficult to unravel the legislative tapestry of legal fictions with the proper use of a few carefully chosen Constitutional clauses. Congress has the power to "ordain or establish" inferior courts. Yes, the Supreme Court shall have jurisdiction with exceptions "and under such regulations as the Congress shall make." Yes, those are business issues between those two branches and not authority to grant themselves new powers over citizens, except in cases with interstate or international consequences. Because those are the only laws allowed to be heard in any "Congressional" federal court. Consider that even Article Three courts are limited in jurisdiction to hearing cases affecting the enumerated powers as stipulated in the Constitution.

Art. 3, Sec. 2, (clause 1)

"The judicial power shall extend to all cases, in law and equity, arising under this Constitution..."

Therefore, federal judicial power is limited to the enumerated cases affecting "ambassadors, other public ministers or consuls ... admiralty and maritime jurisdiction ... controversies to which the United States shall be a party ... between two or more States..." The list goes on but there is no jurisdiction over ordinary citizens except when those citizens live in different States. It does say that "The judicial power shall extend to all cases ... arising under the Constitution..." Does that include laws passed by Congress that are not Constitutional, because such deceits have happened? The Constitution provided a litmus test for such laws.

Article 6, (clause 2)
"This Constitution and the laws of the United States which shall be made in pursuance there of ... shall be the supreme law of the land."

The only legislation that is lawful, would be laws made "in pursuance" of the Constitution, and because the Constitution limited the federal government's ability to expand its power, Congress turned to "amending" the Constitution to give themselves more power, thus labeling their expansion of power as "Constitutional." The legality of such amendments is covered later.

Before the War of 1861, the Supreme Court, under the leadership of Chief Justice Taney, was conservative, meaning a strict interpretation of the Constitution, as exhibited in the Dred Scott decision. The Court was not under the influence of the Radical Republicans. The U.S. Constitution did not stipulate how many Judges should sit on the Supreme Court. The first Supreme Court had one Chief Justice and six associate judges; by 1861, there were nine.

After Taney issued his objection to Lincoln's suspension of the writ of habeas corpus in Maryland, Lincoln was put on notice that he was going to have a fight on his hands in the Supreme Court because of his abuse of power. Lincoln realized he had to conquer the Supreme Court, and the way to do that was legislation, instead of continually ordering Taney's arrest under martial law.

There was an important case coming before the Supreme Court (the Prize Cases) which challenged Lincoln's legal right to blockade the Southern ports, including ports in North Carolina, a State which had not yet seceded at the time of the blockade. Fortunately for Lincoln, during his four years as President, several Supreme Court vacancies came up, which he and the Senate promptly filled with like-minded radicals with a like-minded agenda. The new Supreme Court Judges carried the decision in Lincoln's favor by one vote in the blockade case. Lincoln appointed his own vindication.

Lincoln and the Senate went as far as to add a tenth Justice to the Supreme Court which gave the Republican's Transfer of Power schemes an even safer judicial margin, yet sometimes a law can be so conspicuous even the Republican's hand picked "yes-men" must render a Constitutional interpretation. In 1864, Supreme Court Justice Roger Taney died. Lincoln and the Senate appointed a new Supreme Court Chief Justice, Salmon ("State sovereignty died at Appomattox") Chase.

After the war ended, and while Andrew Johnson was President, the Supreme Court chose to make a decision concerning the legality of the use of martial law in areas where civil courts were sitting. Earlier, Justice Taney had been very vocal saying that Lincoln's use of martial law was unconstitutional in the Merryman case in Maryland, but those remarks were overshadowed by the war. But, in 1865, the same question came up without the diversion of war, in the Exparte Milligan case.

"Exparte" simply means that there was only one party in the dispute, L.P. Milligan, who was tried by a military court back in 1864 and imprisoned in Indiana at a time when civil courts were still in place. Well, the "packed" Supreme Court, much to the outrage of the radicals in Congress, found in favor of Milligan. The high court's decision stated that the moment civil order was restored, there can be no martial law. That decision was a major legal setback for the Republican's plan for reconstruction. The Milligan case was particularly upsetting for the radicals because Andrew Johnson had used all of his Presidential power to restore "civil" order throughout the South to deny Congress their "military" rule.

After their radical reconstruction plans were put on hold, Congress again attacked the Supreme Court and continued their power-struggle to gain supremacy over America's third branch of government. They cut the number of Justices down from 10 to 7 by eliminating the Southern Judicial Districts which eliminated 3 pro-Southern strict Constitutionalists. This finally gave Congress a tight fisted (rubber stamp) control over the Supreme Court. In desperation, the House even passed a bill, (but not the Senate) to change the required vote for a Supreme Court decision from a simple majority vote to a two-thirds vote before they could overrule any new laws of Congress. The Radical Republicans were ruthless and unrelenting in their attempts to convert their war-time martial law powers into a peace-time martial law rule.

The Reconstruction Acts of 1867 actually eliminated the physical boundaries of the Southern States and converted them into five new martial law districts. Thus, a State with no boundaries is not a State and as such can have no "civil order." Congress denied Southern States their borders to preclude any claims that citizens of the "Johnson States" had Constitutional rights. Congress thereby usurped the Exparte Milligan decision from being applied to their plans for reconstruction.

There were appeals to the Supreme Court coming from Southern States like Mississippi and Georgia, but the definitive Supreme Court decision concerning the legality of Congress's martial law over the South involved a Mississippi newspaper editor named McCardle who published news and editorials critical of reconstruction. In April of 1867, only one month after the passage of the first Reconstruction Act which eliminated the borders of the Southern States, the Supreme Court ruled that it did not have jurisdiction over the Reconstruction of the South.

The highest court in the land yielded to Congress; only Congressional courts could adjudicate legal challenges emanating from Southern States under the Military Act. First the Executive Branch of the national government abandoned the Constitution, then the Legislative Branch, and finally, by yielding jurisdiction, the Judicial Branch completed the usurpation of America's new Federal Government.

McCardle lost, the South had no Freedom of the Press! Congress had set up its own empire over ten Southern States (Tennessee was back in the Union). Yes, this was it, this was the big switch; the Supreme Court recognized the creation of a peace-time martial law rule. Individual American citizens (in the South) were denied their Constitutional protections under Article III, and later the Article III Judicial Courts would co-mingle with the new legislative Article I (Congressional) Courts.

The words of the deceased (1864) defender of the Original Constitution, Chief Justice Roger Taney, haunted the Southland:

"I can only say that if the authority which the Constitution has confided to the judiciary department ... may ... be usurped by the military power at its discretion, the people of the United States are no longer living under a government of laws but ... at the will and pleasure of the army..."

Consider these prophetic words by George Mason, author of the Virginia Constitution and one of America's great legal minds, concerning the very existence of federal courts. Mason's warning came eighty years before reconstruction:

"When we consider the nature of these courts, we must conclude that their effect and operation will be utterly to destroy the State governments; for they will be the judges of how far their laws will operate.... The principle itself goes to the destruction of the legislation of the States, whether or not it was intended ... I think it will destroy the State Governments."

The Supreme Court decided they would no longer operate in the South; nor would they challenge the new unconstitutional jurisdiction established by Congress. George Mason's haunting prophecy came true when the Southern States were destroyed, first physically from 1861 to 1865; and then "legally" from 1865 to the present.

To add insult to injury, President Johnson was never allowed to nominate a single Justice for the Supreme Court. Yet in April of 1869, only one month after Johnson stepped down and Union General Grant became President, the radical Congress decided to raise the number of Justices up from seven, to nine. This was when Grant nominated the two railroad lawyers. And it was in 1869, that the same "packed" Supreme Court, headed by Chief Justice Salmon P. Chase, ruled that there had been no secession. Was secession legal? Not according to the best legal minds money could buy!

The Legislative-Executive-Judicial power-struggle ended with Congress reigning supreme. Congress is the supreme law of the land. Congress rules over "We the Subjects," Congress rules above the Constitution, Congress is king of America. America changed from being a Constitutional Republic into being a pseudo-democracy! Congressmen may come and go, but the corruption in the Federal Government is immortal!

Federal judges are minions of Congress, half appointed by one party and the other half appointed by the other party, with one moderate wildcard. When judicial decisions seem split, do not assume that justice is at work, it is a roll-call of party affiliation. The Supreme Court Judges follow six paces behind Congress with their heads bowed. And as far as the power of the President, well, when Congress back-slides out of the bankers' hands (from time to time), the powers-that-be install a Lincoln or a Roosevelt into office and use Executive Orders to get Congress back in line. There are times when the Executive is the king, but typically the Transfer of Power is shared as directed from the shadows, by those who are never elected but never leave Washington.

The Executive and Legislative Branches of our government have entered America into the United Nations and into the arena of International Court. Originally, the International Court at the Hague was designed to hear cases of one government against another, but not any more. One hundred and sixty nations met in Rome in July of 1998 to design an International Criminal Court. This court will also operate at the Hague, but it will hear criminal cases of individuals. America's participation in this court could put Americans on trial for crimes against an alien international law. A citizen of the United States could be taken out of this country, to the Hague, tried, sentenced and punished for a U.N. crime.

Currently the Hague is hearing cases of "genocide" from Rwanda or "war crimes" from the former Yugoslavia. In the new "International Criminal Court" there are 18 judges but no Bill of Rights. The vote in Rome of the 160 nations was 120 Nations voting for the court, 40 against (U.S. against). It passed. Now before actually becoming the law over America (through U.N. treaty) it must be ratified by only 60 of those 160 nations (none of which have to be the U.S.). Three U.S. Supreme Court Justices went to observe the European Court in action and suggested that we use their court as a guide for America.

New America should be cautious about exporting its citizens for trials overseas. The Declaration of Independence listed reasons for America's separation, one of which was: "For transporting us beyond the seas to be tried for pretended offenses." The only difference between then and now, is that America's present generation of patriots lacks the courage to demand liberty.

Enter into the 1865 world of the 39th Congress and follow the tracks of their Legislative malfeasance; as they create legal fiction upon legal fiction. Examine their tactics, logic and chronology as they craft their self-empowering legislation: the 13th Amendment, the Civil Rights Act, the Second Freedmen's Bureau Act, the Reconstruction Acts, the 14th and 15th Amendments. The intention of Congress was to pass a deliberate combination of legislation, each built upon the previous, whose cumulative effect, would leave America entangled in an irreversible quagmire of legal fiction (key word: "irreversible").

TRANSFER of POWER

Chapter 12

Irreversible Legal Fiction

The War of 1861 ended in 1865. The military victory belonged to the national government. In the "War between the States and the Federal Government," the States lost, but at the end of the war, the new national government needed to convert their "military" victory into a "legal" victory. The problem for the 1865 Radical Republican Congress was that they never admitted that there was a bona fide war, therefore any new post-conflict "powers outside of the Constitution" would have to be legally explained, including an explanation of any "emergency powers" that continued after the "emergency." The Radical Republicans desperately needed legislation that would sanction their new powers, particularly, Constitutional amendments and subsequent tactical legislation designed to usurp the Constitutional protections guaranteed to U.S. citizens. They specifically needed new Constitutional amendments to give the color of law to their usurpation. This would allow them to claim their new laws fell under the original power-clause of Article VI, (clause 2):

"This Constitution, and the laws of the United States which shall be made in pursuance thereof; ... shall be the supreme law of the land..."

They could eliminate the "legal nicety" of having to prove that their law was "in pursuance" of the Constitution if they made it part of the Constitution itself.

President Johnson, though he tried to help the South, was also guilty of treason when he used his war-obtained powers over the Southern States to force them to rewrite their Constitutions. Neither did Johnson allow former "Confederates" to participate in the Constitutional Conventions of their States. By Executive Order, Johnson called the government of Virginia null and void and appointed the "Lincoln nominated" Virginia turncoat Francis Pierpont to be the Governor of Virginia in May of 1865.

The following resolution is an example of how it was politically incorrect to call the War of 1861 a war; consider the careful wording of the very first resolution by the Virginia General Assembly after it fell under Federal control. Joint Resolution One; February 6, 1866:

"Resolved by the General Assembly of Virginia, that the people of the Commonwealth ... accept the result of the late contest, and do not desire to renew what has been so conclusively determined ... but we rely on the intelligence and integrity of those who wield the powers of the United States government..."

President Johnson may have had good intentions, to do whatever it took to return the Southern representatives to Congress before the 39th Congress convened, but in America, no government is Constitutional without the "consent of the governed," and no President, no person, no group, nor any radical majority can deny the right of suffrage without due process. Yet despite Johnson's abuse of law, his intentions were to bring the Southern States back to Congress unfettered, to wield the necessary power, as a Democratic majority, to undo the five years of radical violations against the Constitution. But the radical Congress, knowing Johnson's intent, acted with deliberate speed to create a series of irreversible legal fictions as well as a secret plan to prevent the return of the South into the 39th Congress.

They devised six pieces of legislation to change America forever. These pieces of legislation were crafted to build one upon the other; the passage of one made it "legal" to pass the next. The treason is found within each law, but it is the cumulative effect that provided them with an irreversible legal fiction which became America's new law of the land. Here are those laws as they were passed (or enacted) in their tactical chronological order:

13th Amendment	December	1865
Civil Rights Act	April	1866
2nd Freedmen's Bureau Act	July	1866
Reconstruction Acts	March	1867
14th Amendment	July	1868
15th Amendment	February	1870

It was the radical 39th Congress that began this irreversible legal fiction. Backing the Radical Republicans was the "big money" of the eastern establishment with its ties to British banks. The goal was the transformation of the Original "States United" into one "United State." The national and State governments were to be converted into corporate-style governments where the state corporations served the central corporation of Washington D.C. This was the observation as stated by President Johnson:

"Your States are sinking into mere petty corporations ... mere satellites of an inferior character, revolving around the great central power here in Washington. There is where your danger is."

The new government would then become corrupted by the giant private corporations. This was the conclusion as stated by President Lincoln:

"I see in the near future a crisis approaching that unnerves me and causes me to tremble for the safety of my country; corporations have been enthroned, an era of corruption in high places will follow ... and the Republic destroyed."

The 39th Congress followed the European models of Marx, the French Revolution, and the Young Europe movements that concealed their lust for power in altruistic claims dedicated to the dignity of man, but in America they hooked their wagon to the freed slaves. Their strategy did achieve new national powers, but their tactic of playing the Negro-card insured racial trouble in America up to today.

There were two preliminary bills in this strategy that were passed by the previous (38th) Congress. Those two bills initiated the radical plan of creating an irreversible legal fiction. The more sinister of the two was the 13th Amendment Act which, after certain unconstitutional procedures (fraud) were used to achieve its passage, was sent to the States to be ratified, but was not ratified during the 38th Congress.

The last Act of the 38th Congress created the First Freedmen's Bureau on March 3, 1865, the day before Lincoln started his second term of office.

The Freedmen's Bureau was set up to be a transitional instrument to work with the freed slaves and lead them into having useful lives. It was not very radical, it actually seemed very practical, but in the political strategy of the Radical Republicans, the Freedmen's Bureau was their first tactic toward obtaining the Southern Negro vote. The First Freedmen's Bureau lasted only one year, and President Johnson let it die a natural death. It was replaced in July, 1866 by a much more politically intrusive version: the Second Freedmen's Bureau.

The 13th Amendment, was very carefully worded to include an "irreversible" power-clause that would be used by Congress to prevent Article Three courts from ruling over Congressional legislation. The last sentence of this Constitutional Amendment would provide Congress with new powers beyond any "checks and balances" from the Judicial Branch and forever place the new Federal Government over the States. This "power-clause" allowed for the unchecked creation of an unlimited bureaucracy with power over individual citizens. The powers of the Federal Government, up to that time, had to be stipulated in the Constitution; but after the 13th Amendment, the powers became unlimited. Any hopes for a restoration of America's original liberty can only come by a genuine understanding of how that liberty was stolen!

The 13th Amendment

"Neither slavery nor involuntary servitude, except as a punishment for crime where of the party shall have been duly convicted, shall exist within the United States, nor any place subject to their jurisdiction.

"Congress shall have power to enforce this article by appropriate legislation."

Objectivity requires a person to remove the moral issue of slavery from his examination of this Amendment to reveal the clause that is intended to delegate new powers to Congress. The treason is found in the last sentence: "Congress shall have the power to enforce this article by appropriate legislation." Congress shall have the power – isn't that just what they wanted, power? And this was not just an ordinary law, it was a so-called amendment to the Constitution; a permanent change in our National Compact.

"Congress shall have the power to enforce this article by appropriate legislation." What does it mean? Previously, the Constitutionality of a new law would be judged by Article Three courts as being legitimate only if it were "necessary and proper" and within the stipulated powers of the Compact. But, when legislation stemming from this Amendment was legally tested, Article Three courts decided that the term "appropriate" is a "political term" based upon political interpretations, therefore, any review of such "appropriate" legislation allows the Legislature itself to determine what is politically appropriate, and to serve that very purpose, Congress established its own court system.

The 13th Amendment took the Article Three judicial power, and usurped it with Article I Congressional power regarding all legal matters relating to any legislation serving the appropriate needs of the 13th Amendment and the guardianship of the "freedmen." This system began by controlling the South, but when a "freedman" went to California, or any other State, the Federal Government went with him, jurisdiction and all, thus is cases involving the "ward" of the Federal Government, federal laws trumped State laws. Remember, prior to this time, the national government had no jurisdiction over the citizens of States, except in interstate or international matters, or in serving those specific other "Constitutionally delegated" activities. The 13th Amendment gave Congress judicial, legislative, and police powers beyond those given to the Executive or Judicial Branches. Congress could expand its powers by claiming jurisdiction of its own "appropriate legislation" into any State that had "freedmen," which was later deemed "appropriate" to apply to the freedmen's descendants, and thus implemented perpetual racial politics to maintain unconstitutional powers.

Many patriotic Americans who studied to find the truth in history believe that the 14th Amendment is the death knell of the Constitution, but in reality, it was the "appropriate clause" of the 13th Amendment that provided "Constitutional credibility" to the progression of assumed powers taken by the national legislature. Without the "power-clause" of the 13th Amendment, the 14th Amendment would not have been possible.

The physical "military" treason started when Lincoln sent those ships to Fort Sumter to insight a war among the States, but the "treason-at-law" began when Congress used those military powers to obtain unconstitutional legislative powers.

The beginning of the postwar legal fiction was the 13th Amendment and the subsequent and tactical "appropriate legislation" includes the Civil Rights Act of 1866, the 2nd Freedmen's Bureau Act, the Reconstruction Acts, and the 14th and 15th Amendments, all of which created specific new legislative jurisdictions for Congress.

The "power-clause" at the end of the 13th Amendment, from which Congress claimed totalitarian enforcement rights, is also found carefully tucked into the 14th, 15th, 19th, 23rd, 24th, and 26th Amendments. Consider the venues of these amendments with the perspective of the power-clause; Congress can intrude into State jurisdictions on all matters emanating from all of these amendments, and write further legislation however it deems "appropriate," or said plainly: unlimited national power. The power-clause was also in the proposed (women's) Equal Rights amendment of the 1970's, though never ratified. If that were law, for example, Congress would have given itself the power to legislate and adjudicate laws wherever there were women. It is not about power to Negroes or power to women, it is about power to Congress; expanding the power of the Federal Government at the expense of the States.

The "Other" 13th Amendment

The 13th Amendment to the Constitution eliminated slavery, but there was an earlier 13th Amendment not to eliminate slavery but to guarantee the institution of slavery in States where it existed. This was "the other 13th Amendment."

After the secession of seven Southern States, Congress passed the "first" 13th Amendment in March of 1861 and sent to the States to be ratified, but the nation went to war in April and no ratification occurred.

In an 1862 Proclamation to raise more troops, the Governor of Virginia, John Letcher accused the national government: "They have permitted an illegal Legislature...." He was speaking of the Lincoln sanctioned bogus Pierpont "restored government" of Virginia with its bogus General Assembly complete with Senators and Delegates. It was the "Lincoln-loyal" Virginia Legislature that ratified "the other 13th Amendment" on February 13th, 1862. Question: If the war was over slavery, why would Lincoln's puppet government (hiding in western

Virginia) ratify a Constitutional Amendment that would prohibit any future national legislation from interfering with slavery. Yet this "first" 13th Amendment was ratified by "Lincoln's Virginia" after eleven months into a so-called "war to free the slaves?" The Pierpont General Assembly ratification of the "other" 13th Amendment reads:

"No. 11. - Joint Resolution in reference to amendment of the Constitution of the United States.

"Passed February 13, 1862.

"Whereas, in pursuance of the 5th Article of the Constitution of the United States, the Congress adopted the following joint resolution, which was approved March 1861, viz:

"Resolved by the Senate and House of Representatives of the United States of America in Congress assembled, That the following Article be proposed to the Legislatures of the several States as an amendment to the Constitution of the United States, which when ratified by three-fourths of said Legislatures, shall be valid to all intents and purposes as part of said Constitution, viz:

"Article Thirteen

"No amendments shall be made to the Constitution which will authorize or give to Congress the power to abolish or interfere, within any State, with the domestic institutions thereof, including that of persons, held to labor or service by the laws of said State.

"Upon consideration whereof,

"Resolved by the General Assembly of Virginia, that the said proposed amendment be, and the same is hereby ratified, and declared to be valid, to all intents and purposed as part of said Constitution when ratified by three-fourths of said Legislatures."

First Lincoln's "New Virginia" ratified a 13th Amendment to

forever allow slavery in February of 1862, then later in February 1865, Lincoln's "New Virginia" ratified the opposite 13th Amendment to prohibit slavery. "Lincoln's West Virginia" also ratified the second 13th Amendment. These legislative deceptions leave only one conclusion: The 13th Amendment was never lawfully proposed or ratified. This conclusion renders all subsequently derived "appropriate legislation" to be null and void.

The 39th Congress Takes the Helm

In December of 1865, President Johnson had nearly completed his hope (and Lincoln's hope) of returning the Southern States back into the Union with their civil governments in place and ready to take their seats when the 39th Congress convened.

The "Johnson States" had rewritten their Constitutions to eliminate slavery and their voters and elected officials were only taken from men who had not been officials in the Confederacy nor had been Officers in the Confederate Army. By December 4th, 1865, and the convening of the 39th Congress, Texas was the only Southern State that had not conformed to Johnson's plan for re-admittance into the Union, but President Johnson's zealous efforts had not gone unnoticed by Radical Republicans while Congress was adjourned.

Thaddeus Stevens had planned on how the Radical Republicans could thwart the readmission of Southern States into the December 1865 Congress. Stevens, the leader of the House, wrote letters to his Senate counterpart, Charles Sumner, trying to devise ways to reverse the progress of the "Johnson States." Thaddeus Stevens wrote Sumner:

"Is it possible to devise any plan to arrest the government in its ruinous course? When will you be in Washington? Could we collect men bold enough to lay the foundations of a party to take the helm of government, and keep it off the rocks?"

"Is there no way to arrest the insane course of the President?

Senator Charles Sumner then prepared his own program for dealing with the "Johnson States" as revealed in his statement:

"It is difficult to measure the mischief which has already ensued from the 'experiment' which has been made ... it is a terrible failure. It will be for Congress to apply the remedy ... nor do I doubt its duty to see that every pretended government organized by recent rebels is treated as a present nullity."

Those two men, as leaders of the House and Senate, set the mood for the 39th Congress. They crafted an essential parliamentary slight-of-hand in a Congressional power-play to establish a new legal fiction as the law of the land. As odd as it may sound (but was normal then), the 39th Congress was elected in November of 1864, but wasn't seated until December of 1865. If the returning Southern States were denied their Congressional seats then there would be a Republican majority, if the Southern States were allowed to take their seats, the Democrats, North and South would be the majority. Stevens and Sumner had to pervert the will of the electorate.

Johnson had all but Texas ready to legally take their seats at the opening session of the 39th Congress in December of 1865. Those Johnson States had prohibited slavery within their States as required. The returning Southern States even brought their 13th Amendment Ratifications with them to Washington, as was required to "rejoin" the Union. Remember, it was the 13th Amendment that outlawed slavery (as a cover) but actually contained the much coveted "appropriate legislation" clause that would empower Congress to destroy the States. The stage was set, the reunification of North and South was to occur as the gavel sounded at the 39th Congress. The Radical Republicans set their plan into motion.

Congress convened on December 4th. As was the tradition then, the President would open the first session with a prepared speech, but the Republicans had their own agenda which they set into motion before Johnson was given the podium and before he could deliver his speech about mending the nation.

This very moment marks the beginning of the Congressional coup against the postwar Southern States and against the Constitution of the United States. The Clerk of the House, Edward McPearson, omitted the names of the Southern Congressmen from the roll call which denied them their seats and refuted their credentials. Edward McPearson committed legislative treason.

The next order of (pre-scripted) business was performed by Congressman Thaddeus Stevens. Stevens immediately created a "Committee of Fifteen" to review the admission of the Southern States into Congress. Nine of the members were Republican while six were Democrats, and with the votes going strictly down party lines, the Republicans controlled reconstruction. Stevens headed the committee. The Republican members of the Committee of Fifteen were radicals who endorsed the Stevens agenda. The Committee of Fifteen was often compared to the Committee of Public Safety of the French Revolution, under which Robespierre inflicted his Reign of Terror on France. The French Revolution, only 70 years earlier, was cognizant in the minds of Americans; and there were some definite occult political connections between these two conflicts. Radical Republicans were also called Jacobins, recalling another memory of the French Revolution.

The next action by the radical Congress revealed their hypocrisy and total disregard for maintaining any semblance of lawful process. Yet, it was probably unavoidable to use such effrontery at this most-historic juncture in America's Transfer of Power. The 39th Congress accepted as valid, the 13th Amendment ratifications brought to Washington by representatives of the Southern States and used them to officially ratify the amendment, yet denied those same Southern Congressmen their seats. How could that be?

The Southern States WERE NOT States on December 4th, when they came to take their seats in Congress, but the Southern States WERE lawful States on December 18th, when the Secretary of State accepted their ratifications of the "Congress empowering" 13th Amendment. If the Southern Representatives were not lawful Congressmen, (contrary to Article Five of the Constitution) then their States could not be States, and as such, the 13th Amendment was never lawfully ratified. President Johnson concluded that because the Southern States were denied Statehood, their ratification of the Amendment could not be lawful:

"...their concurrence cannot be considered as having been legally given, and the important fact is made to appear that the consent of the three-forth's of the States, the requisite number has not been obtained to the ratification of that amendment, thus leaving the question of slavery where it stood before the amendment."

This particular fraudulent lust for power goes back to when the Amendment was a bill introduced in the 38th Congress on February 1st, 1865. Lincoln allowed Senators from the bogus state of Virginia to vote on the 13th Amendment as it went through Congress at the very time when Richmond was the Capital of the Confederacy, seat of the Confederate Congress, and location of the "White House of the Confederacy." When the 13th Amendment went to the States to be ratified, it was the bogus General Assembly, (having moved to Occupied Northern Virginia) under Governor Pierpont that ratified the Amendment on behalf of the State of Virginia on February 9th 1865, Add to this fraud, the "ratification" by "West" Virginia; a State created under Lincoln's martial law in collusion with the bogus "Pierpont" Virginia government. The ratification of the 13th Amendment includes two "ratifications" by Virginia, while the genuine Commonwealth of Virginia was at war with Congress.

The radicals desperately needed the power-clause of the 13th amendment to create their "New America" and were willing to do anything to get it, whether fraud, treason, murder and actually insurrection! These crimes against the Original Constitution were necessary tactics to destroy the America of Jefferson and Madison. Added to the list of ratification irregularities is the fact that the Southern States were ordered under martial law to ratify the Amendment through their legislatures which were regulated by Union Generals. Was Thaddeus Stevens very cleaver, or just ruthless?

The foremost question of law regarding the status of any State after 1861 is: Were the Southern States - States?

If they seceded, then Congress had no declaration of war and no peace treaty.

If they didn't secede, then after the war, they should have been seated in Congress.

If they as States, could actually amend the Constitution, why were their Congressmen denied their seats in Congress?

If, according to the Supreme Court decision in Exparte Milligan, there could be no martial law where any civil government and court exists, and after the Commander-in-Chief of that martial law, President Johnson, proclaimed that the insurrection was at an end and that peace was restored, and all States but Texas had civil governments, how could the South be denied its Constitutional rights of Article Five?

Were they States or were they not States? It has to be ONE or THE OTHER, it cannot be both. "Claiming both" would be legal fiction; and that is exactly what Congress chose for America: legal fiction. Actually it was Edward McPearson and the Committee of Fifteen that gave "carte blanch" to a new national power, to the Federal Government we know today. No one could stop that 39th Congress, and no one did. The infamous 39th Congress gutted the Constitution, altered American citizenship and jurisdiction, and forever empowered themselves with unlimited legal fictions.

Racial Citizenship

The subject of "race" has been presented to Americans as a legal question of equality, and a social question of tolerance. In today's social climate, the establishment media and political parties and institutions of learning present ONE interpretation of America's racial history and sociology. Governmental racial policies stand as edicts, serving as a barrier between themselves and any challenges to the origins of the "New America." Whereas the media provide the public with repetitious stereotypical social portrayals psychologically keyed to either justify an "entitlement mentality" (40 acres and a mule), or assign guilt to those attempting to pierce the vail of politically motivated altruism. The government and media stand as co-guardians of New America and will not allow other voices into their establishment media or political arena if those voices undermine the essential dogma of "political correctness," the dogma that conceals their historic and unlawful Transfer of Power.

The truth behind the War of 1861 requires those who seek the truth to challenge certain misinterpretations of history, even if they become the brunt of the well-rehearsed rhetoric of racial guilt assignment. The fact to uncover here is that the Republican usurpers fabricated a "social camouflage" to conceal their treason-at-law: tyranny disguised as racial justice. They needed a humane cause that appealed to a person's sense of justice; but their high profile "defiant service to altruism" was, and still is, only political theater as performed in the corporate media.

If the legal fiction derived from political theater can morally replace the Constitutional "Law of the Land" without due process, then we are forever subject to political fluctuations of attitudes that serve avarice and greed. How could Congressmen ever lawfully destroy the government they swore to uphold? How could Congressmen amend or legally negate the freedoms guaranteed under the National or State Constitutions? These are the questions that were avoided in the 1860's because the radicals in the national government disguised their political coup as a fight for social justice, and all who opposed them on Constitutional grounds surely must accept their guilt assignment: "they are filled with hate." Very cleaver Thaddeus.

One point-of-law involved in the cover-up of the 1861 travesty was the creation of a federal "racial" citizenship. As mentioned earlier, the new "empowering" legislation was passed in a sequential order where one law was built upon a previous law which was built upon a previous law. The legality of each subsequent law depended upon the expansion of powers created by the previous law, the more laws, the more power. First, expand Congressional power in a war belatedly dubbed a war to free the slaves, followed by a Constitutional Amendment to secure and expand those powers however deemed "appropriate." Next, make the slaves citizens and the citizens slaves, and in doing so, create more "appropriate" powers for Congress as secured by another Constitutional Amendment. Next, disallow suffrage to the prewar electorate and give the vote to the 14th Amendment "Federal Citizens." The Radical Republicans used "Negro (Republican) suffrage" to extend their party's power in Congress and used the suffrage amendment to secure powers of federal intervention into State elections.

Today, the average school student learns that America (meaning the United States) was always intended to be a nation where "all men are created equal" including Negroes. American children are taught that the Declaration of Independence was provided as a path in time for the equality of all, and if they are kindhearted and fair-minded students, they should condone the legislation that brought justice to Negroes. Most students blindly accept this distortion as historical and legal fact. Any voices to the contrary would insight riots, thus Americans today, seeking to avoid any further establishment-induced feelings of guilt, choose to ignore or auto-discount any "opposing opinions," in the illusion that racial troubles will vanish. But racial troubles are required to keep the citizens from questioning the unlawful origins of the New

America. And so ironically, it is their guilt assuaging blindness to the destruction of the Original Constitution that perpetuates racial problems in America and negates any lawful remedies.

If a blatant tyrant entered American politics and became the leader of the majority party and used that power to dismantled the present government, would today's school students demand the legal scrutiny of the usurper's "so-called laws" used to dismantle the existing government? And if the tyrant shared his wealth with the media, who then dressed his treason up in causes "noble and just," would those students suspect treason and deceit in the media and reject the tyrant and refute his attempt to play their "heartstrings" to his tune of treason? Give today's students the benefit of the doubt, and say yes! So why is there so great a hesitation on the part of today's students (and graduates) to at least question the lawfulness of the postwar legislation of the 1860's which is the foundation of today's intrusive unconstitutional Federal Government?

It should be noted that the earliest forms of "nations" were familial tribal nations; the Negro tribes in Africa were "all black" nations, the Chinese tribes in China were "all Chinese" nations, and the Indian tribes in America were "Indian nations." Tribes were paternal, which in a general sense means the community had the same ancestral father, or patriarch. The word "patriarch" is the root word of the word "patriot." Citizenship of these nations, and especially regarding ascension to their thrones, whether in Africa, China or among the American Indians, was racial.

This natural worldwide development was no less true of the Europeans, especially true of the Royal Houses of the European monarchs. The word "nation" comes from the root word: natal, meaning by birth, thus the first nations and nations up to and beyond the 19th Century were generally extended families. Kindred nations revealed their natural racial self-preference. An objective person would agree that the corporate media has chosen to portray ONLY the "White" race as being socially "exclusive" which is a blatant lie; ethnic self-preference was universal.

Was the Original United States government and the Original thirteen American State governments of the 18th Century racial nations? Yes. What about the "all men are created equal" statement, in the 1776 Declaration of Independence? That Declaration was written by Thomas

Jefferson. Jefferson owned slaves, those slaves were not equal in law, therefore Jefferson's Declaration did not include Negroes, free or slave. It is best to start with facts, and admit them as facts.

It is important in solving America's racial problems that a person understand that Negroes were never covered under the "all men are created equal" statement. If Americans could accept that as fact and keep searching for the truth beyond that, there may be hope to deny the present government its unlimited powers. Such social candor could reveal that the Radical Republican laws of the 1860's were then, and are today, fictitious. Such candor could expose that Congress simply politicized the Negro to achieve unconstitutional political power while promising to give someone else's 40 acres and mule to their created voting block.

Jefferson's intent in his "all men are created equal" statement is further documented by a law passed by the first Congress of the United States, the 1790, U.S. Naturalization Act, written by Thomas Jefferson. This Naturalization Act established America's first immigration policy, stating who could become a citizen in the United States. The requirements written by Jefferson and passed by Congress read: "Any alien being a free White person ... may be admitted to become a citizen..."

There is no doubt that Jefferson meant "all White men are created equal." And no matter what a person may think of that statement, it is part of the foundation of America's laws, and any legal remedy for Negroes must begin there or it is revolution. And if it is revolution, then call it revolution! If the so-called legal remedy resulted in the overthrow of the American Constitution, then openly tell every American and see if they are willing to forfeit their Original Law of the Land and all the liberties therein guaranteed or would they prefer to revoke a handful of usurpations and the subsequent system built upon that legal fiction.

Jefferson was the second Governor of the Nation of Virginia, following Patrick Henry. As Governor of Virginia, Jefferson knew and was oath-bound to uphold the 1776 Virginia Constitution which stipulates the qualifications of voters: "Every White male citizen of the Commonwealth, of the age of twenty-one..." And because State Constitutions are a lawful party to the National Compact, they are included in America's national Law of the Land.

Consider the preamble to the Constitution: "We the people of the United States." Yet, as it is taught in schools today, the preamble is said to have referred to "all peoples." What can be gained by teaching a lie; and how can the status of the Negro be improved by teaching lies and living a lie? The Negro can be helped; the Negro can be free. The Negro can command his own destiny and obtain Liberty; but not based on lies. And considering how the new Federal Government can change its laws, money, and international entanglements with a change of attitude or corporate gratitude, what American can truly be safe. Until the lies of the 1860's legal fictions are exposed and revoked American Negroes will remain Federal chattel.

The famous Dred Scott decision of March 1857, gave the Supreme Court's definition of the "We the People" clause in the Preamble as stated by Chief Justice Roger Taney:

"The question is simply this; can a Negro, whose ancestors were imported into this country, and sold as slaves, become a member of the political community formed and brought into existence by the Constitution of the United States, and as such become entitled to all rights and privileges, and immunities, guaranteed by that instrument to the citizen? ... The words 'people of the United States' and 'citizens' are synonymous terms, and mean the same thing ... 'the sovereign people' ... The question before us is, whether the class of persons described in the plea in abatement comprise a portion of this people and are constituent members of this sovereignty? We think they are not, and that they are not included, and are not intended to be included, under the word 'citizen' in the Constitution, and can, therefore, claim none of the rights and privileges which that instrument provides for and secures to citizens of the United States.

"The men who framed this declaration were great men, high in literary acquirements, high in their sense of honor .... They perfectly understood the meaning of the language they used, and how it would not in any part of the civilized world be supposed to embrace the Negro race, which by common consent, had been excluded from civilized Governments and the family of nations...."

Black's Law Dictionary quotes the Dred Scott decision for its definition of the word "citizen," to say "citizen" is synonymous with "the People."

Jefferson Davis, representing Mississippi in the United States Senate, gave a farewell speech to the Senate after his State seceded. In that speech he touched on this same issue, he spoke about a political deception still used today: the misinterpretation of U.S. documents to usurp the Constitution:

"...the sacred Declaration of Independence has been invoked to maintain the position of the equality of the races .... The communities were declaring their independence; the people of those communities were asserting that no man was born, to use the language of Mr. Jefferson, booted and spurred to ride over the rest of mankind; that men were created equal – meaning the men of the political community ... When our Constitution was formed ... we find provision made for that very class of persons [Negroes] as property; they were not put upon the footing of equality with White men ... but so far as representation was concerned, were discriminated against as a lower class, only to be represented in the numerical portion of three-fifths. Then, Senators, we recur to the compact which binds us together ... which thus perverted, threatens to be destructive of our rights, we but tread in the path of our fathers when we proclaim our independence, and take the hazard."

The founding fathers and brave men like Jefferson Davis and Roger Taney who remained true to the Constitution, knew that citizenship meant men of the White race. Today that sounds so racist, but to solve the racial/social/legal problems of today, we must insist on starting with the truth; without which, we would be unable to unravel the Gordian knot of Congressional legal fiction. Brainwashing school children with politically motivated emotional lies does not offer cultural peace. Students trained in deceit, have also been trained to be intolerant of opposing interpretations. Yet who should expect We the People who know the truth, to accept a lie in order to avoid the mantra of scripted public outrage.

Answers can be found, and truth can be realized, and justice can be served for all; but only after we agree upon the true Law of the Land. America must return to its foundation of the Original Law so we might first restore the America we lost in 1865. Americans must start there to rid our nation of any and all legal fictions. Legal fiction threatens our land more now than in 1861! Only when America eliminates the "big lie" of 1865, can there be any lawful transition toward a true social peace for all.

Is the United States today "a land of laws not men?" America was not established as a land of capricious legal fictions based upon fluctuating political interpretations; how would that be any better than living under King George? One of the many media slogans of today being used to cloak the federal assumption of power is to say that "the Constitution is an evolving document." That is misleading. The Constitution prohibits the "evolving" away from liberty. Notice that the Original Bill of Rights, also called the first Ten Amendments, did not change the Constitution at all and it did not expand the national government at all, it further constrained it. That is the measure of a true Amendment, to negate an abuse of power. There were no "riders" on the Bill of Rights containing power-clauses. The Constitution can grow by amendment, yes, but only with additions that don't diminish any existing liberties, violate the Original Compact between States, or usurp the Original State Constitutions.

Chapter 13

Legal Fiction

The Legislation

The Civil Rights Act of 1866

The first consequential Act of Congress that dealt with the postwar South was the First Freedmen's Bureau Act, which addressed the welfare of the freed slaves. This act thus provided Congress with new powers within individual States, a precedent heretofore denied by the Constitution. The first legislative act with major Constitution-altering consequences was the bill proposal for a 13th Amendment, introduced in January 1864 which fraudulently passed through Congress and adopted by the "States" (under martial law) in December of 1865. The 13th Amendment put an end to involuntary servitude in all of the United States. That Amendment also contained a perpetually expanding power-clause giving Congress the power to "enforce this article by appropriate legislation."

The use of the term "appropriate legislation" removed from Article Three judicial review, all laws based upon that Amendment, and prohibited any review of laws based upon any legislation that was "built" upon that Amendment. In other words, the 13th Amendment was the cornerstone of new State-intrusive laws free from judicial review by the Supreme Court. This is the source of the expanding power of the new Federal Government who is only answerable to the legislative courts of Congress. But because this new power was, and continues to be, based upon the "well-being" of the freedmen (which includes their descendants), the expansion and perpetuity of the Federal Government's new powers requires the expansion and perpetuity of racial disorder, the presence of which, from that day forward, has been "verified" by a cooperative news and entertainment media.

International law recognizes the necessity for nations to have a separation of their "legislature" from their "judiciary." One branch makes the laws, while the other judges the violations and/or legitimacy of those laws. The system created by the 13th Amendment permitted lawmakers to judge their own legislation. After the "adoption" of the 13th Amendment in December of 1865, the first such "appropriate legislation" was introduced on January 5th, 1866. It came in the form of two bill proposals: the Civil Rights Bill, and the Second Freedmen's Bureau Bill.

The Civil Rights Bill would create a citizenship for all persons born in the United States, citizenship heretofore had been a determination of the State thereof. The Civil Rights Bill was passed by the Senate on February 2nd, and passed by the House on March 13th; after which, the bill went to the President to be signed. Johnson vetoed the bill, but Congress overrode the veto. This was the first time in American history that a major piece of legislation passed over a Presidential veto.

President Johnson, went along with abolishing slavery but thought that allowing citizenship to the Negroes would violate the Constitution and thus void the perpetual compact with the States and their posterity. Johnson said:

"I repeat, the expression of my willingness to join in any plan within the scope of our Constitutional authority which promises to better the condition of the Negroes in the South, improving their morals, and giving protection to all their rights as freemen. But the transfer of our political heritage to them would, in my opinion, be an abandonment of a duty we owe alike to the memory of our fathers and the rights of our children."

The Civil Rights Bill was made law on April 9, 1866. The Civil Rights Act read:

"Be it enacted, that all persons born in the United States and not subject to any foreign power, excluding Indians not taxed, are hereby declared to be citizens of the United States."

The Civil Rights Act created a Constitutional dilemma. Citizenship was by State, based upon each State's requirements; that was the basis of the Original Compact. Therefore the federal Civil Rights Act (as an act of Congress and not a Constitutional Amendment) attempted to supersede State Constitutions. The 13th Amendment permitted "appropriate legislation" to remedy slavery, and Congress used that clause, via the Civil Rights Act, to alter citizenship, suffrage and supersede State Constitutions.

The Civil Rights Act, did not give the vote to Negroes, it attempted to grant citizenship to Negroes but failed because an act of Congress cannot override the Constitution. Congress was able to use the Civil Rights Act, as appropriate legislation, to grant citizenship to Negroes but only in the Southern States. Congress could use the Civil Rights Act to flex their muscle in the Southern States, but only as long as they maintained that the Southern States were not States (martial law).

One absolutely crucial factor which developed at that time deals with the creation of a "parallel citizenship." There can only be three theories as to what Congress attempted with their passage of the 13th and 14th Amendments, and the Civil Rights Act:

Theory One:
Congress wanted to make all men equal, and was the savior of America and the Negroes.

Theory Two:
Congress, in 1861, having destroyed the U.S. Constitution and the Rights therein, had no intention of giving full Constitutional Rights to any newly created citizens, but would instead create a second class citizenship, lower than that enjoyed by the White citizens (at that time). Or ...

Theory Three:
Congress, having destroyed the U.S. Constitution in 1861, was in no way going to give Constitutional Rights to any new citizens, but would instead create a second class citizenship for Negroes and later strip Whites citizens of their Constitutional status and place them under Congressional jurisdiction.

Theory Three is the correct answer. To refute theory one, that Congress was the savior of the American Negro, it is crucial to make plain the politics behind so-called "civil rights."

The term "civil rights" simply means "the Rights of citizens." Yet most American law dictionaries make a distinction between the "rights of citizens" and "civil rights." This American definition of "civil rights" is a distinct Federal form of citizenship of which all subsequent "civil rights" legislation is written.

Black's Law Dictionary:

Civil Rights: [Rights to Citizens] "Also a term applied to certain rights secured to citizens of the United States by the 13th and 14th Amendments to the Constitution and by various acts of Congress made in pursuance thereof."

This legal definition is the official definition used today in the Courts of America. Take careful notice what the 38th and 39th Congress did: They created a "Congressional Citizenship" whose rights are not "Constitutional Rights" except as interpreted through the postwar 13th, 14th, and 15th Amendments and the appropriate legislation. And notice, Black's Law Dictionary makes the connecting of these Amendments to the expanded powers of the "various acts of Congress made in pursuance thereof." These are not "Constitutional Rights" of the Original Document, but are instead rights "granted to" a Federal Citizenship, rights that fluctuate with the prevailing political winds of self-serving "Congressional attitude."

What was the political reasoning behind Civil Rights? The Radical Republicans of the 39th Congress simply needed votes, Negro votes, to keep them in power. The Radical Republicans claimed to be the savior of the Negro, yet betrayed him with a second class congressional citizenship. If the Negro was to be freed, and surely he was, he would have been so much better off if his new freedom was authored by men who respected the Constitution, men whose motives were not political "ownership" of an entire people. The motive of the Radical Republicans was to get the Negro into an institution of servitude to a single political party, where they remain today (though a different party).

The First Freedmen's Bureau Act

The 38th Congress created the "Bureau of Freedmen, Refugees and Abandon Lands" simply called the "Freedmen's Bureau" one month before the war ended. This was the first notable postwar legislation because as soon as the war ended, the Bureau went South with the Army. The Bureau was created within the War Department. It was headed by General O. O. Howard, and many of the Bureau agents were double-dipping Union soldiers. This "concern for freed slaves" revealed that Congress intended to use the Freedmen's Bureau to place the South under military rule. Accompanying the Freedmen's Bill in Congress, came a request from the Joint Committee that President Johnson cease his attempts at reconstruction until Congress reconvened in December of 1865. However, Johnson, did not cease his gallant attempts to save the States.

The altruistic goal of the Freedmen's Bureau was to deal with problems facing former slaves. Included in its charter, was an added power that Congress would provide for the welfare of the Negro refugees entering the Northern States, thus expanding Congressional jurisdiction into other-than Southern States. The Act also gave Congress the power to redistribute the so-called "abandoned lands" in the war-torn South. These mandates seemed noble enough, but the less-than-altruistic motives became all too quickly apparent.

The Radical Republican Congress was attempting to transfer ownership of the slaves, in a political sense, from their former masters to the Republican Party. They put Negroes on the "welfare" system hoping that they would vote for the hand that feeds them. After the war, the North provided 21 million food rations to the destitute South in two years; 15 million of those rations went to Negroes. White Southerners were starving and malnourished because they voted Democrat.

The Freedmen's Bureau was given the authority by Congress to redistribute the "abandoned lands." What were the abandoned lands? The abandoned lands were the lands owned by Southern Whites which were taken by the Federal Government with the Confiscation Acts. Remember the words of Thaddeus Stevens: "Hang the leaders; crush the South; arm the Negroes; confiscate the land;" "every foot of ground they pretend to own." The Freedmen's Bureau was the quasi-military fulfillment of the evil dream of Thaddeus Stevens. The Republicans introduced a plan to give every adult Negro male forty (confiscated) acres and a mule. Republicans were buying future votes with land taken from Southerners.

The Freedmen's Bureau was also given authority to protect the Negro refugees fleeing the South. This meant that if a slave went to Ohio, Congressional jurisdiction went with him to protect him in Ohio and whomever mistreated him in Ohio was subject to the new Congressional judicial system (not fully established). The Freedmen's Bureau Act was an attempted legal device to impose Congressional "Article I" jurisdiction into all States where the "freedmen" went. That was an attempted "civilian usurpation" to the Supreme Court's Milligan decision regarding the use of "military courts" in States with civil governments in place. The new Congressional system had not yet fully developed its legal fiction, and not yet plugged all of the Constitutional "loopholes" between them and their "New America."

This "refugee clause" was the precursor to later legislation which would again use the location of the Negro's "person" to establish Article One (Congressional) jurisdiction. Congress eventually installed "civil rights" on all Negroes, and where the Negro went so did Congressional jurisdiction to enforce the nation-altering "appropriate legislation." A 20th Century example would be the 1954 Supreme Court case of Brown verses the Board of Education, and the 1964 Civil Rights Act. When the Federal Government forced "integration" on the local school systems, it brought those "local" schools under "federal" jurisdiction, based upon "racial" criteria; something that the South and the Constitution opposed.

In 1968, federal power extended into every work-place with the "equal employment and opportunities" legislation. Through the mandatory integration of the American workplace, the Federal Government gained jurisdiction over all "local" businesses, something it did not have before the appropriate legislation coming out of 1865. Remember, wherever the Negro goes, there too goes Congress brandishing all of its appropriate legislation, old and new. Playing the race-card was a cleaver tactic by Congress to get their legislative foot into the (previously) sovereign States.

The Second Freedmen's Bureau Act

Congress began their progression of legal fiction with the 13th Amendment Act; followed by their creation of the First Freedmen's Bureau; followed by the unlawful enactment of the 13th Amendment using the ratifications of the captive Southern States. Next, with the Civil Rights Act, Congress claimed jurisdiction over the Negroes to create a citizenry all unto themselves. Congress then extended the 1st Freedmen's Bureau Act with the more powerful 2nd Freedmen's Bureau Act. Remember, each Congressional Act was built upon the previous acts in a strategy to create their empire: New America.

The 2nd Freedmen's Bureau was empowered to enforce the Civil Rights Act that was passed three months prior. Congress systematically built its new empire piece by piece, all of which was built on the cornerstone of civil rights, racial justice and Congressional citizenship and jurisdiction. The Bureau, under the First Act, was to protect and support former slaves, but under the Second Act, the Bureau was empowered to convene military tribunals to enforce the unconstitutional "appropriate legislation" designed to perpetuate Federal powers over States' Rights.

Next, the Bureau elevated the newly created Civil Rights of Negroes to be, not equal but superior to the Constitutional Rights of the Southern White citizens. The struggle to impose a national jurisdiction over State Constitutional jurisdictions would pit the unconstitutional "federal citizen" against the lawful "State citizens." Remember, this policy was implemented before the 14th Amendment "federal citizenship" was foisted upon the whole country. The citizenship provided by the "Civil Rights Act" was only a martial law citizenship imposed upon the Southern States.

Wherever a federal martial law citizen was denied any right enjoyed by State citizens, a military tribunal would try, convict and punish the person or persons who denied the validity of a "Federal citizenship." Congressional rhetoric claimed that they had granted Negroes Constitutional Rights, which they had not. The 2nd Freedmen's Bureau legislation was yet another expansion of military jurisdiction and a prelude for the destruction of American Constitutions, National and State.

When the war ended, Confederate money and Confederate

bonds were proclaimed worthless, and with no money, the South was destitute. Into this economic climate came civilians from the Northern States with money. At that time, in the North, suitcases were made out of a carpet-like material and so those who came South (with their luggage) to gain economic dominance over Southerners were called carpetbaggers. Carpetbaggers kept close relations with the military governors for protection and to devise and implement new "opportunities."

When the civil controls (by the military) combined with the economic controls (by the carpetbaggers) corruption was rampant. Military governors ran up enormous debts in the name of the local and State governments. Each State incurred millions of dollars of reconstruction debt, and the Federal Government used that debt as a bargaining tool against State sovereignty. If States would cooperate and "voluntarily" sign-away their States' Rights, some of that bogus debt could be forgiven. If "federal citizens" were elected to State and local governments; if Southern railroads were sold to Northern bankers; if State Constitutions were amended to accept the "New America," if favorable laws were passed by the puppet regimes, then yes, some of that debt could be forgiven (or simply put: extortion).

The Freedmen's Bureau was openly used by the Republican Party to secure future voters using land give-aways; but land give-aways required more "abandoned" lands. Just how did that land become abandoned? When the Southern States were driven into debt, the military governors used a real estate tax to pay that debt. Remember Lincoln's Lieber Code, Section II, Article 31:

"The title to such real property remains in abeyance during military occupation, and until the conquest is made complete."

But Southerners had no money to pay the real estate tax, and so their land was sold for taxes owed; but if there were no buyers, the land was "abandoned." So the Freedmen's Bureau took the birthright inheritance of the South and gave it as a political bribe to buy the Negro vote. This established a perpetual policy of issuing government entitlements to create a racial voting block; a practice that continues today with 95% of the Negro vote endorsing a single party; but today it's the Democrat Party.

The Federal Government is prohibited under Article One, Section 9, (clause 4) of the Constitution from imposing a "direct tax" within States. This was violated when federally appointed generals and civilians ruled over the South and thus these federal agents "directly taxed" the Southern States. Federal governors ran up State indebtedness and then "directly taxed" within the States whereas prior to such "appropriate legislation," Congress could not. Regarding cases where Southern widows and orphans, and the old and infirm could not make the tax payments to the federal governors, their lands were "abandoned" and "confiscated" to fund the corruption or bribe Negro voters.

The federal tactics performed against the South by the martial law minions created an extreme racial resentment against the occupation obliging federal Negro citizens. The Federal Government politically pitted the White Democrats against the Republican Negroes to divide and conquer the Department of the South. President Johnson, being a Southerner, and a Constitutionalist, vetoed the 2nd Freedmen's Bureau Bill but it passed over his veto. His comment concerning the martial law provisions of the bill:

"I cannot reconcile a system of military jurisdiction of this kind with the Constitution."

Johnson believed that giving the Bureau such unlimited powers, both military and judicial, over the civil matters was unwarranted and unconstitutional. The bill passed into law over his veto and the Bureau began its symbiosis with the Army of Occupation. The Army was not the political force behind the Bureau, only its protector. The political direction was supplied by the Radical Republicans, who created their own civilian strike-force for the political domination of the South: the Union League.

The Union League

The Union League began its operation in 1862, in Philadelphia (though some say Pekin Illinois). Although the Union League was a racially White, and predominantly Republican organization in the North, in the South, it developed into a political organization that almost exclusively recruited Negroes. The overt mission of the Union League during the war was to boost soldier morale and encourage enlistments, both White and Negro. The Union League followed the Union Army into the conquered regions of the Confederacy which after the war included all Southern States. The Union League was the driving political force behind, and manpower within, the Freedmen's Bureau. Therefore, the Republicans' political "Union League" controlled the Congressional Freedmen's Bureau which after the war controlled the Army of Southern occupation.

Membership cross-overs were commonplace; there were Union League-Freedmen Bureau-Army soldiers. To make matters more confusing, there was also a shadow of a mystery which followed the Union League into the South: Negro masonry.

Negro masonry is usually called Prince Hall, after its Negro founder, Prince Hall. It is instructive to introduce the Union League and Prince Hall at the same time to point out their similarities, and considering the earlier Masonic connections to this war, it seems relevant. The Philadelphia and Boston Prince Hall Lodges, acting concurrently to the activities of Rob Morris to unite White masonry, attempted, in 1847, to create a National Grand Lodge. Its first Grand Lodge was in Boston, its second was in Philadelphia, third New York, forth Maryland and the fifth Grand Lodge was the "Union" Grand Lodge formed in Washington D.C. in 1848. Prince Hall lodges spread throughout the North, but not in the South.

The most influential of the Union Leagues were located in New York and Philadelphia. In 1863 the Union League created its Grand Council in Washington D.C. The League was aided by a flock of Northern Ministers, mostly Methodist, who followed the conquering Army into the South to save the Negro and get him to vote Republican. The Union League organized "secret lodges" in the South as they conquered the South.

Prince Hall had Grand Lodges in New York and Philadelphia. They were led by a flock of Negro Ministers, many of whom were Methodists. As the Northern Army conquered the South, Prince Hall Lodges were established in the South. The "Union" Army conquered New Orleans, on April 25, 1862, the first "Southern" Prince Hall Lodge was established there in January, 1863. When the war ended and the Union Army took control of the remaining States, the formation of

214

Prince Hall Lodges followed suit: Virginia, October, 1865; Kentucky and Missouri, 1866; South Carolina, 1867; North Carolina, Georgia, Tennessee, and Florida in 1870; then Alabama, Mississippi, Arkansas and Texas in 1875.

Prince Hall member, and later Grand Master of Missouri, Reverend Moses Dickson had, with eleven others, created a "secret society" called the "Knights of Liberty," years before the war. Consider the "coincidence" that the Knights of Liberty was a secret militant group, and the Knights of the Golden Circle was a secret militant group, and later, even the Knights of the Ku Klux Klan was a secret militant group.

The Union League "secret society" recruited well over 50% of the adult male Negroes (some estimates are as high as 90%). In North Carolina alone, there were 80,000 members. In the Prince Hall "secret society" there were 47,240 Knights of Liberty.

The primary purpose of the Union League was to get Negroes to vote Republican. Before the war ended, the Union League was successful in the 1864 election of Lincoln, by helping deliver 78% of the soldier vote to the Union (Republican) Party. The Union League was also successful in recruiting regiments of soldiers.

Hiram Revels, of Prince Hall, was a Negro Methodist preacher from Baltimore, a chaplain in the Army who recruited a regiment of soldiers into the Union Army. He became a carpetbagging Republican in the political arena of the New South. In 1870, he filled the same U.S. Senate seat for Mississippi that Jefferson Davis resigned in January, 1861. The first Negro Senator was welcomed in D.C. by Senate leader Charles Sumner and the Radical Republicans with much political fanfare. Revels was also responsible in creating hundreds of African Methodist, Baptist and Protestant Churches in the South.

Salmon P. Chase, founder of the Freedmen's Union, toured the postwar South, and in every city where he promoted the Republican cause he was greeted by the loyal Union League Negroes. The Union League distributed five million pamphlets. However, after the war, the Union League dissolved in the North because its mission was to harvest the Southern Negro vote. When the Freedmen's Bureau and the Union League came South, they established schools for the Negro children. What an opportunity to heal the wounds; but instead, they came to teach hate. The Union League promised the Negroes that everything that the "Whites" owned was theirs to take in reparations and entitlements, a sentiment still echoed today; different political party, same political "chattel."

The political results of the combined efforts of the Union League, the Freedmen's Bureau, and Prince Hall paid off. The postwar South Carolina Legislature was composed of 50 Negroes and 13 scalawags. Both of Mississippi's U.S. Senate seats were occupied by Negroes. The Louisiana Lt. Governor and 29 State political representatives and party officials were Negroes. There were very similar results throughout the South. The first racially mixed jury in America was called to sit in judgement in the trial of Confederate President Jefferson Davis. However, Chief Justice Salmon Chase intervened and the Federal Government decided to avoid a trial and the potential Constitutional embarrassment.

The Union League, while pretending to have the best interest of the Negro at heart, was a political strategy and nothing more. From its conception, the Union League calculated ways to recruit the Negro vote. They hired a psychologist who specialized in the Negro race to devise a plan to organize the Negroes into the Republican ranks. The psychologist decided to create a "secret society" within the Union League to be predominantly Negro, and eventually, for Negroes only. In this secret society, members were given mystery oaths, secret passwords, flamboyant ceremonies, and night meetings with guards.

Negroes who did not join were ridiculed. The controllers of the Union League even arranged for Negro women not to marry or associate with non-members. This "social motivation" caused the ranks of the League to grow throughout the South. Their doctrine was anti-White with promises of guns and domination over the South. This was the point where the postwar racial environment became very dangerous for the White residents. Hate crimes and anti-White terrorism became commonplace. In some States, as many as one-forth of the Union League members formed military clubs. And to make matters worse, the reconstruction Governors reinstated the State Militias, in which ex-Confederates could not serve, thus creating almost entirely all-Negro Militias. Also added to this mix, was the military arm of the Negro Masonic Knights of Liberty. Even in today's Army, there are no "White" Masonic lodges, only Negro lodges. Is there a force on stand-by for future ventures into the venue of a racially motivated martial law; a replay of Reconstruction?

This gave the Negroes a real sense of physical power; a power they abused. The Union Leagues, and occult organizations, taught the Southern Negro to hate White people. Negro militia soldiers would get drunk and club to death anyone who looked at them cross-eyed; they even used their bayonets to kill old men. They would bust down doors to private homes, insist on being fed, and then, at their pleasure, beat, kill or rape their unfortunate host.

This was a nightmare for everyone except the carpetbaggers and scalawags. Scalawags were Southerners who supported the Union occupation. Perhaps the worst of these violations of law and crimes against humanity were directed against the widows of the war and their small children. There were situations so bad as to avoid description here. Yes, it was that bad! Noble men who came to the defense of these widows and orphans were often killed on the spot, or worse, dragged out of town, tortured and then killed. All of this evil was done with federal impunity. And never forget, one-third of the soldier-age Southerners were either dead or wounded, leaving the women and children to be defended by "grandpa," but grandpa did what he could and died like a man!

The original Ku Klux Klan started out with noble intentions to right these wrongs condoned by the Federal Government. The illegal activities of the Klan, retribution against White and Negro thugs, had immediate results. Confederate General Nathan Bedford Forrest was one of the South's shining stars during the war and after the war. He led the first Klan. His Klan did not cover their faces, nor hurt innocent Negroes.

Forrest quickly ended his involvement with the Klan when newer branches of the Knights Klan resorted to socially abhorrent tactics; the latter tactics were used as justification for more Congressional interventions over the South. History must record that the first Klan was born out of a desperation to stop the horrible, unending abuses inflicted by the Negro Militias, the Union League and Knights of Liberty.

It must be noted that the South itself had been trying to rid itself of slavery, but with the deliberate resurgence of the pro-slavery sentiment from Britain during the 1830's, a subversion of the South took place. When the war came to the South, there was a cry among Southerners: "Rich man's war, poor man's fight." Add to this the fact that the industrial age was starting to replace "slave labor." Perhaps if slavery was allowed today, there would likely be some idiots who would have slaves; thus slavery is a determination of human awareness and morality.

Slavery should have been outlawed; but how? The legal dilemma centered on the axiom that possession is nine-tenths of the law. Who would compensate for the loss of "property?" Why should non-slave owners pay taxes to pay to slave owners? Why should a Southerner who grows and harvests his own cotton pay taxes to compensate the slave-owning cotton producers who have "unfairly" competed against him?

Various methods of emancipation were suggested by many Virginians before the war, but with the deliberate delay and pro-slavery advocacy funded by European mentors operating in the South, and the lack of money to buy it out of existence, slavery remained. Therefore the British funded operatives in the North used the Union League and other radical instruments to take possession of the Southern Negroes and deliver them into yet another deplorable state of humanity: government dependency and second-class citizenship.

Today's political machine would want to label the preceding statements as racist, but only because such statements reveal the roots of their continued abomination. They prefer that all Americans pretend the elevated status of Negroes today was achieved Constitutionally. In other words, today's Democrats pay lip service to Negroes, calling them equal in law, when in fact Congress never gave them equality, and because Congress claims that they have, it means they never will. Thus, the Democrats of today, like the Republicans of the 1860's must label anyone who says otherwise "racist" and certainly no one will listen to a racist. Will Americans ever come forward to restore the Constitution? Do Americans cherish the Constitution more than they fear being called a racist? Patriotic Americans are willing to die to preserve liberty, but they are not willing to fight to preserve liberty if it means being called a racist! Who will dare attempt to restore the Originial Constitution if it means being called a racist? Long-live the Federal Government!

When the slaves were freed, it meant that the Negro slaves had to leave their homes. Yes, they had homes. What kind of home would you call a slave-shack? Maybe not much of a home compared to today's homes, but take a look at Lincoln's childhood home, or the home of President Andrew Johnson when he lived in North Carolina. Not every American lived in prestigious homes like Mount Vernon, Monticello, or the Hermitage. Most early Americans lived at today's poverty level. The plantations were only a miniscule percentage of American homes, and a slave's home might look small within the shadow of a plantation mansion, but there wasn't a 200 square-foot difference in the size of a slave-shack and the early homes of several American presidents.

The slaves were freed, and by federal mandate, had to leave their homes, which they did for a while, but "freedom" was just another word for nothing left to lose. So they went back to their homes only to be told once again: "You have been freed, you must leave the home you've known and start your new life." So, the Republicans forced them out of the only home they ever knew. Somebody should have kicked Charles Sumner out of his house and called him free.

This martial law mandate led to roaming bands of Negroes; unemployed and hungry. When the male Negro slaves were set free many of them abandoned their wives (yes, they had wives), and turned to moonshine and crime. The Negro women who were abandoned, had to resort to hanging around the Union Army camps, where they were denigrated and abused by Union occupation troops. This was the sad fate of Negro women under the reconstruction policies of the Radical Republicans; abandoned lands and abandoned women. One tragic effect was that the Union Army was responsible for the births of countless mulattoes (mixed race) children, yet modern history falsely blames such "issues" on their former "masseh."

The Republicans then cruelly offered the desperate Negroes a doctrine of hate and terrorism; which the Negroes took: hook, line and sinker. The Republicans established a political divide when they recruited Negroes into a block-vote in opposition to the political party of their fellow Southerners, the institution of racial politics. They allowed the uneducated to rule over the educated which resulted in social devolution, political regression, and fiscal mismanagement. The Radical Republicans, using their "secret societies" to get the Negro to push the White man too far, resulted in a political backlash and the formation of the Ku Klux Klan and the onset of postwar civilian bloodshed.

The racial strife that exists today is a creation of the legislation passed during and after the War of 1861. Things haven't changed much. Negroes still cling (almost entirely) to one party, the party with the anti-White rhetoric and the Party passing out the "rations," while the White citizens, not voting racially, split their votes between parties. Today's

Democrat racial rhetoric has one distinct and familiar theme exposing its Republican roots: "The Negro is the victim of prejudice and must forever have federal help to survive." If the lie works why change it, and if "New America" is built upon racial legal fictions, they must perpetuate racial strife. Politicians (and Hollywood) are forced to make the charge of "racism" the most evil accusation that can be heaped upon an American, so as to prevent any close scrutiny of the legislative foundation of their Transfer of Power.

The Radical Republican solution has proved, over the past 135 years, to be a complete failure in achieving its aims. It did not create "equality" it did not end prejudice; it did not secure the blessings of peace and tranquility for the Negro or the White. The government has used taxation to "transfer wealth" from Whites to the Negroes, and some believe that to be a step toward justice; when in fact, it is just the opposite. The Republicans bought the Negro vote during reconstruction, and the Democrats buy it today. Perhaps the time has come when politicians should stop buying and selling humans.

The time has come to address the serious problems which now threaten the liberty of all Americans. The time has come to stop making a mockery of justice and demand that the Federal Government relinquish its unconstitutional powers. Maybe then, we could return to being a Land of Laws, not politicians. The time has come for the Negro to stop voting for retribution and make a new compact with those he has been taught to hate: the liberty-loving posterity of the Founding Fathers.

A word to the Negro: Observe the motives of those who patronize you, their politically motivated words are so shallow, let them now become transparent. Instead of flattery, seek a justice that can only begin within the truth of the Original Constitution. No longer accept the legal fiction that "set you free," for that "freedom" is only a "permission" allowed you by the Federal Government. They escaped the control of the Original "We the People," do you really believe that they will surrender their ill-gotten power to you at some point in time when you finally ask for the all of the liberty in the Original Constitution? Don't let your hate and prejudice blind you, you have been taught to hate the wrong people. Don't settle for using the servants entrance in the Democrat Party; stop being flattered by the media's advocacy for you; their words are vanity and deceit.

Back to 1867: The Union League of New York, in July of 1867, concluded that the Union Leagues in the South were very successful and wanted to establish one in every town in the South. So even in the midst of Southern anarchy, the radicals were pushing to achieve a continued political domination over the Southern Negroes. The "appropriate legislation" clause of the 13th Amendment gave Congress the power to deny a judicial review of their power grab.

The Civil Rights Act gave Congress "possession" of three-and-a-half million Negroes to politically shape. The Freedmen's Bureau passed out government money to bribe Southern Negroes to politically align with the Republican party. The Union League provided directives in hatred and terrorism, but the Radical Republicans needed more: the assurance to a permanent throne, an irreversible power over the States if or when the Democrats regained control of Congress. They knew that the Southern Whites were getting closer and closer to regaining their citizenship and thus their Democrat vote. The time to secure Republican power was running out, so Congress invoked their next tactic in their longer legislative strategy to guarantee the permanent death of the Original Constitution.

The Reconstruction Acts

1st: March 2, 1867
2nd: March 23, 1867
3rd: July   19, 1867

Before Congress passed the Reconstruction Acts, they passed the 14th Amendment Bill and sent it to the States, but because it was not "enacted" until after, and because of, the Reconstruction Acts, it is necessary to review the Reconstruction Acts first.

In December of 1863, Lincoln introduced his plan for readmitting Southern States back into the Union. It was simple. He would pardon all but the high ranking Confederates; require an oath of allegiance; and when 10% of each State's qualified voters (who were voters in 1860) took that oath, the State would return to its "proper practical relation" to the Union. In opposition to Lincoln's compassionate "re-Union" terms, Congress passed the Wade-Davis Bill which raised the required number of oath bound Southerners to 50%; and each State had to rewrite its Constitution, repudiate the war debt and ratify the 13th Amendment. Lincoln pocket vetoed the bill, and it died.

When Johnson became President he merged the two plans, reducing the Wade-Davis requirement from 50% loyal voters back to Lincoln's 10%. By the time the 39th Congress convened all but Texas had achieved these requirements. The "Johnson States" came back into the Union but were denied their seats in December, 1865.

In the Congressional progression of legal fiction, the 13th Amendment was then adopted and made law by the "States that didn't exist." The "appropriate legislation" clause of that 13th Amendment allowed Congress to write legislation to help the freed slaves; thus the Civil Rights Act of April 1866 issued forth to provide (only) Southern Negroes a new Congressional type of "U.S." citizenship. This second class citizenship could only exist under martial law. The strategic legal fiction was not yet complete, the Civil Rights Act only provided Negro citizenship. The Reconstruction Acts were needed to subdue the Southern States long enough to allow the Republican Congress to harvest the 400,000 Southern (Republican) Negro votes.

President Johnson advised the Southern States to reject the 14th Amendment, and by the summer of 1866, it was apparent the Southern States had refused ratification. The one exception was Johnson's own State of Tennessee, which did ratify the Amendment and was the first Southern State admitted back into the Union, in July of 1866.

Because Congress did not allow the Southern States to reenter Congress in 1865, the election of 1866 provided the Radical Republicans the necessary two-thirds vote needed to override President Johnson's vetoes. Congress could rule over the South with an iron fist; they had defeated Executive veto power, and their "appropriate legislation" had usurped the Supreme Court review of their legislation. Also consider that at this time, Supreme Court Chief Justice Salmon P. Chase was touring the South rallying Negroes into the Republican Party. The Constitutional checks and balances among the three branches of government had all but vanished.

Despite the best laid plans of Congressional mice, month by month, the Southerners were getting closer to regaining their seats in Congress. When the 13th Amendment freed the slaves and the martial law Civil Rights Act gave them citizenship, Congress inadvertently created a temporary setback for their Republican strategy. In the U.S. Constitution, the House of Representatives was proportioned by population; of which, non-citizens counted as 3/5th's of a person. Congress had given the former non-citizens citizenship, which had an adverse political effect: it increased Southern representation in the House of Representatives by 20%, yet their new "U.S." citizens could not vote. This 20% increase in Southern Democrats would reverse the Republican majority in Congress. The Republicans had to scramble before the 1868 elections to create a legal fiction that would insure them holding on to their Congressional majority power.

On March 2nd, 1867 the first of three Reconstruction Acts was passed by Congress. It was politically necessary for Congress to continue in the legal fiction that assumed that the Southern States did not exist, despite earlier proclamations by Presidents Lincoln and Johnson. Lincoln had declared on April 2nd, 1865, that the insurrection had ended and told Generals Grant and Sheridan that as soon as the Confederates surrendered, they were to be allowed back in the Union. President Johnson declared on May 10, 1865 that the insurrection is virtually at an end. In April 1866, when Congress voted on the Civil Rights Act, in a failed attempt to prevent any further Congressional impositions against the South, President Johnson proclaimed:

"The insurrection which heretofore existed ... is at an end and is henceforth to be so regarded."

Yet Congress passed the Civil Rights Act that April, yet by the summer of 1866, when it was apparent that the States would not ratify the 14th Amendment, President Johnson feared more radical legislation was at hand. And so again in August, 1866, while trying to negate a blood thirsty Congress, President Johnson issued another proclamation:

"I do further Proclaim that the said insurrection is at an end and that peace, order and tranquillity, and civil authority now exist in and throughout the whole of the United States of America."

Johnson used words such as "peace" and "tranquility" and "civil authority" to counter the Constitutional verbiage used by Congress as their justification to extend martial law: the Preamble: "...insure domestic tranquility" and Article 4, Section 4: "protect each of them ... against domestic violence." Johnson chose words that would invoke the Exparte Milligan case which stated that the existence of "civil authority" voided the use of martial law. The Executive and Legislative branches were in a legal war of words for the soul of the South and so Constitutional words like "life," "protection," "peace" and even "necessary" became weapons. Examine their choice of words in the First Reconstruction Act:

"Whereas no legal State governments or adequate protection for life or property now exists in the rebel States of Virginia, North Carolina, South Carolina, Georgia, Mississippi, Alabama, Louisiana, Florida, Texas, and Arkansas; and whereas it is necessary that peace and good order should be enforced in said States until loyal and republican governments can be legally established: Therefore, be it enacted ... that the said rebel States shall be divided into military districts ... it shall be the duty of the President to assign the command of each of said districts an officer of the Army not below the rank of brigadier general ... he [the general] may ... allow ... civil ... or ... military ... tribunals."

Section Five of the First Reconstruction Act lists the "requirements" to obtain Statehood:

1. Create a Constitutional Convention to rewrite the State Constitutions to be approved by Congress.

2. Allow Negroes to vote, and to be delegates in these conventions.

3. No Confederate soldier or government official can participate as a delegate, nor vote in the convention.

4. The new State Constitutions must give Negroes the vote. (Something not required of Northern States)

5. Ratify the 14th Amendment.

When the Supreme Court was brought into the question of the legality of the Reconstruction Acts, Chief Justice Chase, and the "packed" Supreme Court declined jurisdiction.

Black's Law Dictionary says of reconstruction:

"Reconstruction: it presupposes the nonexistence of the thing to be reconstructed as an entity."

President Johnson said of reconstruction:

"There is no such thing as reconstruction. These States have not gone out of the Union."

Congress grew tired of President Johnson's interference. The Congressional problem with martial law was that it fell under military control, and the Commander-in-Chief was the President. So along with the Reconstruction Acts in March of 1867, Congress also passed legislation, which led to Johnson's impeachment: to deny Johnson's Presidential powers as Command-in-Chief of the Army. The purpose of this act was to guarantee that the new military control over the South was not in the hands of Johnson. Johnson called the Reconstruction Acts the "legislative machinery of martial law."

Johnson's veto of the Reconstruction Act of March 2, 1867 stated:

"The veto of the original bill of the 2nd of March was based on two distinct grounds, the interference of Congress in matters strictly appertaining to the reserved powers of the States, and the establishment of military tribunals for the trial of citizens in time of peace."

The Reconstruction Acts passed over Johnson's veto. Union Army brigadier generals became the governors of the five military districts, which were the 10 Southern States. (Tennessee was back in the Union; Kentucky and Missouri were never acknowledged to be out of the Union.) It was Thaddeus Stevens' plan to erase the State borders, it was Charles Sumner's plan to seize Southern property and give it to the Negroes; Congress delivered both.

The first order of business for the "governor-generals" was voter registration and supervising the elections. These governors could remove State officials and replace them with their own choice of scalawags. These governor-generals had total control over drafting new

State Constitutions. Delegates to the Constitutional Convention were mostly comprised of Negroes, Northerners, Scalawags and foreigners; and the Constitutions of the "New States" were drafted by Republicans. In the Original America, a Constitution was intended to be the voice of the people governed, but that nation, "died at Appomattox."

There was one common factor in all of the reconstruction plans, whether Lincoln, Johnson or Congress: All of the White Southerners who aided the Confederate Government, or aided any "insurrectionist" State was denied citizenship and denied the right to vote until they took the "iron clad" oath of loyalty. Yet none of the Negroes who aided the Confederacy, and there were thousands, was ever denied his citizenship or suffrage by Congress. New America sanctioned anti-White racial bias, a policy which continues today in the "appropriate legislation" of the various equal opportunities acts that allow and promote the denial of jobs or college entrance to persons of White.

It was the 15th Amendment that gave "Northern" Negroes the vote, but it was the Reconstruction Acts that first granted Negro suffrage (in the South only). Reconstruction suffrage was admitted to be of no legal effect as deduced in the wording of the 14th Amendment:

"But when the right to vote at any election for … President and Vice President … Representatives in Congress … officers of a State … is denied … the basis of representation therein shall be reduced in the proportion…"

If for some reason, a State might eventually disallow "federal citizens" the vote, Congress would disallow the Negro population to be counted toward Congressional representation in the House. Their own legislation proves that the First Reconstruction Act created unconstitutional voters, and it was those voters who wrote and ratified the new State Constitutions and elected the "new government" officials. The results of those unconstitutional elections remain in place today and affect every State in the Union.

The Reconstruction Acts ordered each Southern State to rewrite their Constitutions "legalizing" Negro suffrage. And the last four Southern States who didn't return to the Union until after the passage of the 15th Amendment, had to ratify the 15th Amendment (national Negro suffrage) or remain under martial law. Virginia had to grant Negro suffrage three separate times: the First Reconstruction Act, the State Constitution, and the 15th Amendment; such legislative multiplicity reveals Congressional malfeasance at law and political desperation to use the Negro vote toward obtaining unconstitutional powers and making those powers irreversible.

In June, 1868, seven of the remaining ten Southern States ratified (under military duress) the 14th Amendment. But as also stipulated in the Reconstruction Acts, the States that did ratify the 14th Amendment would still not be allowed back into the Union until "all" of America, ratified the 14th Amendment. Yet all of America (North or South) was not going to ratify the 14th Amendment. Even the military mandate on the Southern States to ratify did not deliver the necessary three-forth's of the States into the Congressional entrapment because the Northern States rejected it. So in July, 1868, in another gigantic usurpation of power, the 14th Amendment was simply said to be "enacted."

Upon the enactment of the 14th Amendment, seven more Southern States were allowed to take their seats in Congress. Virginia, Mississippi and Texas did not ratify the 14th and were kept out. Georgia, in a home-grown political coup, expelled all of the Negro members of its legislature, and so Georgia reentered the Union only to be kicked out. These four "rogue" States remained under the military duress of the Reconstruction Acts and would now be required to ratify the 14th and 15th Amendments before being allowed to join New America. The reuniting was achieved State by State, from January to June, 1870.

It was the conformity of those seven States in 1868, to the Reconstruction Acts which allowed them to return to the Union just in the nick of time for the Presidential elections. Did the returning of the Southern States to the national election return a Democrat majority to Congress? No, because "Confederates" still could not vote. There were however, 400,000 Negro votes in the South, Negroes who had been taught by the Union League that the Republicans are their friends, Negroes who were promised 40 acres and a mule and Negro supremacy in government.

The "reconstructed" South delivered 400,000 Negro votes into the 1868 national elections. In the popular vote, Republican candidate Grant, beat Seymour by 309,000 votes. The Republicans put their puppet-general in the White House. Very well planned and very well executed; and all it took for the Republicans to stay in power was to destroy the Constitution and all of the States. Congratulations Misters Grant, Sumner, Stevens, Lincoln, Trumbull, Fessenden, Butler, Stanton, and the Radical Jacobin Republicans; you killed America.

The Reconstruction Acts delivered the South prostrate at the feet of Congress, but still, as Georgia had proved by evicting the Negroes from their State House, all of the legal fiction up to the Reconstruction Acts was still reversible, but would not be after the 14th and 15th Amendments were passed. And so Congress kept their eyes on the prize (and booty). Thaddeus Stevens finally died in 1868.

The 14th Amendment

The 14th Amendment to the U.S. Constitution was supposedly written to provide citizenship to non-White persons born in the United States. The Amendment was drafted by Salmon P. Chase, who became the Chief Justice of the Supreme Court. Chase, on more than one occasion, had run for the Republican nomination for President. Where is the "Separation of Powers" when the Chief Justice of the Supreme Court is adjudicating the Constitutional legislation that he drafted? He should have recused himself. Every aspect of the 14th Amendment is contrary to the Original Law of the Land.

When the 14th Amendment to the Constitution was being pushed through Congress by the Radical Republicans, everyone knew that the vote would be too close to call. A pre-vote survey revealed that the 14th Amendment bill would have been a tie, which meant the bill would be rejected. The Republicans were counting every vote. In seeking to tilt the vote in their favor, the radicals in the U.S. Senate removed one New Jersey Senator who they knew was going to vote against it. That obvious act of political chicanery left one New Jersey Senatorial seat empty during the critical vote, and because of that one missing vote, the Amendment passed through Congress and went to the States to be ratified in June of 1866.

During this Congressional session, to make the two-thirds vote work in the Republicans' favor, the Southern States "did not exist." But after getting the bill through Congress, the radicals knew that the Northern State legislatures would not ratify the 14th Amendment by the necessary three-fourths majority, so they decided to again include the

Southern States in the ratification of the Amendment (the "missing States" were found). With the Southern States under martial law, the Radical Republicans could mandate their ratifications. It was under President Johnson's guidance that the Southern States ratified the 13th Amendment, after which Congress still denied them their seats in Congress.

The radicals wanted to play the same game again for ratification of the 14th Amendment. This time the Southern States "didn't exist" when the 14th Amendment was going through Congress, but "did exist" if they could be used to ratify the Amendment. Congress sent the 14th Amendment to the States to be ratified, but the South, having been tricked once, refused to ratify the 14th Amendment. The radicals responded with the use of force, Senator Doolittle of Wisconsin told Congress:

"The people of the South have rejected the Constitutional Amendment, and therefore we will march upon them and force them to adopt it at the point of a bayonet, and establish military power over them until they do adopt it."

The next legislation did just that, the Reconstruction Acts, in which the radicals prescribed that for a "rebel" State to be admitted to the Union, it must ratify the 14th Amendment. Congress waited from July 1866, when the States first rejected the 14th Amendment, until July of 1868 for the Amendment to pass, but it didn't. Seven of the Negro scalawag Southern State governments did ratify the Amendment, but three-forths of the United States did not.

The all important election of 1868 was quickly approaching and the Republicans needed those 400,000 Negro votes in the national election to stay in office, so they admitted the seven Southern States that ratified the 14th Amendment. Two of those States did not vote for Republican Grant in the election: Louisiana and Georgia; thus Georgia was thrown out of the Union. Georgia was the last Southern State to be readmitted in to the Union in June 1870.

Even though seven Southern States did ratify the 14th Amendment individually, according to the Reconstruction Acts, those States were not to be allowed back into the "Union" until the Amendment was nationally ratified, and it was not. Therefore the votes from those States in the 1868 election of Grant were void, by their own legislation; yet Republican Grant won. What happened to that great nation of laws not men? Consider the observation made by Mark Twain:

"The eight years in America, 1860-1868, uprooted institutions centuries old, and wrought so profoundly upon the national character of the people that its influence will be felt for two or three generations."

The radicals could only let the Southern States back into the Union, as written in the Reconstruction Acts, upon the national ratification of the 14th Amendment, and not upon each State's ratification of that Amendment. The radicals needed the Southern Negro votes in the 1868 election. So, if the radicals let them back into the Union, (for the sake of re-electing Grant) then the 14th Amendment must have been ratified before their return, right? Wrong! Here are the numbers.

The Union flag that was taken down by Major Anderson at Fort Sumter in April 1861 had 33 Stars. Kansas had joined the Union in January, 1861 but in United States flag protocol, the star representing a new State was not added to the flag until July 4th. So, counting Kansas, and saying that States couldn't secede there were 34 States in the Union. West Virginia, through the legal fiction of martial law, became the 35th State in June of 1863. Nevada became the 36th State in October, 1864. The 13th Amendment "adopted" in 1865 require 27 States (2/3s of 36). Nebraska became the 37th State in March 1867. There were 37 States in the Union when those seven Southern States were reseated in Congress.

Being that there were 37 States in the Union, and the Constitution requires three-forths of those States voting in favor of ratification for an Amendment to pass, it would require 28 States voting to ratify the Amendment. Even though Virginia, Texas and Mississippi were not seated in Congress, they were being counted in the ratification process of the 37 States. The final numbers were 22 voting in favor; 12 voting no; and 3 not voting. There was no 28 State three-forth's majority. The 14th Amendment did not get the number of ratifications required to pass; it failed. But to get those 400,000 Negro votes into the critical 1868 election, the Republican controlled Congress usurped the Constitution (again) and ordered the confused Secretary of State William Seward to declare that the 14th Amendment was "enacted." Was this

Constitutional, or just more appropriate legislation? Is this America, the nation of laws, not men? No, this was the "New America," a nation of politicians, not law!

There was also some contention concerning what to do about certain State legislatures, Oregon, Ohio, and New Jersey. who rescinded their ratifications prior to the national adoption of the Amendment. Is that lawful? Even if these were granted the affirmative, the 22 votes would become 25 votes and would not equal the required 28 votes; but remember, those States did rescind their ratifications prior to its national adoption. The New Jersey State Senate-House Joint Resolution to rescind their approval stated that the Amendment would:

"place new and unheard of powers in the hands of a faction, that it might absorb to itself all executive, judicial and legislative power, necessary to secure to itself immunity for the unconstitutional acts it had already committed, and those it has since inflicted on a too patient people."

New Jersey was right; the Amendment gave Congress Executive, Legislative, and Judicial powers, immunity from prosecution. The Amendment failed. Congress had to resort to deceiving human nature as expressed in the axiom: "The bigger the lie, the more people will believe it." Congress was selling the legal fiction that the 14th Amendment was "ratified" when actually it was "enacted" by the Secretary of State. This was not only a Congressional fiction of law, it became part of the Constitution. Lawfully, it was not a part of the Constitution then or now. But remember, the real goal of Congress was to introduce enough irreversible legal fiction to make it impossible for Americans to restore the Original Constitution of Madison and Jefferson.

It is important to insightfully read the text of the 14th Amendment to realize the hidden agenda of Congress and Chief Justice Chase. The 14th Amendment is possibly the most wordy and most powerful (so-called) Amendment of the Constitution; carefully consider these selected excerpts:

Part one states "All persons born or naturalized in the United States, and subject to the jurisdiction thereof, are citizens of the United States and of the State wherein they reside. No State shall make or enforce any law which shall abridge the privileges or immunities of citizens of the United States; nor shall any State deprive any person of life, liberty, or property, without due process of law; nor deny to any person within its jurisdiction the equal protection of the laws."

In this portion of the Amendment, the Federal Government created "national" citizens and claimed to make a mandatory co-citizenship in each State. This was the imposition of federal law to supersede the State laws which controlled citizenship. This is the reason State Constitutions had to be rewritten under the Reconstruction Acts prior to the adoption of the 14th Amendment.

This article employed the usual Constitutional language to legitimize their usurpation of powers. The First Amendment of the Constitution PROHIBITS CONGRESS from "abridging the freedom of speech, or of the press...." The 14th Amendment PROHIBITS STATES from enforcing "any law which shall abridge the privileges or immunities of citizens of the United States..." The clause continues with this wording taken from the 5th Amendment: "deprived of life, liberty, or property, without due process of law..." This verbal linkage to the Original Constitution was to give credibility to the citizenship being Constitutional, but more importantly, it was included to codify federal power over State powers in the ever-expanding jurisdiction of racial politics.

The "privileges and immunities" phrase in the 14th Amendment was designed to attach itself to Article 4, Section 2 of the Constitution: "The citizens of each State shall be entitled to all privileges and immunities of citizens in the several States." The 14th Amendment was attempting to merge national and State citizenships into one, to bring all citizens under federal control; a power heretofore not given to the national government except as stipulated in the Constitution.

After the Amendment was enacted, and "Republican fever" was waning, the Supreme Court and State legislatures began attempts to restore the damage done to the Constitution and to the States. These attempts were usually in reaction to further "civil rights" legislation with its assumption of more powers over State citizens based upon race. Whether 1865, or 1965, civil rights acts were intended to expand federal power over State citizens. One such example was the Civil Rights Bill of 1875. As the bill was making its way through Congress in 1874, the General Assembly of Virginia passed a Resolution in opposition, quoting a U.S. Supreme Court decision that limited the expansion of federal powers over State citizens.

Consider that even though Virginia remained under the martial law of reconstruction at the passage of this resolution on January 5th, 1874, the General Assembly was dissecting the true intentions of the 14th Amendment, which was, and is, the federal intrusion into State affairs. January of 1874 brought in Virginia's first postwar Governor who wasn't a Lincoln puppet, or a Union General, or New York resident. Virginia's acknowledgement of the 14th Amendment was required to regain Statehood and was required to end martial law, thus the wording of the Resolution somewhat patronizes the Amendment, but the defense of Virginia citizens from the expanding powers of the Federal Government stands clearly in opposition.

"Joint Resolutions

"Reaffirming the third Resolution of the Conservative Platform of 1873, and Protesting against the passage of the Civil Rights Bill, now pending in the Congress of the United States. Agreed to January 5, 1874. [abridged]

"Resolved by the General Assembly of Virginia....

"That this General Assembly recognize the Fourteenth Amendment to the Constitution of the United States as a part of that instrument, and desire good faith to abide by its provisions as expounded by the Supreme Court of the United States. That ... it is only the privileges and immunities of the citizen of the United States that are placed by this clause under the protection of the Constitution, and that the privileges and immunities of the citizen of the State 'whatever they may be, are not intended to have any additional protection by this paragraph of the amendment' and that the 'entire domain of the privileges and immunities of the citizens of the State as above defined, lay within the constitutional and legislative power of the States, and without that of the Federal Government.'"

The quote within the quote above is from the U.S. Supreme Court in a decision concerning the 14th Amendment. Here the Supreme Court makes the distinction between the two types of citizenship.

The Supreme Court, in the 1869 case of Plessey verses Ferguson, established a policy of "separate but equal" which revealed that there was a difference between the two types of citizenship; they were "separable," meaning Original (common law) State citizenship was distinct from the new 14th Amendment national citizenship. Even after the 14th Amendment had been "enacted" as law, there were legal minds able to force the courts to recognize the limited jurisdiction of the 14th Amendment.

The Civil Rights Bill of 1875, which called for the integration of the schools was vetoed by President Grant in an effort to persuade Southerners to vote Republican (not for a hundred years). Martial law in the South was lifted in 1877. Plessey verses Ferguson (a.k.a. "separate but equal") was reversed by the Supreme Court in the 1954 case Brown verses the Board of Education of Topeka, on the claim that the segregated schools were not "equal."

Part two of the Amendment says that if a State denies "citizens" the vote, then their State's representation will be reduced in proportion to the disallowed voters. It is most odd that there was a clause in the 14th Amendment to say that if a State chose not to let Negroes vote then the penalty would only be a reduction in its representation in Congress; meaning that there was no enforcement beyond that; no guarantee of "equality to vote" which again showed that it did not and could not provide a Constitutional "State" citizenship, but that it did provide a lesser national "United States" citizenship; Federal Citizens.

Part three prohibits former "Confederates" from holding federal offices, with exceptions allowed by a two-thirds vote of Congress on each individual. This violates Article One, Section 9, (clause 3) of the Constitution: "No bill of attainder or ex post facto law shall be passed." A bill of attainder is a "legislative act" that punishes an individual without a trial. The 14th Amendment "punished" Americans who served in the Confederacy without providing individual trials; therefore, Article One of the Constitution makes the 14th Amendment unconstitutional.

Part four prohibits any repayment of war debts by the States. Didn't that hurt the European bankers who had investments in the South? Yes, but why only have "investments" in the South, when you could own it? Besides, the Rothschild bankers sued the State of Virginia after the war and recovered their losses from the burning of Richmond.

Part five is the same power-clause contained in the 13th Amendment: "The Congress shall have the power to enforce, by appropriate legislation, the provisions of this article." This violated the separation of powers of the Constitution, and violated Article 6, (clause 2) of the Constitution requiring all laws to conform to the Constitution: "This Constitution, and the laws of the United States which are made in pursuance thereof..." The 14th Amendment, as a law of Congress, was not made in pursuance of the Constitution, but in spite of it.

The 14th Amendment was an attempt by Congress to bring all of the United States under the legal fictions that had subjugated the South. The citizenship of the 14th Amendment was a re-make of the citizenship of the Civil Rights Act and of the Reconstruction Acts. It was the unlawful tampering of the electorate to serve their political lust. This Amendment was in no way done for the benefit of the Negro. When Chase wrote the Amendment, he knew it had an ulterior purpose: to serve interstate business. The legislative preference shown to favor "national" governance over State, and "national" banking over State, also had corporate applications. The 14th Amendment was the legal mechanism to centralize the American economy.

The 14th Amendment was worded so that lawyers could take the words "All persons born or naturalized" and apply them to corporations. The legal definition of "person" was written to include corporations and therefore made all corporations beneficiaries of the 14th Amendment. This was particularly applied to the postwar boom of interstate corporations trying to evade the control of State laws. The 14th Amendment was a powerful tool for the railroads. In the first 40 years following the "enactment" of the 14th Amendment, there were 604 cases brought before the courts. Only 28 of those cases dealt with the Negro and his rights. The 14th Amendment was written to give corporations legal impunity to violate State and local governments and confiscate their economies. Supreme Court Chief Justice Chase drafted the Amendment and sat in judgement of it. Should it be assumed that this former Treasurer of the United States, and author of national banking legislation did not know that his 14th Amendment was corporate law?

The 14th Amendment, a product of the Radical Republican Congress, was placed before America (by a corporate media) as a beacon of justice but in reality, it wasn't even law. Even conceding that if this legal fiction were law, look at its use. It is a corporate shield disguised as an opponent of the Jim Crow laws. It is not a beacon of justice but a distress flarc of liberty. If the slave was freed 134 years ago; why are their descendants still begging to a political party for equality and rations? The Confederate government isn't around to blame; and the Sovereign State governments aren't around to blame. Should we blame the Southern people? Or blame White people? Or blame Whites who aren't liberals? Or are we to only blame the White voters who aren't Democrats?

The racial problems of today are with us because the 14th Amendment was not drafted to cure America's social ills, it was the "appropriate" treason to achieve political supremacy and provide economic centralization. It established second-class citizens and created a corporate nobility. The political deception that the 14th Amendment was properly ratified adds insult to injury for the American Negro. American non-Whites were never granted Constitutional citizenship, and because the political "Powers that Be" cannot now admit their lie, the future status of Negroes will continue to be a political ward of Congress. The big lie may be taught in schools as fact, and believed by the uninformed, but the Original United States was a "Land of Laws, not men."

Does it serve any good purpose to turn away from truth? Does it serve any good purpose to pretend that something is law, when it is fiction? What is the fate of those who seek the truth? Can this country ever abandon the political curse called legal fiction which has robbed us of our liberty and justice? Is the legal fiction born out of the War of 1861 really irreversible? Has that unconstitutional Transfer of Power forever taken away America's "perpetual" rights?

The 15th Amendment

"The right of citizens of the United States to vote shall not be denied or abridged by the United States or by any State on account of race, color or previous condition of servitude.

"The Congress shall have power to enforce this article by appropriate legislation."

The 14th Amendment spoke of United States citizens, which was a new creation because up to that time, citizenship was a power of the States. But the "powers not delegated to the United States" which were Constitutionally "reserved to the States" were in fact being taken by the national government. President Johnson was impeached for making such predictions: "Your States ... are sinking into ... mere satellites of ... the great central power here in Washington." And in this radical agenda to create a "New America," the strategy required a new citizenship, a second class citizenship, and the future Negro (Republican) voters were the intended recipients. Citizenship alone was not enough to make the power grab irreversible. They needed more; they took more.

Congress, in February 1869, introduced the 15th Amendment and sent it to the remaining "outlaw" States to be ratified, this was the legislated cost of admittance back into the Union. Those outlaw States were Virginia, Mississippi, Texas and the "on again - off again" State of Georgia. The purpose of the 15th Amendment was to force Negro suffrage on the "Northern" States who refused it. The 15th Amendment was also to give "Constitutional" credibility to a temporary martial law suffrage that made the 15th Amendment possible. The 15th Amendment is another Amendment ending with the same power-clause that provides Congress the legislative carte blanche to pass any "appropriate legislation" that would be free of review by Article Three courts.

The 15th Amendment was another Amendment passed in the fashion of the 14th, as prescribed by Wisconsin Senator Doolittle:

"...we will march upon them and force them to adopt it at the point of a bayonet, and establish military power over them until they do adopt it."

This abuse of power was not condoned by all Northerners; after Lincoln's wartime suppression of the press ended (with the ending of Lincoln) voices from his own State spoke out against the vengeful usurpation of law in the occupied South. One article in the Chicago Chronicle even exposed the vengeance and fraudulent alteration of the Constitution to make the tyranny permanent:

"The Fifteenth Amendment to the Constitution grew our of revenge, for the purpose of punishing the Southern People. It became a part of the Constitution by fraud and force to secure the results of the war."

Thus, another unlawful amendment. International law states that laws passed under martial law cease to be laws when the martial law is lifted. Therefore, when martial law was lifted in 1877, all laws passed while under it, including the 13th, 14th, and 15th Amendments, and elections that counted votes of non-citizens, are null and void.

With the 15th Amendment, Congress achieved the goal of an irreversible legal fiction, unless the nation revoked all of the martial law legislation. That did not happen for many reasons: 600,000 dead Americans died for what; there had to be the pretense that it was for something. How does a nation undo citizenship? Americans were destitute and wanted the whole political catastrophe to simply go away. And the insurgent Congress wanted to cover their tracks of treason. These questions of law could not be settled by a war-exhausted and demoralized people, they could only hope that a future generation could right the wrong. The destruction of the Constitution remained ever-present in the minds of those who knew the truth; as expressed by the (imprisoned) Confederate President, Jefferson Davis:

"A question settled by violence, or in disregard of law, must remain unsettled forever."

Consider the observation (or warning) from U.S. Supreme Court Chief Justice Day on June 3, 1918:

"If Congress can regulate matters entrusted to local authority, the power of the States may be eliminated, and thus our system of government be practically destroyed."

This was not a war of North against South, it was a war by the Federal Government to destroy State governments, State citizenships, and State Constitutions. These thoughts were expressed in a speech before Congress, directed against Congress, on March 23, 1872 by Indiana Congressman Dan Vorhees:

"From turret to foundation you tore down the government of eleven States. You left not one stone upon another. You not only destroyed their local laws, but you trampled upon their ruins. You called conventions to frame new Constitutions for the old States. You not only said who should be elected to rule over these States, but you said who should elect them. You fixed the quality of the voters. You purged the ballet box of intelligence and virtue, and in their stead you placed the most ignorant and unqualified race in the world to rule over these people."

The evidence herein provided to show the illegality of the war and postwar legislation reveals that there has not been a single piece of Constitutional legislation passed since April, 1861! All laws since that time are legal fiction, and to this day the Constitution has not been restored.

If you discovered today, that your that your great-great grandfather left you a million dollars in a bank in Washington D.C., and when you went to claim it, the banker said they wrote a "new bank law" that gave them your inheritance, and you are left with nothing, would you seek justice? Did this petty corporate "bank law" override your property rights and inheritance? Did the passage of time make the bank right?

America's Founding Fathers left us something much more precious than a million bucks, they gave us liberty within a federation of State governments. That "perpetual" liberty is no longer on deposit in Washington in our names, new laws were written. In today's New America, where political pet minorities grab for reparations and entitlements, how can it be wrong for "We the People" to seek to "secure the blessings of liberty to ourselves and our posterity" by re-establishing the Original Constitution, and by refusing to live under the capricious, fluctuating, and unnatural laws of the Federal Government?

Chapter 14

The Federal Government … continued …

The Constitution is dead.
Long-live the Federal King!
(much too long)

The Treason of 1861 began long before that fateful year; the roots of treason can be found much earlier in Massachusetts, Louisiana, Charleston, London and Germany. But in those earlier years, incubating in the shadows of a hidden agenda, the treason did not claim to be "THE" U.S. Government; that assertion began in April of 1861, when Abraham Lincoln declared martial law.] By February, 1862, he issued (Presidential) Executive Order #1. That first Executive Order was the beginning of a tyranny that continues to this day.

The Treason of 1861 is not just an interesting nugget of history from America's distant past. The roots of the 1861 treason have brought forth the bitter fruit of America's present social and economic disfunction. It would be remiss if this discourse brought forth the truths of the causes and results of the War of 1861 yet did not provide the direct linkage from that historic evil to the current Federal Government. Therefore, the following chapter reveals some aspects surrounding the further usurpations and expansions of powers that occurred as the Federal Government continued….

One of the most conspicuous links from the tyranny of 1861 to the tyranny of today is the use (and abuse) of the Executive Orders. The "pre-emergency" scripting of Executive Orders are offered as evidence that there exists a continuation of Lincoln's martial law. Lincoln issued the first Executive Order and drew powers outside of the Constitution, and though Lincoln died, the number of Executive Orders has continued to increase over the past 135 years.

The number of Executive orders is staggering. On May 14, 1998, President Clinton issued Executive Order #13,083. Emergency powers have come a long way since April of 1861. Their intended expansion of powers can be revealed by the content of the Executive Orders, and the expanse of their intent is measured by their creation of entire governmental departments to serve each expanded power. The "war-time" departments that were created in World War I remained in place after the war ended. Ten examples of modern Executive Orders designed to implement "Emergency Powers" are:

Executive Order Number:

10995: (1962) Gives the control of all communications in America to the Federal Communications Commission "Emergency" Broadcast System, which has recently been changed to the "Emergency Activation System." Is there an Emergency Activation scripted for our future?

10997: (1962) Gives control of all energy production and resources and distribution to the Secretary of the Interior.

10998: (1962) Gives the control of all food storage, production and distribution to the Secretary of Agriculture.

10999: (1962) Gives the control of all transportation and seaports to the Secretary of Commerce.

11000: (1962) Drafts all citizens into a work force under the control of the Secretary of Labor. (Benjamin Butler would be proud.)

11001: (1962) Gives control of all health, welfare and education to the Secretary of Health Education and Welfare [Department of Education].

11002: (1962) Assigns the registration of all citizens to the Postmaster General. [The mailman knows where everybody lives.]

11003: (1962) Gives control of all airplanes and airports to the Federal Aviation Administration.

11004: (1962) Gives control of all housing; designating communities to be abandoned, and communities to be relocated, to the Department of Housing.

11005: (1962) Gives control over all railroads, inland waterways and public storage facilities to the Interstate Commerce Commission.

11051: (1962) Gives control of all of the previous "emergency" Departments to the Office of Emergency Planning in the Executive Office of the President. [FEMA & NSA]

11490: (1969) Combines the above Executive Orders into one order (11,490) which can imposed all order at once.

Those are but a few Executive Orders, but those few can combine to change the present "subjects" of the Federal Government to "prisoners" of an unannounced agenda. With those Executive Orders listed above, the "Union Army" can take all your food, let someone of their choosing live in your house, draft you into a slave camp, deny you transportation out of America, move you to Alaska's outback, not allow you to communicate with anyone, and take over all business and jobs and your back yard garden. They will likely claim it is done out of "necessity" and for the "public safety" and claim it to be "appropriate legislation." When they did this from 1861 to 1877, the American South suffered its greatest oppression. Next time, both the North and the South will suffer, and suffer worst than our grandparents did during reconstruction!

Distrust of the Federal regime is becoming commonplace in America today. Even some of the media which are owned by the carpetbaggers are now beginning to see the "not so hidden" tyranny and are speaking up, a squeak at a time; only to be removed as a talking head. One of these Johnny come lately media outcries came when President Clinton issued Executive Order #13083.

In this Executive Order it allows for the usurpation of State powers in favor of Federal controls:

1. When there is a need for uniform national standards. [take over local education]

2. When States have not adequately protected individual rights and liberties. [Remember the wording of the Reconstruction Acts: "Whereas no legal State governments or adequate protection for life or property now exists in the rebel States…."]

3. Whenever State attempts to decentralize the Federal government would result in an increase the costs of local government thus imposing additional burdens on the taxpayer. [expanded Federal authority through creative bookkeeping]

4. When a matter relates to federally owned or managed property or natural resources or international obligations. [The national debt owed overseas to be redeemed through the IMF by the sale of our national forests or sovereignty?]

The Johnny-come-lately media concluded this story: "It is astounding that a President with as little moral authority as Clinton could attempt such a power grab." The article was titled "When a 2nd-Term Prez Sought to Repeal the 10th Amendment." The 10th Amendment: "The powers not delegated to the United States by the Constitution, nor prohibited by it to the States, are reserved to the States respectively, or to the people."

The carpetbag media has finally come around to the question of "States Rights," about 135 years too late. When the Pretender to the Throne no longer needs to pretend, the Boys in Blue should rally side-by-side with the Boys in Gray to demand and restore the liberty that our Constitution guarantees.

"Twice as Equal"

The Civil Rights Act of 1866 created a new citizenship: a "United States citizenship" for non-White citizens. These citizens were then, and are today protected separately (distinct from White citizens) by the Federal Government. If a crime was committed against a "federal citizen" in a State, the State (or locality) would try the case and render a verdict. If that verdict was not accepted by the Federal Government, the case could be tried again in a federal court (for the federal citizen). This violates the Fifth Amendment: "nor shall any person be subject for the same offense to be twice put in jeopardy...." If "Original" State citizens can "be twice put in jeopardy" for an alleged offense against a federal citizen, it would appear to make federal citizens "twice as equal."

There was a famous, fairly recent incident of some Los Angeles policemen beating a Negro man (Rodney King). The police were put on trial to find their guilt or innocence. They were found not guilty. As a result of the "not guilty" verdict, the City of Los Angeles was victimized by race riots and burning. The Federal Government put the U.S. military on the streets of Los Angeles. Remember, the Constitution prohibits the use of soldiers against its citizens. The Federal Government claimed its authority to use soldiers against citizens was based on an "old law from the civil war era." That "old law" must have been the Civil Rights Act of 1866, which authorized the use of land and naval forces on U.S. soil for the enforcement of that Act. And it remains in force for the federal citizens of today, but not for all Americans.

Wherever the federal citizens go, they are protected by the U.S. military in addition to the local law agencies. As mentioned earlier, federal courts, prior to 1861, had no jurisdiction over State citizens except in acts or crimes as specifically stipulated in the Constitution. The "civil rights" (appropriate) legislation that came a hundred years later (1960's) expanded federal jurisdiction into all American schools and businesses, thus putting those schools and businesses under the control of the Federal Government and its military.

And when those Los Angeles policemen were found not guilty, the Federal Government turned right around and tried them a second time for the same "acts committed" but they worded it as alleged violations of the Negro's "civil rights." This case is only one of thousands that proves the "New America" is not the old America because "civil rights" legislation supersedes the Constitution. Many Americans wondered: How can those policemen be tried twice? Most Americans don't understand the double judicial system of Article III courts under the Constitution and Article I courts under civil rights legislation.

The protection, defense, and advocacy of the "New America," whether governmental or civil, is evident today in the endless propagation of anti-White narratives. These narratives have labelled "racism" as the worst offense of all humanity. The corporate media methodically reinforces this "guilt assignment" on a daily basis in both entertainment and news. Political rhetoric demands these evils be crucified. These tactical (emotional) defense mechanisms are keyed on race because the treason against the Constitution is cloaked in racial legislation. Any attempts to restore the Constitution will be extinguished in shouts of racism. Admit it, very cleaver, and it works.

As long as the Federal Government and their satellite state governments continue to use racial politics to deny "We the People" our Constitutional liberties, there will be racial animosity. What is needed now is for non-Whites to remove their consent of the Federal Government's usurpation of the Constitution; and go back to 1861 politically and legally to repair the nation without sacrificing the nation. To achieve this, guilt-ridden White Americans must reject the "self-esteem" granted them by the agenda-driven media for their adherence to the tactical dogmas of "inclusion, tolerance, equality, etc." that serve as the cloak for the Federal Government's assumed powers.

Bankers & Industrialists
The Federal Government
Federal Citizens and Aliens
and We the People
(in the order of their power)

The War of 1861 proved that money can buy nations. After buying America, the "big money" advocates revealed a much larger plan. The bankers of Europe migrated to the United States and used their newly acquired centralized Federal Government to fulfill a dream as old as time: to rule the entire known world. There are so many "tracks" in the sands of time between 1861 and today, and this effort is but a short book, there is only space enough to briefly touch on a few of the "players and deeds" to show the connections from the Transfer of Power of 1861 to the global insurrection of today.

Remember how European money brokers used Salmon P. Chase to destroy America's Constitutional money, and create the National Banking System? Well Mr. Chase got in on that act himself and endorsed the founding of Chase Bank.

Remember how the European Rothschilds financed both sides of the War of 1861, well among their operatives in America were the German bankers Kuhn and Loeb. Also consider, John D. Rockefeller, the man who during the War of 1861 cut a deal of "rebate scamming" with the railroads that allowed Standard Oil to control 95% of America's oil refining by 1895? Well, Kuhn Loeb managed Rockefeller's buy-out of Chase Bank. The Rockefellers became the "American Rothschilds."

Remember how John Slidell's nephew-in-law, August Belmont was an agent for the English House of Rothschild? Well, that British House was headed by Lionel Rothschild, who, in 1858, became a member of Parliament. Lionel Rothschild trained Max Warburg, the patriarch of the German Warburg banking family, in the international application of banking. Max sent his son, Paul Warburg to America where he became a partner at Kuhn Loeb, (Rothschild's War of 1861 agents) marrying into that family. As an American operative, the German Paul Warburg wrote a book in 1907 titled "Plan for a Modified Central Bank" for the United States. Salmon Chase created the National Banking System and Paul Warburg took over where Chase left off, on behalf of the same international bankers.

An American player named Colonel Mandel House, whose father was a representative of British banking in Texas joined into the scheme. Colonel House was responsible, more than anyone, for getting Woodrow Wilson into the White House in 1913. Colonel House introduced Paul Warburg's banking ideas to President Wilson. Warburg wrote the draft of the "Owens-Glass" bill which created the Federal Reserve Bank in 1913. Paul Warburg was later appointed head of the Federal Reserve Bank. One of the controlling member-banks of the New York Federal Reserve was (and remains) Kuhn Loeb, the Rothschild agents who financed the debt of the War of 1861. It was the Federal Reserve Bank that completed the international takeover of America's banking system, a takeover that began with Salmon P. Chase in 1863, under Lincoln, (for the Rothschilds).

When President Franklin Roosevelt declared an "Economic Emergency" in 1933, his tactics were taken out of the playbook of Lincoln. Emergency powers are the peacetime version of martial law. Roosevelt used the "Banking Holiday Act" to invoke those emergency powers; that Act was written by the Federal Reserve Board. So, the private international bank known as the Federal Reserve wrote the Act which brought the American Economy under peacetime martial law. The emergency powers granted in that Act put absolute power over the American economy into the hands of two men: the President of the United States and the Secretary of the Treasury. Those were the two most powerful men in the world, made so, by an Act written by the Warburg created Federal Reserve Bank.

At the end of the Second World War, the United Nations created the International Monetary Fund to control the World economy. Today the U.S. Secretary of the Department of the Treasury is also the U.S. Governor of the IMF. It is evident that the Rothschilds, who helped cause and finance the War of 1861, trained the man who wrote the Federal Reserve Act, now control the management of both the American and World economies.

Back to the 1880's. Lionel Rothschild's son, Nathaniel, took over his father's operation and became a member of the House of Lords. Lord Rothschild was co-founder of a secret British organization called the "Round Table." The Round Table was created in 1891, the year that the Massachusetts Confederate General Albert Pike died (and passed the "illuminated" torch). The Round Table adopted as its goal, the specifics of a plan developed by Albert Pike to deliver all nations into a World Government.

The goal of the Rothschilds in the War of 1861 was to centralize the United States. That required the end of State sovereignty. It is easier for tyrants to control one "head" (national government) than 34 (or 50) heads (State governments). The ancient dream of a "World Empire" is as old as Nebuchadnezzar and Babylon. Destroying the sovereignty of the United "States" was just a prerequisite in a world strategy: the destruction of all sovereign national governments. Having succeeded in America in 1865, the British family bankers continued with their more grandiose plan: to merge all nations into a world government. That became the mission of Britain's Round Table.

World War I, was instigated and run by members of the Round Table. The war ended with the Treaty of Versailles. Representing the United States at Versailles, was President Wilson and Rothschild associate Colonel House. A week after the British announced that the war should end with the creation of an international association of governments, President Wilson, on January 8th, 1918, announced his now famous Fourteen Point Peace Plan, which called for "The establishment for a general association of nations." The Peace Process would take over a year.

Assisting the President at Versailles, were his Secretary of State Robert Lansing and Lansing's two nephews, John Foster Dulles and Allen Dulles, relatives of John D. Rockefeller. Lansing was responsible for including Wilson's plan for an "association of nations" as a mandatory part of the Treaty of Versailles. The wealth of the German colonies was to be divided up between the nations that would sign the peace treaty, but if a Nation signed that treaty, it also joined the League of Nations. In other words, if you want a piece of Germany's empire, you must join the "World Government." That Treaty was signed on June 28, 1919 and created the League of Nations.

Remember the goal of the Round Table was simply the global version of that American experiment we know as the War of 1861. Karl Marx and Mazzini's Young Europe groups attempted a European version with the "United States of Europe" movement, but fell short. These three campaigns had the same amalgamation strategy: create a war to pit several sovereign States against each other, inflicting the maximum possible devastations, the sovereignty of those "independent" States would be subverted into a centralized government. That was true in the War of 1861, World War I, World War II and it is true among the third world nations being sacrificed for the approaching New World Order: the final and strategic fait accompli.

Those relatives of Rockefeller and members of the British Round Table who created their prototype "world government" in Versailles in June of 1919, had met one month earlier in Paris in a Round Table session hosted by Colonel Mandel House. At that meeting, the Dulles brothers were instrumental in the creation of the Council on Foreign Relations (CFR), which was the Round Table's American counterpart in the mission to create a world government. Although officially formed in 1922, the CFR was conceived at the Round Table meeting of May 19th, 1919.

By 1919, Round Table activist Lord Nathaniel Rothschild had died, his son Lionel carried on for the House of Rothschild. J.D. Rockefeller bought the Harold Pratt House in New York City to be the headquarters of the Council on Foreign Relations. So the "tracks" which are found leading from our War of 1861 can be followed through the Rockefellers and the Rothschilds leading us (by the nose) into a global centralization.

The greatest plans of mice and men sometimes go awry. The U.S. Congress refused to approve President Wilson's plan to join the League of Nations and so the U.S. did not join the great world government after World War I. But after another World War, the League of Nations in Switzerland was superceded by the United Nations to be headquartered in New York, on a building site bought by John D. Rockefeller for 8.5 million dollars. The tracks of the treason leading from 1861 continued step-by-step toward its destination: world government. When the U.N. came into existence on October 24, 1945, forty-six of the U.S. founding delegates, were members of the Council on Foreign Relations.

Officially, two months after the U.N. came into existence, it created the International Monetary Fund (IMF); in reality the IMF a.k.a. the World Bank was created in 1944. Consider, the Rockefellers, Rothschilds and Warburgs are bankers and the IMF was their instrument to control national economies, and thus control those nations. Voting power in the IMF is a graduated voting power based on a nation's money reserves on deposit in the IMF. The two most powerful members in the

IMF are the U.S. and Britain (of course). Money is a great persuader for usurping sovereignty, but it also takes men in the shadows.

Remember the two Dulles brothers at the Round Table meeting of May 1919? Well, Colonel House impressed upon John Foster Dulles the importance of religion in international persuasion. John Dulles, a trustee in the Rockefeller Foundation, joined the Federal Council of Churches, which was also financed by John D. Rockefeller. This "religious front" was simply a repeat of the religious activities that accompanied the War of 1861.

As a member of the Executive committee of the Federal Council of Churches, John Dulles worked on a committee called the "International Round Table of Christian Leaders." In that capacity he drafted a message titled: "A Christian message on World Order." In 1945, John Dulles published a report titled: "The Churches and the World Order," in which he said:

"We call upon our government to accept the international laws as are adopted by the United Nations."

He called for its soldiers to wear U.N. uniforms and swear allegiance to the U.N. John Foster Dulles made these remarks in January of 1945, before there was a U.N.

In 1949, before changing its name to the National Council of Churches, the Federal Council of Churches was comprised of 142,000 congregations with over 28 million American members (20% of the U.S. population). This prompted J. Edgar Hoover to testify that he had "real apprehension so long as communists are able to secure ministers of the Gospel to promote their evil." Hoover's analysis was a little simplistic, he called it "communist." John Dulles went on to serve as Secretary of State during the Eisenhower Administration. His brother Allen served in a different capacity.

Allen Dulles became one of the "men in the shadows" working toward global governance. Allen Dulles became a leader in America's World War Two era secret intelligence network called the O.S.S. The American OSS was the counter part to British Intelligence. In fact British intelligence trained our OSS. The British agent in charge of training our OSS agents was Harold Kim Philby. It was revealed in the 1980's that Philby was, while training Allen Dulles and the OSS, a

NKBD agent. The NKBD was the predecessor to the KGB. It is also obvious that Philby was not just a double agent but a triple agent. That meant he was misleading the NKBD as well as the OSS, using American and Soviet intelligence networks to serve the agenda of the British.

Working for the British came naturally to Allen Dulles, having been in the Round Table and founder of its American spin-off the Council on Foreign Relations. Allen Dulles served the OSS in Switzerland during World War Two with fellow OSS and CFR member James Warburg, son of the architect of the Federal Reserve Bank, Paul Warburg. Allen Dulles created and staffed the Central Intelligence Agency, and every Director of the CIA except one, since its beginning has been a member of the Council on Foreign Relations. In 1950, Allen Dulles became President of the Council on Foreign Relations and during the Eisenhower Administration, while his brother John was Secretary of State, Allen was Director of the CIA.

That information is necessary to understand the linkage of the past to the present. The Rothschild's financed our War of 1861. The Rockefellers came onboard during that war and became America's financiers for the centralization plan of the international bankers. Rockefeller became Chase bank. These banking families financed the Round Table and the Council on Foreign Relations and the United Nations. British Intelligence trained and recruited CIA and KGB agents to be their spies working in the shadows for globalization.

In the 1970's George Bush became the Director of the CIA; while his counterpart in Russia, Mikhail Gorbachev, became head of the KGB. As global fruition improved, George Bush became President of the United States, and Mikhail Gorbachev became Premier of the Soviet Union. After playing the role of the "Evil Empire," the Soviet Union dropped the "evil" and dissolved the "Union" of Soviet Socialist Republics to be pieces picked up by the expansion of Karl Marx's belated European "Union."

The "collapse" of the Soviet Union left the United States (home of the U.N.) to be the single remaining "Super Power." The U.S. and all other U.N. Nations entered into a treaties that downsized their "national" military muscle while increasing their "international" financial muscle.

Gorbachev then moved to San Francisco, birthplace of the U.N., and founded the Gorbachev Foundation; a think tank. The U.S. base in San Francisco, the Presidio, fell victim to the U.N. mandated military down-sizing, and the Presidio was shut down just in time for the Gorbachev Foundation to locate its offices at the Presidio. When Gorbachev established his headquarters at the former U.S. military base he said:

> "This is a symbol of our irreversible transition …
> to a new world order."

This irreversible transition is akin to the irreversible "legal fiction" of America's "reconstruction" which America has yet to clearly define, much less reverse.

George Bush (former CIA) joined with Mikhail Gorbachev (former KGB) in the Gorbachev Foundation's "State of the World Forum" in a presentation titled: "Toward a New Civilization: Launching a Global Initiative."

George Bush said of his relationship with Gorbachev:

> "Out of these troubled times a New World Order can emerge … this is the vision I share with Mr. Gorbachev."

This plan wouldn't be complete without a word from a Rockefeller of today; David Rockefeller:

> "This present window of opportunity during which a truly peaceful and interdependent World Order might be built, will not be open for long."

He implied that the culmination of centuries of work is now reduced to a brief "window of opportunity."

The mystery of today's chaotic world can be solved by looking more closely at the Treason of 1861. It goes further back than that, but that is far enough to get the picture. The key to restoring the American National and State Constitutions and the liberty and justice therein, is to be found by unraveling the legal fiction of America's reconstruction. However, caution is required: legal fiction is not defenseless; but it is vulnerable, vulnerable to the truth and to the letter of the law. The liberty guaranteed by the Constitution will only belong to the people again if and when "We the People" claim it.

Fast Forward....

The war that began against the American people in 1861 by certain persons within our government, has not ended. Those persons indeed have died, but the hidden agenda has perpetuated to this day. The military war ended in 1865, but then it transformed into a war of law. The power in Washington D.C. has never openly admitted that the Constitution is overthrown, and that is a chink in their armor. Technically, we will not be a conquered people until they openly abandon the Constitution. They could try to live in the quasi-Constitutional status forever and maintain a high degree of control. But avarice and greed are never content with leaving loose ends that could reverse their powers no matter how remote that possibility might be.

Any final strategy to conquer America must include the destruction of any remnants of our Constitutions. This attempt will likely come through international treaties that will yield America's national sovereignty "voluntarily" to a world government. After Karl Marx observed the War of 1861 and upon its conclusion, he stated that the world revolution would best be served operating from the United States. But national and world revolutions require maintenance; tyranny is not automatically perpetual, even collective tyrants have had setbacks.

When the War of 1861 ended, and after martial law was lifted in 1877, despite the best efforts of the federal iron fist, liberty began to return. Lincoln and the radical stooges gained more power over America than any predecessor, then Congress exceeded Lincoln's military treason by crafting irreversible legal fictions; yet that radical Congress died off and newer members of Congress were elected who were not privy to the deliberate dismantling of the Constitution. Although the legal mechanism established by the 13th Amendment voided the body of the Constitution, legal arguments were made that State citizens still had rights guaranteed under the Constitution.

As the war politicians retired to their graves, the Supreme Court tilted more toward the conservative interpretation of the law. But make no mistake, the bankers who had caused this trouble were still around, in the persons of their dynastic children. And whenever America gets too close to repairing the Constitution, the bankers step in, hire new politicians and repeat the political tactics, establishing more effective controls through the further expansion of Federal powers.

The best way to express that statement is to give a comparison of Lincoln's assumption of powers to Roosevelt's assumption of powers in the 1930's. Roosevelt's actions were scripted by international bankers, to achieve the second major phase of a plan. Lincoln conquered the government, Roosevelt would conquer the economy.

Comparison One:

Lincoln began his war, by issuing Executive Order #1, which suspended the Constitution and gave him martial law powers to enforce a naval blockade of Confederate ports and North Carolina, a State that had not seceded.

When Franklin Roosevelt became President he decided to declare "war" on the economic depression caused by the same bankers who scripted his economic remedies. So on March 6, 1933, he declared an "economic emergency," invoking emergency powers, and that, with or without Congress, he would take emergency actions to defeat the economic threat to America.

Comparison Two:

Lincoln, operating under martial law, ordered Congress back into an emergency session, giving him power over Congress.

When Roosevelt became President, he issued Executive Order # 2038, and called Congress into an emergency session.

Comparison Three:

After Lincoln printed his "greenbacks" there was a run on the banks to exchange them for "Specie" (gold coins) but there wasn't enough specie to back the "paper" so he suspended the use of specie.

After the Federal Reserve Bank declared to Roosevelt that there was a run on the banks to exchange the paper "gold certificates" for the real gold, Roosevelt outlawed the redemption of paper into gold. Roosevelt used the exact same law (the very same wording) that was written for Lincoln to suspend the use of specie.

Comparison Four:

When the Supreme Court was going to hear a case in 1863, which questioned the legal standing of Lincoln's power to blockade the State of North Carolina before they seceded, Lincoln stacked the court and won. This was also the case when the Supreme Court ruled against Lincoln's use of martial law, Exparte Milligan (1864), after which, the Court was again stacked before hearing the Exparte McCardle case which would have ruled on the legality of reconstruction. Lincoln's "New America" Supreme Court declined jurisdiction in the McCardle case.

The Supreme Court ruled in the 1935 case of Butler verses the United States, that Roosevelt's "New Deal" policies had no Constitutional power over individual States. Roosevelt followed the Lincoln play-book and stacked the Court so that in 1937, Roosevelt's "New America" Supreme Court reversed the decision. In the Butler decision, because Roosevelt had declared "war" on America's economy, the Supreme Court ruled that Article III courts cannot decide on what is a state of "war," that was a political question. The Supreme Court declined jurisdiction.

Comparison Five:

Lincoln stated that the "old Union" cannot be saved and that a "new Union" must be established in its place.

Roosevelt said: "We will never go back to the old system."

So the Roosevelt regime updated the work of Lincoln and Thaddeus Stevens, but the "New Deal" got more permanent and more specific and made the entire American economy federal business.

The legal mechanism used to make the Federal Government overseer of all American businesses was a Congressional Act from World War I: the "Trading with the Enemy Act." That Act took to possession of all "trade and property" of anyone in America trading with Germany. Roosevelt's allies in Congress took the exact wording of that Act and subtracted the reference to "enemies" and inserted the "people of the United States." Meaning: this war was economic, and the enemy in this war was the American people, and so to win this economic war, Roosevelt and his advisors at the Federal Reserve Bank stepped in to control those "enemy trading Americans."

This Act implied that we no longer had a "personal" standing in court because we spend money, and spending money was a threat to the economy, thus the remaining status of Constitutional citizenship was reduced to a commercial status. This tactic of making citizens a party to an "economic" war, created the legal fiction to "justify" the use of "war or emergency" powers and thus blocks a citizen's access to Constitutional legal remedies.

This is the basis of authority for the government to require the many licenses for everything that affects the economy, and this is where a person's deeds to intra-state property became subject to federal controls. Meaning, under rules of war, all property can be seized for "public use," even to support our national debt.

When Roosevelt began his assault on American liberty it did not go unnoticed. There have always been Americans who were concerned enough to pay attention and willing to speak out in the face of tyranny. One such example is found in a statement made by Congressman Beck in 1933 as he spoke out against the assumption of powers by Roosevelt; Congressman Beck:

"I think of all the damnable heresies that have ever been suggested in connection with the Constitution, the Doctrine of Emergency is the worst. It means that when Congress declares an emergency, there is no Constitution."

The Lincoln-invoked, Congressionally extended, martial law powers ended in 1877. Question: How long have the 1933 Roosevelt-invoked "emergency powers" lasted? Answer: In 1973, U.S. Senator Frank Church led a Senate committee called the "Special Committee on the termination of the National Emergency," to study Nixon's use of emergency powers. Senator Church stumbled into something much bigger than he expected. The report of the Committee stated:

"Since March 9, 1933, the United States has been in a state of declared emergency ... hundreds of statutes delegate to the President extraordinary powers ... This vast range of powers, taken together, confer enough authority to rule the country without reference to normal constitutional processes.

"Under the powers delegated by these statues, the President

may: seize property; organize and control the means of production; seize commodities; assign military forces abroad; institute martial law; seize and control all transportation and communication; regulate the operation of private enterprise; restrict travel; and in a plethora of particular ways, control the lives of all Americans."

Senator Church said:

"If the President can create crimes by fiat and without Congressional approval, our system is not much different from that of the communists...."

Senator Church and his committee voted to end the national "emergency" but left in place, Section 5, which was the Trading with the Enemy Act as amended to apply to citizens spending money which is the core of all post-Roosevelt Executive Orders with their Washington bureaucratic administrations. In other words they did nothing to end the emergency powers. Those extra-constitutional powers remain in place today. If Senator Church truly eliminated the emergency powers, it would have resulted in an "emergency" (Catch 22). This determination makes Roosevelt's usurpation of the Constitution, by their interpretation, irreversible. Lincoln and the Radical Republicans created their "irreversible" treason; and Roosevelt and the radical Democrats created their own version of "emergency irreversible" treason.

It should be noted here that the transition from the Radical Republicans to the radical Democrats was done beginning with "Virginian" Woodrow Wilson. Wilson's Presidency began in 1913. The Republicans version of the Federal Reserve Act, the Aldrich bill, failed because American's were well aware of the collusion between the Republicans and the bankers. The bankers switched parties, recruited two Democrats to reintroduce it as the Glass-Owen Bill and the Federal Reserve Act passed with President Wilson's blessing and signature. The switch had occurred, but only at the highest levels in Washington. The bankers needed to merge elements of the Republican Party into the Democrat Party.

The South, resentful of the Transfer of Power of 1861, continued to vote Democrat, in what came to be known as the Southern Democrats. The Republicans could not implement its revolution fast enough because the Southern Democrats were standing as a block in opposition. President Roosevelt was the administration to accomplish this "party switch" promoting big government intrusions. Roosevelt was elected to four terms as President and though he died in office in his 12th year, it was enough time to complete the transition of "big brother" from Radical Republicans to radical Democrats.

The economic emergency that the bankers provided to Roosevelt allowed him to introduce his big government socialistic ideas into an economy that he controlled through his ill-gotten emergency powers. The "federal citizens" that were once the "possession" of the Republicans became the voting "chattel" of the party that created higher levels of entitlements with patronizing rhetoric claiming to compensate for historical victimizations. The Southern Democrats turned to a third party, the States Rights Party (Dixiecrats) but it fell short of competing with the monied parties. The Democrat South migrated into the Republican Party.

What can be said about the historic position in which we find ourselves in today? Are we the posterity of our Founding Fathers only by our bloodline or can we be their equal in our deeds? The majority of Americans refuse to question the existing authority, they are slaves to their possessions, jobs and cowardice. What is the fate of a Democracy whose majority has been bought off with the trinkets of daily life? If the majority submits to such domestic tyranny, can we expect them to rise up when the global tyranny ascends to the throne, offering trinkets and altruisms. As these evils surely come to fruition, does liberty's last brigade have a single workable option?

Chapter 15

Proclamation for Liberty

When in the course of human events it becomes necessary for one people to dissolve the bands that tie them with another, it is prudent for that people to list the grievances which have caused this course of action.

Our lawful needs have already been established by our forefathers and because there has been no war against us nor subsequent treaty with us to explain our loss of Rights, legally we cannot, and have not been deprived of those Rights. The Rights which we were given by our forefathers were non-revokable Rights. And no legal fiction, whether presented as a Congressional bill, Executive Order, or Constitutional Amendment, or any other illegally obtained legislation, judicial review, treaty or compact can separate the liberty established by our forefathers from us, their posterity.

Ours is not a conflict of one people against another, but a conflict devised by certain persons within our government to divest We the People from our guaranteed Cultural Sovereignty. The usurpation of our Rights by our own Executive, Legislative and Judicial Branches of government through acts of legal fiction are not to be accepted as the legitimate Rule of Law by We the People. Therefore, any claim of governmental authority over the Original Citizens of the States derived from such attempts at legal fiction cannot be accepted as a de facto Rule of Law.

This challenge to all legal fictions perpetrated against the posterity, that is, the heirs of the Constitution, is written to be exact and concise enough to leave the perpetrators with nowhere to hide. Their deceptions at law are no longer able to conceal their agenda of avarice and greed. They will no longer be able to successfully hide behind the pretense of their self-proclaimed justifiable cause whether masquerading as a "national emergency," or to protect the so-called "public safety" or "civil order," or to suppress any contrived "insurrections or rebellions," or enforce any so-called "appropriate legislation" in defense of human rights. None of these cleaver tactics can usurp the Law of the Land nor excuse their legal evasion of this challenge at law.

Neither does the Pretender to the Throne have the option to ignore or refute our lawful claim or deny our proclamation of grievances based upon their claim that our actions are feigned because of our entanglement in or benefit from the socialistic network that they have created. There is no legal slight-of-hand that can assert that "We the People" have been removed from our Constitutional Rights by force or by legal submissions. This claim is Constitutional and can be proved to be true. But where can it be proved in court? Both Article III and Article I Courts have become tributary courts serving the Pretender to the Throne and therefore are by their present nature hostile and prejudiced against We the Posterity? There is no justice to be found among them; we know them by their fruits.

Legal fictions have been used to subvert our rights and create a myriad of national courts and bureaucracies superior to, yet unauthorized by, the Constitution. The federal consolidation of the sovereign States unto itself has had the effect of reducing the American people to the subservient condition as feared by the author of the U.S. Constitution James Madison as stated in his Virginia Resolution of 1798:

"...this Assembly doth explicitly ... declare that it views the powers of the federal government ... as limited by the plain sense intention of the instrument constituting the compact ... and that in case of a deliberate ... and dangerous exercise of other powers ... the States ... are in duty bound, to interpose for arresting the progress of the evil ... That the General Assembly doth also express its deep regret, that a spirit ... has been manifested by the federal government to enlarge its powers ... so as to consolidate the States by degrees, into one sovereignty, the obvious tendency and inevitable consequence of which would be to transform the present republican system of the United States, into an absolute, or at best a mixed monarchy."

How much more authoritative judgement could Americans require that these words from the Father of the Constitution. If any other authority were requested, it would likely be a solicitation from the minions who wield the new powers; and so let them judge their assumption of powers by the words of the author of the Declaration of Independence, Thomas Jefferson, in his warnings against the assumption of powers by the federal government of 1798, in his Kentucky Resolution:

"Resolved, That the several States composing the United States of America, are not united on the principle of unlimited submission to their general government ... and whensoever the general government assumes undelegated powers, its acts are unauthoritative, void, and of no force ... that the government created by this compact was not made the exclusive or final judge of the extent of the powers delegated to itself; because that would have made its discretion, not the Constitution, the measure of its powers ... each party has an equal right to judge for itself...."

The following paragraphs are a review of the chronological legal fictions that methodically usurped the "delegated powers" and "consolidated the sovereign States" and "transformed the republican system" into one federal government, which has made itself the "final judge of the extent of the powers delegated to itself." With the States at present destroyed, Madison would surely claim that this situation now leaves the Posterity of the Original Citizens "duty bound, to interpose for arresting the progress of this evil." The litigious parade of Congressional treason against the Constitution begins:

The 13th Amendment: The power-clause contained within the 13th Amendment allows Congress absolute power over anything dealing with freedmen (Negroes) because Congress is controlled by their own interpretations (and enforcement) of appropriate legislation, and not by Article III Judicial reviews. The Congressional passage of the bill for the 13th Amendment contained elements of fraud (West Virginia voting). The ratification of the 13th Amendment contained elements of fraud (Pierpont's bogus "New Virginia" ratified it; and West Virginia ratified it) and the Southern States ratified under duress, at a time when Southerners were under martial law and denied their right to vote without due process of law (with no bill of attainder), and were denied their seats back in Congress until after they ratified the 13th Amendment. Even after having ratified such under duress, those same States were denied their seats in Congress, thus making all legislation of the 39th Congress null and void.

The Civil Rights Act of 1866: This legislation was deemed "appropriate" only by the assumed powers derived from the illegal 13th Amendment, passed by the illegal Congress, thus making this Act "unauthoritative, void and of no force." It created a separate legal venue, a Southern citizenship for non-White inhabitants, thus Congress attempted to create a new political power-base in a contraposition to the Constitutional citizens of that region. Citizenship was a matter for the States. Congress "assumed undelegated powers" thus again making this Act "unauthoritative, void and of no force." Any subsequent elections or legislation using these "voters" is also void.

The Freedman's Bureau Acts: This Legal Fiction placed military jurisdiction over civil law in cases involving former slaves (the entire South). Military jurisdiction cannot override civil law (where the President said that civil authority was in place) but did through a legal fiction achieved by politically defining the actions of the Southern States as being violations of the (unconstitutional) 13th Amendment, leaving five million White Southerners without the benefit of Article III judicial hearings. This Act was also under the umbrella of the "appropriate legislation" of the illegal 13th Amendment.

The Reconstruction Acts: These Acts divided the Southern States into five martial law districts, eliminating the boundaries of ten Southern States. They suspended all Constitutional rights without Due Process of Law. They gave suffrage, a State's Right, to the "Congress-created federal citizens" while denying suffrage to most of the Constitutional citizens. These Acts voided the State Constitutions and "authorized" Union Generals, carpetbaggers, scalawags and "federal" citizens to re-write State Constitutions. The Acts also mandated that the Southern States could not return into the Union unless they ratified the 14th Amendment, and then only when that amendment passed nationally. The Reconstruction Acts were passed under martial law, meaning that any legislation passed under martial law expired when martial law was lifted (1877) as stated in Exparte Milligan.

The 14th Amendment: This legislation attempted to give national and permanent credence to the citizenship of the non-Whites, to supersede the temporary Civil Rights Act that was in effect only in the

South. The Amendment was illegal because the Federal Government assumed a power not stipulated in the Constitution and as such reverted to the 10th Amendment: "Powers not delegated to the United States by the Constitution ... are reserved to the States...." This Amendment was never lawfully ratified but was "enacted" by a Congress that had over-stepped its Constitutional restraints. Any pretense of ratification is still based on the coercion of the Southern States, and voting by non-constitutional citizens. The 14th Amendment is not a Constitutional Amendment at all, but only more illegally passed "appropriate legislation" whose authority is derived from the illegality of the 13th Amendment and subsequent legislation.

The 15th Amendment: This legal fiction attempted to give suffrage to non-Whites in Northern States as well as giving Constitutional credence and permanence to governmental alterations already imposed on the South under the Reconstruction Acts. The 15th Amendment, like the 14th Amendment is an assumption of power through the martial law of the Reconstruction Acts, which is not Constitutional legislation.

The combination of all of these legal fictions, erroneously being accepted as law, leaves us with one overwhelming conclusion: All legislation after the 37th Congress is null and void, as well as all war legislation.

The Posterity of the Founding Fathers who are alive today are left in a difficult situation. The Transfer of Power was designed by Congress to be irreversible by altering the electorate thus making any future "lawful" return to the Constitution by a Constitutional "electorate" unobtainable, without disenfranchising the federal citizens, an action that surely would be rallied by the "usurper" toward his "in the street" advantage. Our forefathers have placed upon our hearts, the absolute necessity of eternal vigilance to preserve (or restore) our freedom, even at the terrible expense of being called names!

Circumstances have left us very little room to maneuver; we are left with only one choice if we want to save our freedom. We must step forward as the Constitutional Posterity, and without violating any liberties of the Original Constitutions, draft a plan that will be based upon the true "Law of the Land" and yet practical and generous to all inhabitants of today's America, without divesting any person of anything they own, and with the commitment to draft a settlement that benefits all but the usurper.

If we do reverse our Constitutional standing to that of 1861, would that again make slavery legal? No one owns today's Negroes. There are no slaves now and neither is there the question of "restitution" for loss of property. In 1778, Virginia outlawed the international trafficking of slaves. Today, America can accept the international law prohibiting the trafficking of slaves and thus, America will have no slaves. Slavery would not and could not exist, yet that change would not violate the Original Constitutions.

The Federal Government, to hide its legal fiction, refused to declare war on the South or negotiate a peace treaty, or accept a Constitutional challenge in a court of law. The failure of the Federal Government to "openly" defeat us in a genuine war requires New America to explain its new powers by changes in law, which they have not done, will not and cannot do. Therefore, We the Posterity are left to decide our own fate based upon our commitment to the true unabridged Law of the Land and our love of liberty and duty to posterity.

We the People must continue toward our own destiny, apart from the current agenda to amalgamate all nations into one. Allow other nations the continuance of their culture and peculiar laws that they deem appropriate, and thus allow We the People the destiny of our own culture. As an identified "posterity" of the Founding Fathers, we are bound to claim the liberty and birthrights that preceded our coming to America. We should never forget our Original America or our Original States, and neither should we forget the sacrifice of our dear Confederacy.

Time and events require us to make a bold commitment to restore liberty in our lifetime, or surrender our perpetual rights and forever accept the servitude to ever-changing legal fictions. We must hold fast to the organic principles of our Original Constitutions but sadly may have to abandon the geographic boundaries and specific structure of those governments, if they will not return. There will be no convincing today's dictatorship by the deceived majority to allow all of America to be restored; they prefer avarice and greed over liberty and the Rule of Law. Perhaps our only salvation is to plant ourselves and the liberty of our Constitutions into an autonomous rural setting apart from the jurisdiction of the existing legal fictions.

Our fathers gave us this land in a perpetual covenant, and we have every right to restore our liberty here in America. But to lay claim to all of America would alter the lives of all Americans and because most Americans know nothing of these truths, their ignorance would be politically manipulated against us. And because the foundation of "New America" is based upon racial legislation, the corporate media would claim that efforts to restore the Law of the Land would be a resurgence of bigotry, racism, and even slavery causing all federal citizens to rally 'round the Pretender to the Throne. Therefore, we must humble ourselves and accept only a small piece of America where we will proclaim our Cultural Autonomy. And if our restoration is refused, even in its humbled and diminished jurisdiction, then true America will either Stand or Die.

We have every right to regather somewhere within the boundaries of this nation which currently calls itself the United States. There is no other place on Earth where we could go to have a claim as valid as here. Many Confederates left the South after the War of 1861, they went to South America and elsewhere, but where are they today? What promises to they have for their posterity? We cannot afford to run away in attempts to create a "play-America" conclave in some Spanish speaking province nor attempt to establish "Constitutionalist segregated" neighborhoods under the jurisdiction of the usurper.

Somewhere in North America, between the Atlantic and the Pacific, with our liberty intact, we can set out once again to become a nation of brothers, but this time we will not allow the corporate money-loving parasites to follow. And considering that race is the power basis of the current evil Federal Government, it would be a clear and present danger to invite any of their 14th Amendment citizens into our land, least they will bring with them all of their "appropriate legislation" and the Federal Government itself. We should support efforts for those federal citizens to truly free themselves and also establish their own autonomous land unto themselves here in America, where they can abandon their much abused "federal culture" and establish a new culture based upon their own realities and their own choices.

And to that troubled nation that we leave behind, that nation which hates us so, we wish a peaceful farewell. And when at last we are absent from among them, the remaining Americans will quickly discover that it wasn't the liberty loving White man causing the racial problems, it was a centralizing system of legal fiction and corporate greed attempting to fulfill an ancient dream of world domination. After the "Founding Remnant" finally leaves the land of federal occupation, will we still be blamed for all of America's social ills? Probably yes, but that's their problem.

Down through the ages, this people called "Europeans" have had to flee the hand of tyranny over and over again, but now there is no ocean to cross, and no wilderness to enter. We must make it here or die. We are faced with the dilemma that if we don't "come out of Babylon" one more time, we will abandon the living remnant of our ancient culture and abandon our posterity, liberty and Rule of Law that we brought into the world.

Consider the liberty that is being denied you here and now in today's so-called United States. Who has convinced you that you cannot have the liberty guaranteed by the Constitution? Think about it; have Americans accepted defeat out of ignorance? If so, then exactly who has tutored the ignorance and convinced America to accept defeat? The voices have been so many and have been so subtle for so long a time, who does know? Was it our education; was it the media's entertainment and news; or was it both? We are the cultural link between our grandfathers and our grandchildren; and today we are a very weak link. We are weak but have not yet failed. America's national tyranny will soon pass its crown to a global tyranny, thus our restoration and preservation fall upon this generation. May God forgive us if we fail.

Proclamation of the Governor of Virginia
John Letcher; June 1862
[abridged]

The General Assembly of Virginia, impelled by the sacred obligation to protect the citizens of this State from the usurpations and tyranny of the Government of the United States, having passed "An act to authorize a force of 10,000 men to be raised for the defense of the Commonwealth" it becomes my duty to execute that act . . .

The people of Virginia, by overwhelming majorities of their convention and Legislature, have solemnly announced to the world the purpose of this Commonwealth under no conceivable circumstances again to acknowledge allegiance to or unite the destinies of our people with those of the United States . . .

Will you not rally to . . . give . . . the force necessary to make the law effectual? Will not all Virginians aid in this noble purpose? If anything other than the love of country and obedience to the call of your mother Virginia be wanting, it will be found in the execrable acts of the Lincoln government.

A recital of a few of these acts, which are undeniable, will suffice for the justification in the eyes of the world. The course they pursued previous to the war was more than sufficient to justify our separation from them, but their disgraceful violations of the Constitution and of plighted faith since the war, their utter perversions of truth, their reckless disregard of justice and of the rights of property, and their departure in numerous instances from the usages of civilized warfare, the invasion of our homes, and the murder of our peaceful citizens renders a connection with them in [the] future odious to our sense of honor and abhorrent to our feelings. It has produced an estrangement as enduring as if there was an impassable gulf between us.

The Constitution, as they interpret it; the contempt of its provisions . . . the laws made . . . in direct conflict with its plainest provisions . . . are equally approved by them; the men who have been the instruments to execute their power and vengeance, and the hirelings who have pillaged our land, desecrated our churches, polluted our fair fields, sacked our towns, and insulted the innocent and helpless, render them alike detestable to us and disgraceful to humanity. They were bound by the Constitution to guarantee to us our rights and protect us against invasion. They have invaded us themselves with the avowed object to subjugate and overwhelm us, to confiscate our property, and banish us from our domain . . .

They have refused to permit us to obtain with our own means even the medicines necessary for our sick and wounded - articles never hitherto considered contraband by any civilized nation. They were prohibited from forming or erecting a new State within the jurisdiction of any other State. They have permitted an illegal Legislature, not acknowledged by the constitution or laws of this State or by a majority of our people, to profess to establish a new State within the jurisdiction of Virginia, acknowledging the acts of the Governor of that State, receiving its Representatives and Senators into the Congress of the United States without the color of law, justice, or right . . .

They were prohibited from making any law respecting an establishment of religion, or prohibiting the free exercise thereof. They have sent their myrmidons into churches and dragged our ministers from the sacred desk for a mere omission to put up a petition to the Almighty for their execrated President. They have shut up our places of worship for the same cause, and prohibited our people from assembling together for the exercise of their religious rights. They were denied authority to abridge the freedom of speech or of the press. They have recklessly imprisoned private citizens, holding no office or position, civil or military, for expressing a mere difference of opinion with themselves, and for fearlessly uttering their sentiments; and even incarcerated our honorable women for similar causes, permitting their armed jailers to watch and insult them in the privacy of their cells.

They have placed the press of the country wherever their power extends under censorship, and in numerous cases prohibited the circulation of papers, broken up their forms and scattered their types to the wind. They were restrained from infringing the right of the people to keep and bear arms. They have disarmed large portions of people within one of the States still in their Union, and hunted and baited those in others who have presumed to keep their own arms against their mandate. They were expressly prohibited from quartering soldiers in any house without the consent of the owner, and not even in time of war but in a manner to be prescribed by law. They have not only thus quartered them, but they have instigated their soldiers, when so quartered, to plunder them of every valuable, and wantonly to destroy what their cupidity could not carry away. They have not only shot down helpless owners, who ought to have been reverenced for their age and sex, but have consumed the owners and their dwellings in one undistinguished conflagration.

With this catalogue of violations of solemn constitutional obligations, well may we say they keep no faith and pervert truth, justice and right. When in the history of civilized nations has it been known that non-combatants, plain citizens engaged only in farming pursuits, were imprisoned for having shown allegiance to their own State laws? When has it been known that wives and pure and spotless maidens have been violated by soldiers without an effort on the part of their officers to pursue the perpetrators with the vengeance of the law? What civilized nation would not blush to conceal its own flag . . . and hoist . . . the flag of its enemy, in order to decoy that enemy into murderous fire, and then glory in the meanness of the deception and the cowardice of the act? What ancient or modern nation ever used a flag of truce to decoy an enemy in battle other than the United States of America? Let history record the disgrace and brand the infamy upon their brow for all time to come.

What ancient or modern nation would openly fire upon a public hospital, in which the sick, the wounded, and the dying are being cared for by the generous and the kind-hearted, the surgeon, and the Sister of Charity?

We brand it as a crime upon the United States, and call upon the historian to record it against them. They were required to guarantee to every State a republican form of government. Wherever their armies have obtained a foothold they have established a military government, and appointed military satraps and provost-marshals to execute laws never sanctioned by the people or the government which they created, and have executed arbitrary power, enforcing it by bayonets and at the mouth of the cannon; these military rulers issuing proclamations . . . compelling obedience by . . . submission or starvation; and by their mere military order causing some of our most patriotic citizens to be ignominiously hung upon a charge of treason, without trial and without law!

Will the people of Virginia tamely submit to such tyranny? If such acts are perpetrated while they have but partial control, what may we not expect when the demons have full sway and authority? Citizens of Virginia, the State appeals to you to . . . redeem our fair State from the hand of the oppressor. Make up the force now called for, and be prompt in your action.

Given under my hand and under the seal of the Commonwealth, at Richmond, this 27th day of June, 1862, and the eighty-sixth year of the Commonwealth.

John Letcher,

Governor of Virginia

Consider reading Elliott Germain's most recent book.

Econarchy

A Salient Critique of Laissez-faire

Econarchy is presented in the same style as Transfer of Power: cut to the bone; get to the root of the problem; tell it like it is - in plain language to be best understood. Econarchy also provides an historical perspective that builds one fact upon another to reveal the multiple yet specific origins of today's economic crisis.

Discover the strategies used to convert America's "fair" enterprise system into a centralized, then international, then global economy.

Gain an understanding of how British bankers used America's gold standard to put America on a debt-based monetary system.

Reveal for yourself, the working relationship between modern capitalists and their Keynesian socialist counterparts; while claiming to be adversaries, they work together hand in glove; one for avarice, the other for greed.

Understand the transition of power from the Federal Reserve Bank to the International Monetary Fund; and how today's economic "collapse" is only a latter day tactic in a long-term strategy.

This book provides an example of the type of economic system that could be an alternative to accepting the collapse of America.

For a copy of Econarchy or another Transfer of Power
Send $20. (includes tax and postage) (two books $35) payable to:

Liberty Nation
P.O. Box 464
Hanover, VA 23069